Sbragia

THE 1992 PROJECT
AND THE FUTURE OF
INTEGRATION IN EUROPE

THE 1992 PROJECT AND THE FUTURE OF INTEGRATION IN EUROPE

John A. C. Conybeare
Russell J. Dalton
Richard C. Eichenberg
David Garnham
Barry B. Hughes
Paulette Kurzer

Leon N. Lindberg
Frances H. Oneal
Frederic S. Pearson
James Lee Ray
Alberta M. Sbragia
Dale L. Smith

DALE L. SMITH and JAMES LEE RAY
Editors

M.E. Sharpe
Armonk, New York
London, England

Available in the United Kingdom and Europe from M. E. Sharpe,
Publishers, 3 Henrietta Street, London WC2E 8LU.

Library of Congress Cataloging-in-Publication Data

The 1992 Project and the future of integration in Europe /
edited by Dale L. Smith and James Lee Ray.
p.   cm.
Includes bibliographical references and index.
ISBN 1-56324-022-X
1. European Economic Community countries—Economic policy.
2. Europe—Economic integration.
3. Europe 1992.
I. Smith, Dale L.
II. Ray, James Lee.
HC241.2.A6156   1992
338.94—dc20
92-13467
CIP

Printed in the United States of America

The paper used in this publication meets the minimum requirements of
American National Standard for Information Sciences—
Permanence of Paper for Printed Library Materials,
ANSI Z39.48–1984.

BB (c)   10   9   8   7   6   5   4   3   2

To our children,
a new generation for a new community

Contents

List of Contributors

John A. C. Conybeare is Professor of Political Science at the University of Iowa. Recent publications include *Trade Wars* (1987); "Voting for Protection," *International Organization* (Winter 1991); "The Triple Entente and the Triple Alliance: A Collective Goods Approach" (with Todd Sandler), *American Political Science Review* (December 1990); and "A Random Walk Down the Road to War," *Defense Economics* (1/4, 1990).

Russell J. Dalton is Professor of Political Science at the University of California, Irvine. He is co-author of *Germany Transformed* (1981), co-editor of *Electoral Change in Advanced Industrial Democracies* (1984), *Challenging the Political Order: New Social and Political Movements in Western Democracies* (1988), and *Politics in West Germany* (1989). He is completing a book-length study of the environmental movement in Western Europe.

Richard C. Eichenberg is Associate Professor of Political Science at Tufts University where he is also the Director of the International Relations Program. His publications have appeared in *The American Political Review, International Security, World Politics*, and many edited volumes. His latest book is *Public Opinion and National Security in Western Europe* (1989). He is now at work on a comparative study of leadership and foreign policy in the United States and Germany, with a special focus on the administrations of President Jimmy Carter and Chancellor Helmut Schmidt.

David Garnham is Professor of Political Science at the University of Wisconsin-Milwaukee. He is the author of *The Politics of European Defense Cooperation: Germany, France, Britain, and America* (1988), as well as articles, book chapters, and conference papers on Western European security issues and U.S.–Western European relations. His current research compares the policy cultures of the NATO-European countries, the United States, Canada, and Japan.

Barry B. Hughes is Professor at the Graduate School of International Studies, University of Denver. He is the author of *The Domestic Context of American Foreign Policy, World Futures, Continuity and Change in World Politics,* as well as other books and articles. His interest in European integration is part of a larger interest in global change.

Paulette Kurzer is Assistant Professor of Political Science at Babson College and has published articles on central bank politics and the European Monetary System. She is completing a book on the transformation of the European political economy from welfare capitalism to neoliberalism.

Leon Lindberg is Professor of Political Science and Environmental Studies at the University of Wisconsin-Madison. He specializes in comparative and international political economy with emphasis on Western Europe and the United States. He has written extensively on the theory of European economic and political integration and on the politics of the European Community. His major EC-related publications include: *Regional Integration: Theory and Research* (co-editor and co-author; 1971); *Europe's Would-Be Polity: Patterns of Change in the European Community* (with Stuart A. Scheingold, 1970); and *The Political Dynamics of European Integration* (1963).

Frances H. Oneal is Assistant Professor of Political Science at the University of Alabama. She is pursuing research on state-level activity in industrial development and export promotion, particularly in Southeastern states. Other research interests include public-sector growth, the measurement of interdependence, and the political causes and effects of government deficits.

Frederic S. Pearson is Professor of Political Science and Director of the Center for Peace and Conflict Studies at Wayne State University. His research, which has appeared in numerous books and journals, has focused on security and conflict studies with a special emphasis on Western Europe.

James Lee Ray is Professor of Political Science at Florida State University, where he has served as Director of the International Affairs program since 1985. His writing has focused on economic integration in Latin America as well as Western Europe; he is the author of *Global Politics,* and articles in such journals as *Journal of Conflict Resolution, International Studies Quarterly,* and *International Organization.*

Alberta Sbragia is Associate Professor of Political Science and Director of the West European Studies Program at the University of Pittsburgh. She is directing the Brookings Institution's Governmental Studies Program's project on the institutional implications of 1992 and, in that capacity, is editing *Euro-Politics: Institutions and Policymaking in the "New" European Community* (forthcoming 1992). She is also engaged in comparative research on American and EC environmental politics and policies.

Dale L. Smith is Assistant Professor of Political Science at Florida State University. He has published in *International Organization* and *Journal of Conflict Resolution*. His work continues to focus on the European Community, particularly the redistributive consequences of the 1992 Project.

List of Tables and Figures

Tables

Figures

Preface and Acknowledgments

Like most projects of this type, ours has had a relatively long gestation period that began in the spring of 1989 when we began to investigate a curious discrepancy between the enthusiasm for the 1992 Project in Europe and the apparent lack of interest in European integration among American scholars. This led to early versions of the study that now appear as chapter 2 of this volume.

As we delved further into that study and presented it as a conference paper, it became clear that not only was there more interest than we had originally thought, but more importantly, the interest was growing at a phenomenal rate. Exploiting this growing trend, we organized a conference to bring to Tallahassee a group of scholars that epitomized this new focus on European integration. The group included both international relations and comparative politics specialists in order to reflect the differing perspectives that each brings to the study of integration. The papers presented at that conference were revised, reworked, and some even reinvented to become the core chapters of this volume.

We wish to thank the Florida State University's Political Science Department and International Affairs Program for their generous support in underwriting the conference. Smith's work on our original study was funded in the summer of 1989 by a research grant from FSU's Council on Research and Creativity and the Department of Political Science. We wish to acknowledge Jürgen Wanke for his able and conscientious research assistance. Finally, we want to thank all the faculty and students at Florida State University who participated in and contributed to the success of the conference.

Dale L. Smith
James Lee Ray

THE 1992 PROJECT
AND THE FUTURE OF
INTEGRATION IN EUROPE

1

The 1992 Project

Dale L. Smith and James Lee Ray

There is a new momentum in Europe. The stagnation and malaise that seemed to typify political and social relations in the 1970s and early 1980s has been replaced by a feeling that Europe stands at the threshold of a new era. The collapse of the communist regimes in central Europe, the disintegration of the Soviet Union, and the unification of Germany have brought an end to the "postwar order" in Europe, and while these changes often garner most of the headlines in the United States, changes within the European Community are likely to have at least as great an impact on the future of Europe. With the ratification of the Single European Act in 1987, the European Community (EC) embarked on its most ambitious attempt to increase the level of integration among its twelve members. If successful, these changes would be felt far beyond these twelve West European states. According to Samuel Huntington (1988–89, 93–94), an integrated Europe "would be a powerful force on the world scene. If the next century is not the American century it is most likely to be the European century. The baton of world leadership that passed westward across the Atlantic in the early twentieth century could move back eastward a hundred years later."

Completing the Internal Market

The term "1992 Project" commonly refers to that portion of the Single European Act (SEA) which commits the EC to the completion of a single unified market by the end of 1992. Though often labeled by Americans as the "Common Market," a number of barriers still prevent the EC from truly reaching that goal, and it is these barriers to the free movement of goods, services, people, and capital that are to be swept away by 1992. The completion of the internal market can be grouped around the removal of three types of barriers: physical, technical, and fiscal.

Physical Barriers to the Single Market

The physical barriers refer to abolition by 1992 of all intra-Community customs checks. With respect to the individual traveler, this means that all passport and immigration controls at borders within the Community will cease. While such a change will certainly make border-crossing less burdensome for the individual traveler, the real economic benefit will be the effect it will have on freight-hauling. Frontier checks have been used for collecting taxes and statistics, licensing certain restricted products, preventing the importation of banned products, and many other time-consuming functions. The economic burden of border delays is seen in the comparison of two 750-mile truck trips. The first, completely within England, takes thirty-six hours, while the second, from London to Milan, takes fifty-eight hours, excluding Channel-crossing time (Emerson et al. 1988, 39). Ultimately, that extra twenty-two hours represents a direct cost to Community producers and consumers that could be reduced with the elimination of customs checks. By 1993, the traveler or trucker should be able to travel from Denmark to Portugal as easily as they travel within their own countries today.

Technical Barriers to the Single Market

While these physical barriers are important, much larger contributors to the "costs of non-Europe" are to be found in the technical barriers that prevent the free movement of goods, services, capital, and people. With the establishment of the customs union in 1968, all tariffs and quantitative restrictions on the intra-Community trade of goods were to have been eliminated. However, there still exists a welter of national, technical standards that prevent the same product from being sold in all EC countries. As explained in a recent EC document,

> . . . cars and televisions have to be altered in innumerable ways to meet all sorts of different national standards. British chocolate simply cannot be sold in some Member States because they use a different definition of chocolate. (Europe without Frontiers 1989, 37)

These differing national standards affect trade in literally hundreds of products, ranging from the maximum allowable levels of automobile exhaust or pesticide residues in food to limits on lawnmower noise. Whether important or mundane, the Community must examine each case and decide whether (1) to harmonize their differing national laws on a single standard or (2) to mutually recognize all national standards. This second path, mutual recognition, is becoming increasingly prominent due to the difficulty of trying to agree on a single standard and would imply, in the previous example, that if one country defines the product as "chocolate," all other states must accept that definition and allow the good to be imported as "chocolate."[1]

The technical barriers that prevent the free movement of people involve differing professional and vocational qualifications across the member-states. Despite intensive efforts over the last thirty years to agree on common standards, many professionals and tradespeople still cannot practice their profession outside their home country. Because of the difficult negotiations that are required to agree on common standards, the Community has decided on the "mutual recognition" approach, whereby any person that is judged competent to practice a profession or trade in one country is also fit to practice it in any other. In this way, the French plumber will be able to practice his trade without undue hindrance in Germany.

With its planned liberalization of capital movements, the 1992 Project moved into a jealously guarded area of national control. Nugent (1989, 213) notes: "for many states, control of capital movements is an important economic and monetary instrument and they preferred it to remain in their own hands." The economics of the situation required, however, that if there was to be a single internal market, then capital must be at least as free as the other factors of production, and so the imperatives of the single market have forced certain national governments to finally reconsider their long-standing reluctance to liberalize capital movements. These changes, combined with the creation of a common market in financial services, should provide both the household and business sectors much broader opportunities for borrowing and investment.

Finally, a common market in services will be established as part of the 1992 Project. While the free movement of goods has been the primary emphasis of the Community for decades, the service sector must also be addressed if a truly unified market is to be realized. This is an obvious requirement, since the service sector now accounts for almost 60 percent of the value-added produced by the member-states. Again, the principle of mutual recognition is being used so that financial, broadcasting, advertising or any other type of service licensed in one state would be able to operate in every other.

Fiscal Barriers to the Single Market

With the physical and technical barriers eliminated, the final set of impediments to the attainment of a single market are fiscal barriers. Here the intention is to approximate the national value-added and excise taxes that exist across member-states. Vastly different value-added tax (VAT) rates lead to artificial price differences between states that can distort competition. As the American experience illustrates, it is not necessary for every state to have identical tax rates, however, some narrowing of the current differences is required to prevent smuggling and cross-border shopping. For example, the VAT rate applied to automobiles in Germany is 14 percent, while in Italy the same car would be taxed at 38 percent (Emerson et al. 1988, 60). Because the ability to determine these taxes bear directly on the fiscal sovereignty of the member-states, the Community's goal of approximating tax rates could well be one of the most difficult aspects of the 1992 Project to implement.[2]

The 1992 Project represents nothing less than an attempt by the EC to reproduce, at the Community level, the free movement of all factors of economic activity—labor, capital, goods, and services—that one normally associates with a national economy. Stretching from Ireland to Greece, the EC, with over 300 million consumers, will be the single richest market in the world. However, the SEA was more than just a commitment to complete the common market. It also includes important institutional reforms, such as increasing the use of majority voting in EC decision making and expanding the powers of the European Parliament, as well as the extension of EC authority into such new areas as environmental policy (see chapter 5). These institutional reforms will prove essential not only in attaining the single market, but also in moving beyond it to economic and monetary union.

Multilevel Games and the Consequences of 1992

The 1992 Project has brought about a dramatic revival of interest in the European Community, and this volume is a product of that revival. Each of the chapters provides evaluations and estimates of the future of the Community and the integration process from the perspective of the various specialists in international relations and comparative politics. Some of our contributors base their analyses of the effects of continued integration primarily on the study of the history of the Community, while others pay closer attention to the most recent trends and developments. Together, we believe, these chapters provide a range of insights and evidence which will serve as a useful guide and reference point for readers who share an interest in the fate of the European Community in the 1990s.

Two themes are shared by the various authors of this book. The first is a view of the process of integration as a multilevel game. Here we see actors at various levels involved in multiple games that both influence and are influenced by the process of integration. These actors range from subnational interest groups and national governments to the supranational Community and even other international actors. The second theme running throughout these chapters is an examination of the consequences of the integration process on either the games or the actors. While many studies are searching for the determinants of "renewed" integration in Europe, this volume looks at the other side by focusing on the possible effects of integration on these multilevel games and the actors involved. We will briefly address each of these themes and, in the final section of this chapter, present the plan of the book.

Multilevel Games and the Study of Integration

Any examination of the 1992 Project must not lose sight of the fact that integration studies are not new. The study of the European Community, as well as regional integration schemes in other parts of the world, influenced a whole generation of scholars in the 1960s and early 1970s. Integration studies were one of the most exciting and dynamic areas within both international relations and comparative politics. In terms of theoretical developments within the discipline, this work represented a clear and important challenge to state-centric realism, the dominant paradigm at the time within international relations (Puchala 1988, 207–211). In terms of actual developments, the integration movement gave many scholars hope that the international system, after the most devastating war in its history, was finally evolving "beyond the nation-state."

However, any optimism generated by regional integration in either Europe or the developing world was relatively short-lived. With the collapse of regional integration projects in the Third World and the apparent stagnation of the process in Europe, interest waned. By 1976, Ernst Haas, one of the founders of the field, pronounced the study of regional integration obsolete in the European context. With the international shocks and instability of the 1970s came what is commonly referred to as the period of "europessimism." Lasting until the early 1980s, these dark days of the EC only confirmed the realists' view that the ideals of political community and supranationality would invariably be sacrificed on the altar of national interest.

One of the most interesting aspects of the work done in the 1960s and 1970s is that the focus on regional integration attracted both international relations and comparative politics specialists. This was a new area, sitting at the nexus of the national and the international, that both fields found they could address. One of the factors that made collaboration between them productive was the dominant theory of the time, neofunctionalism. Originally developed by Ernst Haas, neofunctionalism extended the existing theories in both fields by recognizing important interconnections between domestic and international politics. Going beyond the dominant state-centric approach to international relations, states were no longer viewed as unitary rational actors. The conception of the state for the neofunctionalists became much richer, focusing on subnational groups, political parties, and competition and bargaining over national policy. On the other hand, going beyond the domestic focus of comparative politics, neofunctionalism emphasized how regional and international contexts influenced state policy. National policy was not determined solely by nation-level factors; now transnational coalitions and regional influences became central to the argument.

As our contributors illustrate, we have also attempted to bring together specialists from both international relations and comparative politics. However, this volume employs as its organizational framework a much more recent attempt to link these two spheres of study. In an influential 1988 article, Robert Putnam develops the metaphor of a two-level game to illustrate the interconnections between the domestic and the international. The logic of Putnam's two-level game derives from the view that national leaders are simultaneously playing at two tables, one domestic and the other international. At the national table, the

Figure 1.1. **Putnam's Two-Level Games**

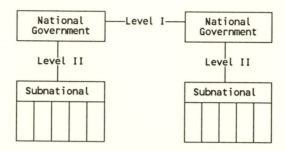

political leader tries to increase his power by building coalitions among domestic interest groups. At the same time he sits at a second table, opposite his foreign counterparts, and bargains to increase his ability to satisfy domestic demands. The international game is referred to by Putnam as a Level I game, while the national game takes place at Level II. Figure 1.1 illustrates these ideas with the international, or Level I, game represented by the links between the two "national government" boxes and the national, or Level II, game depicted by the vertical lines between the "national government" and "subnational" boxes.

Putnam is not offering a theory, but rather a useful metaphor to illustrate the interconnections and feedbacks between domestic and international processes. However, to use Putnam's metaphor as one of the organizing devices of the current volume, two extensions are necessary.[3] First, studies of integration require more than a "two-level" conceptualization. Supranational communities represent a new level, distinct from either the domestic or the international, and by including this new level one is, in a sense, adding a third "game table" with a different set of players. Unlike the other two tables—the national and international—the nature of the game at this third table, as well as the players involved, will change depending on if one is a member of the community. If a state is a member, then the players will include the leaders of the other member-states, as well as Community-level officials. But, if a state is not a Community member, then one's bargaining partners are the representatives of the Community, rather than the leaders of the member nations. Figure 1.2 extends Putnam's two-level game to a multi-level version more suitable for our purposes. On the right side of this figure, we have the four "national government" and "subnational" boxes shown in Figure 1.1, but now above them we have added a "European Community" box indicating both are Community members. On the left side, a third set of boxes has been added to indicate a nonmember state. As in Figure 1.1, the international games between the national governments (Level I) as well as the domestic games between the governments and the subnational groups (Level II) remain unchanged. However, a Level III and IV have now been added to repre-

Figure 1.2. **Multilevel Games: The Logic of Domestic, Community, and International Interactions**

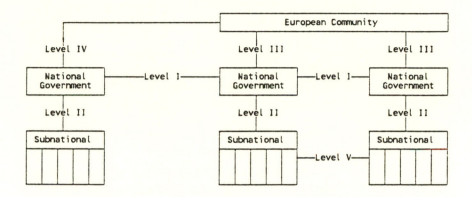

sent, in the first case, Community members negotiating with each other, and in the second, the Community bargaining with outside members.

The second aspect of Putnam's work that we need to elaborate is due to the fact that he ignores the possibility of transnational coalitions developing and influencing negotiations. Again, in most areas of domestic policy one might be able to ignore this extension, but in terms of integration studies, transnational coalitions have shown themselves to be of central importance in affecting the negotiations at both the national and international levels. One example of these nongovernmental linkages would be the European Business Roundtable, a transnational coalition of business leaders that has had, according to most observers, a significant impact on the current program for completing the single market by 1992. In Figure 1.2, these transnational linkages are labeled "Level V" games. Therefore, by extending Putnam's view to include the development of transnational coalitions and the addition of a new level representing the Community, his attempt to link the domestic and international arenas through the metaphor of a multilevel game serves our purposes quite well.

Putnam (1988, 459) concludes his article by noting that "the most portentous development in the fields of comparative politics and international relations in recent years is the dawning recognition among practitioners in each field of the need to take into account entanglements between the two." While true, one must not lose sight of the fact that integration studies have brought together practitioners of both fields in useful collaboration since the 1960s. This volume, along with the conference from which it grew, continues that collaboration. In the 1960s, neofunctionalism was the overarching theoretical framework that tied the two fields together. Though the consensus on neofunctionalism as the appropriate theoretical approach may have evaporated, the multilevel game metaphor provides a useful device for integrating the studies in this volume, since each of our contributors analyzes the integration process by focusing on at least one of these games or the interaction between games at different levels.

It is worth reiterating that the multilevel game we have laid out here is not a theory but a metaphor that allows us to emphasize the different levels of the system and the interactions and bargaining that occurs between them. No author can address all the game tables that affect a single issue or all the issues that are "played" on a single table. Rather, the authors in this volume examine parts of the larger game, and we believe that their shared conception of the process of integration as a multilevel game will assist the reader in understanding how these different studies, focused on different levels and issues, fit together.

The Consequences of the 1992 Project

After an enormously active decade of research, a conference was held in 1969 to reassess the field of regional integration theory. In a concluding essay to a set of articles drawn from that conference, Stuart Scheingold (1971) argues that the field needs to pay much closer attention to the *consequences* of regional integration.[4] According to Scheingold, the focus up to that point had been on the determinants and process of integration, rather than on its consequences. Although Scheingold could only speculate, he believed the focus on the inputs and the process rather than outputs was at least partly a function of the view that

> . . . integration was good by definition since it was directed at economic reconstruction and permanent reconciliation between nations of the world. A "United States of Europe" seemed almost by definition likely to serve the cause of a peaceful and prosperous future. (1971, 376)

Despite Scheingold's call for a focus on the consequences of integration and despite the deepening and broadening of the process of integration over the intervening two decades, his assessment is still valid today. Two of the most prominent recent studies of the Single European Act continue this focus on the determinants of integration.[5]

The studies in this volume take a different approach, focusing for the most part on the consequences of the completion of the single market. Building on our first theme, these studies examine the effects of the 1992 Project on the multilevel games, whether at the national, Community, or international level. Some studies focus on its consequences on subnational groupings, others on the games played between the member nations and the Community. Still others look beyond the Community to examine the effects of the completion of the single market on nonmember states.

Our view of the process of integration, however, is dynamic, with the consequences of one step in that process becoming the determinants of the ones to follow. With all the attention that has been focused on the 1992 Project, it is sometimes easy to forget that this is only one step in a process that has been underway for over forty years and that the consequences of this step will affect future developments.[6] Therefore, distinctions between studies that focus on the determinants of integration and those that focus on its effects are never absolute. One overlaps by necessity into the other, and so we are not simply studying the consequences of a single act, because it is the effects of this step in the process that will determine the ones that follow. If the realities of completing the single market do not live up to the high expectations that currently exist, or if the costs and benefits from the 1992 Project are distributed too asymmetrically, then the momentum to move to the next step in the process could quickly dissipate. From our perspective, the 1992 Project is not an end in itself but only one more step in a very long process; and to understand the direction and speed that process might take in the future, a careful examination of the consequences of the 1992 Project is essential.

The Plan of the Book

We begin in part I of the book with some "theoretical considerations" that go beyond a focus on the 1992 Project, putting this step in the process of integration into a broader perspective. In chapter 2, we examine the development of integration theory as a research program and contrast the "gloomy" academic analyses of European integration that developed in the 1970s with the "rosy" revisionist view of the progress the Community has made over the last forty years. After reviewing both the rise and decline of integration theory and the steady progress of the Community, we posit several factors to explain this anomalous disparity between academic analyses and the reality of European integration.

In chapter 3, Barry Hughes introduces his view of the process of integration in terms of the development of complex governance—"the emergence of multitiered, overlapping structures of government." This is a view that is distinct from either the state-building orientation of neofunctionalism or the nation-building approach favored by Karl Deutsch, for it views the development of the EC as part of a larger process in which various levels of government (subnational, national, and regional) share policy-making responsibilities as they search for the most efficient structures for providing the public goods demanded by the citizenry. It is an image of integration that is similar to our own metaphor of multilevel games in the sense that these multitiered, overlapping structures can easily be thought of in terms of the multiple tables and interconnected games that are played upon them.

Having provided in these two chapters the empirical and theoretical foundation necessary to place the 1992 Project in a broader perspective, part II of the book turns to the consequences of the project.

Russell Dalton and Richard Eichenberg (chapter 4) focus on how public opinion increasingly influences, and is influenced by, the games played at Levels II and III. A strong interactive effect will link the games played between the national governments and the Community and those between these same governments and domestic interest groups. National leaders must bargain at the Community table (Level III) to satisfy domestic groups, while at the same time the opinion those groups express for or against continued integration help frame the government's policies. In terms of the effects of 1992, Dalton and Eichenberg argue that public opinion will play an increasingly important role in the process of integration and examine the public's perception of the benefits that might arise from the single market. If those positive perceptions of this next step in the process of integration are at odds with the reality produced by the 1992 Project, then that discrepancy could have a dramatic effect on the public's willingness to pursue higher levels of integration.

While Dalton and Eichenberg are measuring and assessing the evolution of forces at the "bottom" in terms of changes in public opinion toward European supranationalism, Alberta Sbragia (chapter 5) focuses on forces at the "top," examining the institutional development of the European Community. Although the economic dimension of the Single European Act, in terms of the 1992 Project, has received most of the attention, this Act was also a watershed in terms of the institutional development of the Community and may have laid the foundation for continued political and economic integration. Sbragia contrasts the impressive strides the EC achieved over the last two decades in the areas of legal and monetary integration with problems of decision making within the Council of Ministers due to the rule of unanimity. Finally, with the adoption of the SEA and the introduction of qualified majority voting, the calculus of decision making has changed and with it the bargaining among the national representatives that compose the Council. No longer can a single recalcitrant member halt progress, and so bargaining now focuses on building a "qualified majority" rather than consensus. In terms of multilevel games, Sbragia's interest is with the Level III game between the member-states and the Community. In addition to consequences of this movement away from unanimity, Sbragia's chapter also draws our attention to the expansion of the Community's interests into new areas such as the environment and the effect that might have on the continued development of EC authority.

The 1992 Project's liberalization of capital movements and financial services is the basis for Leon Lindberg's analysis (chapter 6) of the effects it will have on the next step in the process of integration: economic and monetary union (EMU). Focusing on "the bargaining behavior of states and the institutional dynamics of national, intergovernmental and supranational systems," Lindberg's effort is primarily concentrated on the Level I and III games—bargaining among the member-states and between the states and the Community. However, in his effort to explain the Community's renewed efforts toward monetary integration, he also discusses the subnational forces that have proved to be important stimuli.

While Lindberg projects forward from the 1992 Project to EMU, Paulette Kurzer (chapter 7) draws her lessons for continued economic integration from the experience of small countries with the European Monetary System (EMS). Why were these countries willing to sacrifice a significant portion of their economic autonomy to join a system that required restrictive monetary and fiscal policies? And what could be the effects on these countries' policies as the Community moves toward EMU? In terms of multilevel games, Kurzer's discussion of monetary integration is focused on a single table, the Level II game. For her the answer to why Belgium, Denmark, and Holland were willing to sacrifice policy autonomy in this area is rooted in the games of bargaining and coalition-building played between the national governments and certain subnational groups.

In the chapters by John Conybeare and Frances Oneal we have two contributions that focus on international relations beyond the Community, but from very different perspectives. In chapter 8, Conybeare analyzes the effects of the single market on other (non-Community) national actors and, more broadly, the structure of international economic relations. Will it be a force for free trade or lead to the "Fortress Europe" that some fear? While the Europeans proclaim that the single market will not be protectionist, Conybeare raises several reasons why the disappearance of internal barriers could lead to new external barriers. In terms of Figure 1.2, Conybeare's focus is at Level IV, the games between the Community and other (non-Community) national actors.

In chapter 9, Frances Oneal examines a "game" that is not even shown in Figure 1.2. Of all the linkages, identified as "Levels," shown in that figure, there is no direct link between the subnational actors at the bottom and the Community at the top; the linkages shown would imply that all such forces from the bottom are filtered through the national governments. This is an obvious simplification since domestic groups do affect and are affected by the EC. If in no other way, the direct election of the European Parliament is an important channel of influence from the bottom to the top. Oneal, however, looks at the opposite direction of influence, from the top to the bottom, and gives it a slightly different twist by focusing not on intra-Community relations, but rather on the effects of the 1992 Project on subnational actors in another nation outside the Community, in this case, the United States. State development agencies and overseas liaison offices are playing an increasingly important role in furthering the economic interests of the states' business communities, and Oneal's research examines how the American states have been affected by and are reacting to the 1992 Project. In terms of our multiple game tables, Oneal sees the Community sitting on one side of the table, and on the other side sits not a single national actor, but a collection of American states each plotting how best to take advantage of this new situation.

Finally, we turn from the economic to the security dimension with two analyses by Frederic Pearson and David Garnham (chapters 10 and 11). It was the momentum created by the Single European Act in the mid-1980s that aided current efforts to give European supranationalism a foreign and security policy dimension. Both authors acknowledge the impetus that the 1992 Project will have on developing a technologically sophisticated and competitive European defense industry. However, in assessing the future security arrangements in Europe, the effects of the 1992 Project are only one part of a very complex and volatile brew. Games played at other tables, where the issues are declining superpower domination, German unification, and the collapse of the Soviet Union, all affect the prospects for increasing European security cooperation. Given the importance of these extra-Community actors to this process, bargaining among national governments (Level I) and between the member states and the EC (Level III) will help determine the course of these developments. Additionally, domestic interest group coalitions, either within (Level II) or between member-states (Level V), will attempt to influence national governments and the Community regarding the desirability of adding a security dimension to the European movement. While both Pearson and Garnham touch on all four of these games in their analyses, the two authors concentrate on different levels. Pearson's chapter focuses on the domestic and transnational interest groups (Levels II and V) that have developed in the wake of the Single European Act, while Garnham emphasizes the international (Level I) and intra-Community (Level III) influences on European security integration.

In part III, chapter 12, we bring together the analyses of each of our contributors, not only to reach an overall assessment of the 1992 Project, but also to move to the next level and begin to think about the future of the Community.

No single volume could hope to cover the consequences of the 1992 Project in all areas. However, by focusing on public opinion, institutional developments, financial and monetary integration, international effects, and political and security considerations, we believe these analyses provide the reader with a wide-ranging assessment of the consequences of 1992.

Notes

1. The mutual recognition of differing national standards is often referred to as the *Cassis de Dijon* principle, which is explained more fully in chapter 2 of this volume.

2. But there are not only fiscal issues at stake here. Consider the excise taxes applied to cigarettes: in Denmark it is about $9/100 cigarettes; in England, $5; and in France, Spain and Greece, about $1 (Emerson et al. 1988, 61). In the case of Denmark, and other high cigarette tax states, there is more than simply an economic decision behind these rates. These countries have made a clear social decision regarding cigarette smoking, and to try to reach a compromise that would be acceptable to both Denmark and Greece will be very difficult.

3. Putnam (1988) alludes to both of these limitations in his original article, but prefers to limit himself to the two-level case for simplicity of exposition.

4. The papers from this conference were originally published as a special issue of the journal, *International Organization* (vol. 24, no. 4, 1970), and later as a book (see Lindberg and Scheingold 1971).

5. See Sandholtz and Zysman (1989), and Moravcsik (1991).

6. In terms of the perceived significance of the 1992 Project, one could contrast the view of Sandholtz and Zysman, who see the Project as a "disjunction, a dramatic new start, rather than the fulfillment of the original effort to construct Europe" (1989, 95), with chapters 2 and 5 in this volume, both of which see 1992 as a continuation of a process that may have slowed during the 1970s but certainly did not disappear.

References

Cecchini, Paolo. 1998. *The European Challenge: 1992: The Benefits of a Single Market.* Aldershot: Wildwood House.

Emerson, Michael, et al. 1988. *The Economics of 1992: The E.C. Commission's Assessment of the Economic Effects of Completing the Internal Market.* Oxford: Oxford University Press.

"Europe without Frontiers—Completing the Internal Market." 1989. *European Documentation,* 2/1989.

Haas, Ernst B. 1976. "Turbulent Fields and the Theory of Regional Integration." *International Organization,* 30:173–212.

Huntington, Samuel P. 1988–89. "The U.S.—Decline or Renewal?" *Foreign Affairs,* 67:76–96.

Lindberg, Leon N., and Stuart A. Scheingold, eds. 1971. *Regional Integration: Theory and Research.* Cambridge, MA: Harvard University Press.

Moravcsik, Andrew. 1991. "Negotiating the Single European Act: National Interests and Conventional Statecraft in the European Community." *International Organization,* 45:19–56.

Nugent, Neill. 1989. *The Government and Politics of the European Community.* Durham, NC: Duke University Press.

Puchala, Donald J. 1988. "The Integration Theorist and the Study of International Relations." In Charles Kegley, Jr. and Eugene R. Wittkopf, eds., *The Global Agenda,* 2d ed. New York: Random House.

Putnam, Robert D. 1988. "Diplomacy and Domestic Politics." *International Organization,* 42:427–60.

Sandholtz, Wayne, and John Zysman. 1989. "1992: Recasting the European Bargain." *World Politics,* 42:95–128.

Scheingold, Stuart A. 1971. "Domestic and International Consequences of Regional Integration." In Leon N. Lindberg and Stuart A. Scheingold, eds., *Regional Integration: Theory and Research.* Cambridge, MA: Harvard University Press.

PART I

THEORETICAL CONSIDERATIONS

2

European Integration
Gloomy Theory versus Rosy Reality

Dale L. Smith and James Lee Ray

Introduction

On April 18, 1951, a treaty creating the European Coal and Steel Community (ECSC) was signed in Paris. This organization was given the very specific task of coordinating the production and distribution of coal and steel among six European nations, both victor and vanquished, as they attempted to recover from the most devastating war in their history. Today, less than forty years later, the ECSC has evolved into the European Community (EC), expanding the scope and level of its influence far beyond either the original six nations or the coal and steel industries. The number of member-states has doubled, currently encompassing more than 90 percent of the population of western Europe. Its policy-making influence ranges from international trade and monetary matters to foreign affairs and even domestic labor policies, and its institutions include a directly elected parliament and a supranational court. As important as how far the Community has come is where it is going, for with the Single European Act of 1985 the EC set in motion a process that will ultimately culminate in a truly unified internal market by the end of 1992. The momentum has continued with the Maastricht Summit and its decision to move toward economic and monetary union.

If the EC is successful, or at least partially successful, in completing the single market by the end of 1992 then it will have taken another important step toward transforming itself in a short forty-one years from a limited, task-specific organization of six independent nation-states in what has been in modern times the most war-torn continent on earth, into one of the most powerful and influential political actors in the global system. "This change could rank historically with the emergence of the United States and the Soviet Union as superpowers"

(Laurent 1989, 62). Ultimately, it may be even *more* important. According to Samuel Huntington, "a federation of democratic, wealthy, socially diverse, mixed-economy societies would be a powerful force on the world scene. If the next century is not the American century it is most likely to be the European century. The baton of world leadership that passed westward across the Atlantic in the early twentieth century could move back eastward a hundred years later" (1988–89, 93–4).

Despite the considerable achievements of the EC, and its even more impressive potential, academic analysis of the integration process in western Europe, except for some initial enthusiasm, has been dominated by skepticism and pessimism, which, until very recently, was replaced by boredom and an almost total lack of interest. This paper will address this anomalous disparity between the actual development of EC institutions and processes, and the predominance of gloom in theoretical analyses of its status and future prospects that has appeared over the years since its creation. First, we will present our case for the existence of this anomaly. That is, we will attempt to demonstrate that much of the most prominent research and writing dealing with the EC has been consistently pessimistic to an unwarranted degree. We will conclude with an attempt to explain this anomaly, with a view toward deriving "lessons" that might be applied in future theoretical analyses of the European Community.

The European Community:
Toward a "Revisionist" History?

According to Robert E. Osgood, "Historical revisionism—the reinterpretation of events to refute the conventional view of the past—is a recurrent phenomenon. . . . It may reveal reality in a new light" (1971, v). Similarly, J. H. Hexter in *Reappraisals in History* argues that "the need for re-writing history is . . . a function of the increase in actual data on the thing to be written about" (1979, 12). We feel that the launching of the 1992 Project in particular constitutes "new data" that call for a reinterpretation of not only the recent past, but the entire history of the European Community. While our differences with past interpretations will not be nearly as sharp as those radical revisionists had with orthodox historians and political scientists regarding the origins of the cold war, we feel that the time is ripe for a "revisionist" look at the European Community.[1]

From the perspective of the mid-1970s, the gloomy assessments found in the scholarly literature of both the past accomplishments and future prospects of the European Community seemed no doubt well-justified at the time. However, from our current perspective those assessments seem strangely pessimistic. We find significant gains in both the scope and level of integration in Europe. A multitude of comparisons of the EC now with its status in the past lead unmistakably to the conclusion that it is growing in importance and strength and, despite some serious problems along the way, has done so consistently from the beginning.

This can be seen along two basic dimensions: (1) incremental/economic and (2) institutional/political.

From an organization of six states trying to overcome the ravages of the war, the EC has doubled its membership and developed into a community that compares favorably, on several dimensions, with the world's economic superpowers. The original Community of six had a combined Gross Domestic Product (GDP) of $150 billion, which was only about one-third that of the United States. By 1989, the combined GDP of the EC was about $4.7 trillion, 94 percent of that of the United States.[2] In terms of a population to support that economy, the twelve states of the EC combine to number 327 million people, one-third larger than the United States.

However, it is in the international economic sphere that the power of the EC comes into clearest focus. The EC is clearly the largest trading unit in the world, currently accounting for 15 percent of world exports and significantly larger than its next closest competitor, the United States, at 12 percent (CEC 1991, 27). That the EC has become important in the area of international trade is quite beyond dispute. "A common foreign-trade policy . . . makes it impossible for third parties to sign individual trade agreements with any of the EC's twelve members. Negotiations must be conducted with the EC itself. This means that a country's embassy in Brussels, the seat of the EC, may now become more important than its other embassies" (Pompeu de Toledo 1989, 15).

The power of the EC in international economic affairs extends far beyond trade. The Community and its member states are the largest donors of public aid to the Third World. According to OECD estimates, Europe currently provides almost three times as much to the poor of the world as does the United States (CEC 1991, 28). This final point might be more relevant to the future, when the Community does speak with one voice in terms of foreign policy, but all of these indicators provide us with evidence of the remarkable achievements, and enormous potential, of the European Community.

While the indicators up to this point have examined the EC in relation to either the world or other international actors, one of the traditional methods of assessing the level of economic integration has been the examination of trade flows.[3] Taking the current twelve members of the Community and tracing the percentage of intragroup exports to the group's total exports from 1958 to 1989, we find that it has increased from 37 percent to 63 percent. According to this admittedly simple measure, the EC has clearly become more tightly integrated over time.

In a recent economic analysis of the effect of the EC on growth, Marques Mendes (1987) estimates the degree to which "integration effects" contributed to the overall growth of the member countries.[4] In a set of results that would appear counterintuitive, given the pessimism of the 1970s, Mendes finds that the contribution of integration to the overall growth rate for these countries was, on average, higher during his second estimation period (1974–81) than during his first

Figure 2.1. **Integration Effects on the Growth Rates of the EC Countries**

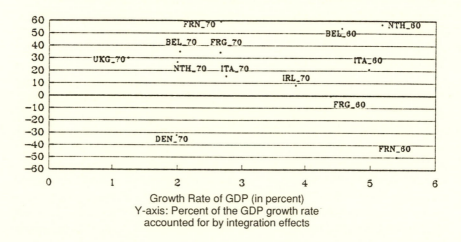

Growth Rate of GDP (in percent)
Y-axis: Percent of the GDP growth rate
accounted for by integration effects

(1961–72). Illustrating his findings, Figure 2.1 plots the actual growth rates for each member during these two periods against the *percentage* of that growth rate accounted for by integration effects. During the 1961 to 1972 period, all of the EC members had growth rates above 4 percent, but the contribution to growth due to integration effects varies considerably. For the BENELUX countries, the EC accounts for over 50 percent of their growth; but for the three larger economies, the EC-induced effects range from a small positive result for Italy to a significantly negative effect on French growth. When the EC's contribution to growth is weighted by the relative size of each economy, the overall effect for the region is very slightly negative.[5]

In Marques Mendes' second estimation period (1974–81) the effects are quite different. As Figure 2.1 clearly shows, the overall rates of growth are much lower in the 1970s, with only Ireland able to average above 3 percent per annum. During this postexpansion period, the contribution of the EC to overall growth is now positive for all members except Denmark. Also note the clustering of the original six members. All the growth rates for the original six are now between 2.0 and 2.75 percent, while integration effects account for between 15 percent (Italy) and 59 percent (France) of overall growth. Interestingly, the outliers in the second period are the new members. As Mendes notes, "the new benefited least in absolute terms relative to all the older members, although in relation to the actual growth rate the U.K. apparently experienced a larger benefit than the Netherlands and Italy" (1987, 98). However, when these integration effects are averaged across the member-states (weighting by the relative size of each economy), the results indicate that during the 1974 to 1981 period one-third of Europe's growth derived from EC-induced effects. In line with our own "revisionist" view of the EC, Mendes' results provide evidence that the Community was more important to the economic well-being of its members in the 1970s than in the 1960s. Appreciated or not during the turbulence of the 1970s, the processes which had been set in motion in Rome in 1957, and expanded in 1972, were becoming increasingly important aspects of each member's economy.

Even more important, perhaps, than this day-to-day, incremental growth of the EC has been the institutional development of the Community. Perhaps the functional and the neofunctional approach that has tended to dominate scholarly analysis of the EC has helped to obscure the steady progress on this front (Pinder 1985–86). Then, too, much of the progress on the institutional dimension is so familiar, and in part so long-standing, that it tends to be overlooked. Although the historical roots of the Community can be traced back to 1500 and beyond, for our purposes it can be concluded that institutionally the Community originated with the creation of the European Coal and Steel Community in 1951. In a manner described quite well by neofunctional theory, that Community spawned two new organizations, the European Economic Community, and the European Atomic Energy Community in 1957. In 1961, the heads of state of the six members formally committed themselves to work toward political union. In 1967, the High Authority of the ECSC and the Commissions of the EEC and Euratom were merged, so that all three Communities from that time on have had one Commission, one Council of Ministers, and one European Parliament. In 1973, Denmark, Ireland, and the United Kingdom joined the Community, followed by Greece in 1981, and by Spain and Portugal in 1986. Those well-known (even mundane) facts alone, observed by some future historian examining the broad sweep of events in the twentieth century, would be seen as indications of steady, even dramatic progress in the growth and importance of the EC's institutional strength. Our detached future observer might, in fact, form a more valid opinion of the evolution of the Community than the more informed, and therefore more jaded, analysts of today.

A more detailed look at the EC's judicial, legislative, and executive organs confirms that impression. The exception to the rule that the Community's institutions have steadily increased in strength and importance might be the European Court of Justice, but only because the Court has been quietly, but very effectively, "supranational" almost from the beginning (Axline 1968). It is *sui generis* among courts of "international law," recognizing individuals as legitimate parties, and overturning rulings of national supreme courts. As Lord Plumb asserts, "Community law is a particularly entrenched form of law. Once adopted, it cannot be amended or revoked by any national parliament, even following a general election. Community law overrides national law" (1989, 114). This is why the Court's ruling in the 1979 "Cassis de Dijon" case, during the time the Community was, and is still often, described as "stagnant," is now commonly recognized as a milestone in its development. In that case, the Court ruled that free access to the market of another member-state cannot be denied on the basis of "national norms"; specifically, it ruled that Germany could not limit the import of liqueur de Cassis from France because its alcohol content was too low to qualify as a liqueur and too high to qualify as wine. This decision reinforced a 1986 "insurance decision" that "established cross-border service delivery as legitimate under the Treaty of Rome for all services" (Bressand 1990, 50).

As Alberta Sbragia (see chapter 5 in this volume) has observed, the contribution of law to the integration process in the EC has been crucial, and it promises to be even more so in the future as the result of the decision in the Community to adopt a qualified majority vote in the 1992 program. Such a procedure should increase the impact of the Court's already substantial supranational powers. Sbragia concludes that even in comparison with the impact of the law and Supreme Court on the integration of the American states during the nineteenth century, the federalism of the Community as exemplified by its legal procedures is quite impressive. This conclusion is reminiscent of that to be found in the *Economist*: "Just as the Supreme Court settles disputes in the federal structure of the United States, so the Court of Justice settles those in the EEC club. Its judgments are final; there is no further appeal. . . . A great part of the court's authority comes from the fact that Community law prevails over national law where there is a conflict between the two. . . . EEC members have no choice but to respect the rulings of the court. . . . " (1989, 48).

The European Parliament's influence in the Community has grown steadily, perhaps especially during what is still universally referred to as the Community's stagnation of the 1970s. "The budget treaties of 1970 and 1975 . . . created what amounts to a bicameral budgetary system whereby . . . Council and Parliament jointly thrash out the Community budget" (Plumb 1989, 114). The second of these treaties was reinforced in 1975 with the introduction of a conciliation process by a Joint Declaration that established that if the Council wishes to diverge from the opinion of the Parliament, the matter should first be referred to a conciliation committee made up of members of the Council and the Parliament. "The Parliament does have an important power of co-legislation with the Council of Ministers in enacting the Community budget," according to John Pinder, "thanks to decisions taken in the 1970s" (1989, 312). And it is well known that in 1979 for the first time the Parliament took what is perhaps its most important step in the direction of real power when it was directly elected. "The direct election of a European Parliament in 1979 is striking," according to Sbragia, "to those who recall that the United States Senate was not directly elected until after the Seventeenth Amendment to the Constitution was ratified in 1913" (1990, 14). The Parliament has taken advantage of the increased legitimacy that results from its direct election. In 1980, as a result of the "isoglucose" ruling of the Court of Justice, the Parliament was given a de facto delaying power in the legislative process. (This may not, on the surface, sound so crucial, but the Council is often in quite a hurry.) The ruling struck down a piece of Community legislation on the grounds that the Council had adopted it before Parliament had given its opinion. Additionally, the Parliament played a key role in getting the Single European Act off the ground, and that Act itself has increased Parliament's powers, first through a *cooperative procedure*, which gives it colegislative power with the Council on legislation having to do with the completion of the internal market, and because of a new *assent procedure*, which requires Parliament's approval for the accession of new states, and for the adoption or revision of association agreements involving trade and economic cooperation agreements with third countries (Plumb 1989, 115).

The allegedly stagnant 1970s also were a time of significant development of the Executive organs and powers within the Community. In November 1970, "the foreign ministers of the Six for the first time emphasized the need for harmonization of voting in the United Nations" (Galtung 1973, 21). Also, in the early 1970s, "two intergovernmental organs were established alongside the Community: the European Council of Heads of State and Government; and the Committee for European Political Cooperation, in the sense of cooperation between the major governments in the field of foreign policy" (Pinder 1985–86, 47). The European Council has been meeting at least twice a year since 1975. In 1978 and 1979, the Community took a couple of important steps toward becoming more "nationlike" when it launched the European Monetary System, as well as the European Currency Unit (ECU). And in the 1980s, the Commission, along with the European Parliament, played a key role in the passage of the Single European Act, and the initiation of the 1992 Project. That Act itself has transformed the executive process within the Community by introducing qualified majority voting in the Council of Ministers.

So, especially in institutional terms, and most especially during the ten or fifteen years before the passing of the Single European Act, that is, during the era of "europessimism," and at a time when the Community was largely ignored, the EC nevertheless experienced dramatic growth (in membership), important developmental advances, and corresponding increases in its influence and importance. As Stanley Hoffmann, not noted for his optimism about the fate of the Community, has admitted recently, "Europe would not now appear so promising if, during the 'dark' years, steps had not been taken to preserve the Community from decay and to strengthen it in some important areas" (1989, 30).

By focusing on where the Community began and where it stands today, we have ignored many of the very serious problems that have threatened its development. Gaullism, with its adamant opposition to British entry, almost tore the EC apart in the 1960s. The collapse of the international monetary regime in 1971 shook the Community and delayed for several years the establishment of a European monetary system. OPEC's boycott in 1973 provoked a real crisis, and the Community, at least publicly, was not very helpful to the Dutch, who were singled out as a special target for OPEC's wrath. The economies of the member countries have, in large part, not yet recovered from the twin oil shocks and inflation of the 1970s, and the recession of the early 1980s that followed.

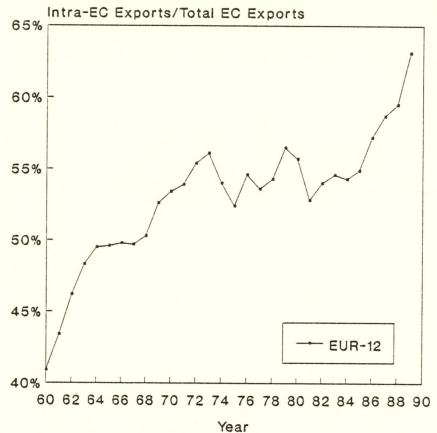

Source: Eurostat, *External Trade: Statistical Yearbook*, 1990.

These events during the 1970s provided a series of external shocks that continually disrupted the process of integration, and their effects are reflected in the
underlying economic developments. For instance, as a indicator of integration
we introduced earlier the level of intra-EC exports relative to total exports,
noting the sharp rise between 1960 and 1989. However, when annual observations on these data are presented as in Figure 2.2, the story becomes somewhat
more complicated. Simply reporting the end points as indicators that the level of
economic integration has increased in Europe over the last twenty-nine years
conceals the most striking element of Figure 2.2: the increases in intra-EC trade
have not been consistent from year to year, but rather are concentrated in two
periods. The 1960s, the formative years for the EC, exhibit tremendous growth in
the relative level of intra-EC trade, increasing from 37 to 53 percent. However,
from 1970 to 1985 the relative level of trade remained within a fairly narrow
band, ranging between 52.4 and 56.5 percent. It is not until after 1985 that this
indicator again moves upward with an almost 8 percentage point jump between

Figure 2.3. **Indices of Total Employment: EC-12, United States, and Japan**

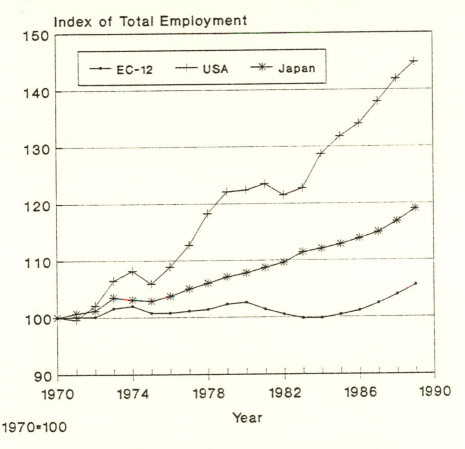

Index of Total Employment

1970=100

Source: Commission of EC, *European Economy*, 46 (December 1990), p. 222.

1985 and 1989. Examining only the first half of the figure, the pessimism of integration theorists in the mid-1970s becomes easier to understand. The dramatic increases in intra-EC trade in the 1960s are followed first by deceleration and then stagnation during the 1970s. When one combines this indicator of the underlying process of economic integration with the dramatic political events of the period, the pessimism of integration theorists in the mid-1970s seems more justified.

While the decade of the 1970s was arguably the most difficult one for the process of European integration, the European economies continue to be confronted with some very negative economic forces, particularly in terms of jobs and growth. On the continent, it is often noted that Europe has not created a job in twenty years. While this is an overstatement, the data confirm that it may not be far off the mark. Figure 2.3 presents indices of total employment for the EC and its two main economic competitors, the United States and Japan. From the early seventies until the late eighties, the picture looks uniformly bleak with the total level of European employment remaining within 2 percent of the level achieved in 1970. And while the economic expansion of the late 1980s led to some increases in employment, European job creation cannot compare with that of either the United States or Japan. Of course, the flip side of these data are the unemployment figures and here we find a seven-year period between 1976 and 1983 when the EC went from less than 5 percent unemployed to over 10 percent, which is roughly where it remained until 1989 when it fell to 8.9 percent.[6]

While growth in all the advanced industrial economies has slowed significantly since the 1960s, the decline for the Europeans, relative to their two main competitors, the Americans and Japanese, has been particularly distressing. In Table 2.1 average annual growth rates in real GDP for each of the decades, the sixties, seventies, and from 1981 to 1989, are presented for the twelve EC members and the United States and Japan.[7] While growth rates in Europe above 5 percent were not uncommon in the 1960s, the EC could sustain an average annual rate of only slightly over 2 percent in the 1980s. However, just as important as the actual rate of growth is how it compares *relative* to the United States and Japan. After growing more rapidly than the United States in the 1960s and 1970s, the EC could not keep pace in the 1980s. The average annual growth rate in the largest European economy, Germany, was over one-third lower than in the United States and less than half the Japanese rate.

So, while the unsettling shocks that plagued the Community in the 1970s have disappeared, all the news is not good, and Europe continues to face significant economic problems against which it has struggled, but without much success, for almost a decade. But even this cloud has its silver lining; economic stagnation was one of the main factors that motivated the Community to implement the provisions of the Single European Act.

And the revolutions in Eastern Europe and the dissolution of the Soviet Union will have an impact on the European Community that is extremely difficult to anticipate. Pressure for economic development funds from eastern Europe might well create serious antagonisms toward the Community within its poorer members, who might otherwise have received some of those funds themselves. Pressure from some eastern European countries (Poland, Hungary, Czechoslovakia) for membership in the EC and fear of the newly unified Germany could ultimately produce significant impediments to the continuation of the integrative process.

But not all the possibilities inherent in the current ferment and instability are bad ones. There is a popular argument that a unified Germany creates an even greater need for a strong European Community, that both Germany and its neighbors will be safer if they are united in such an organization. The leadership in the Federal Republic, so far at least, shows no real signs of being inclined toward neutrality, or exit from the Community. It is also possible that the emerging EC

Table 2.1

Average Annual Growth Rates of Real GDP (EC Members, USA, and Japan)

	BEL	DEN	FRG	GRC	SPN	FRN	IRL	ITA	LUX	NTH	POR	UKG	EUR12	USA	JAP
1961–70	5.0%	4.5%	4.5%	7.7%	7.4%	5.6%	4.3%	5.7%	3.6%	5.1%	6.5%	2.9%	4.8%	3.9%	10.5%
1971–80	3.3%	2.3%	2.7%	4.8%	3.5%	3.3%	4.8%	3.8%	2.7%	2.9%	4.8%	2.0%	3.0%	2.8%	4.7%
1981–89	1.7%	1.8%	1.9%	1.6%	2.8%	2.0%	2.9%	2.3%	3.4%	1.7%	2.6%	2.7%	2.2%	3.1%	4.1%

Source: Commission of the EC, *European Economy,* 46 (November 1990), p. 230.

will be seen as a kind of anchor, a safe port in a storm of political change, and the heart of a new, stable Europe. But ultimately, even in the course of this exercise in optimism, we must admit that so much astounding political change occurred in Europe in the late 1980s that it is impossible to foresee even in broad outlines what additional dramatic changes may occur beyond 1992, and what their impact on the EC will be.

The Pessimism in Academic Analysis of
the European Community

To examine the pessimism that has been dominant in academic analyses of the European Community, it is useful to return to the mid-1950s when the mood was much different. As the titles of the two works that were to influence a generation of scholars indicate, the mood was one of optimism. In their 1957 book, Karl Deutsch and his colleagues wrote about the development of political community in the North Atlantic area, while Ernst Haas, in a book published one year later, focused on the uniting of Europe (1958a). While both works shared an optimistic tone, they brought very different perspectives to their subjects, provided very different explanations of the dynamics of regional integration, and laid the groundwork for the two main "schools" that have dominated the recent study of integration: transactionalism (Deutsch) and neofunctionalism (Haas).[8]

Just as Figure 2.2 shows a sharp increase in the level of economic integration within the EC during the 1960s, there was also a sharp increase in research on international integration. The neofunctionalist argument seemed to be holding for the European experience, and integration schemes in other parts of the world were springing up. Using citations to identify networks of IR scholars, Russett examined the published work of 74 prominent researchers over a three-year period, 1966–68. Factor analyzing these citations, Russett produced twelve clusters, or "schools," within international relations with two of the three largest dealing with international integration. The single largest group was headed by Deutsch and composed mainly of his students and colleagues at Yale. The third largest grouping was led by Ernst Haas. While such studies are subjective enough to invite various levels of criticism, they do illustrate our basic point: by the mid-1960s the study of international integration had become a key focus of interest within the field.

Despite the growth of the field, all was not well. By the late 1960s it was becoming increasingly clear that the predictions of the neofunctionalist model were not coming to pass. The model could not explain de Gaulle and his apparent ability to influence, and even halt, the course of integration. Illustrating both the importance of the field and the controversy within it, the Autumn 1970 issue of *International Organization* was wholly devoted to regional integration.[9] Appropriately, Haas wrote the introduction to the volume, but now the optimism reflected in the title of his 1958 book was beginning to give way to the "joy and anguish" of theorizing about regional integration. Of the six articles focusing on the concept of integration, two presented "revised" models/theories of regional integration (Nye 1970; Schmitter 1970).[10] Attempting to explain the anomalous developments that the original neofunctionalist formulations could not, these models were, by necessity, much more complex and process-oriented. Since the core dynamic of neofunctionalism, spillover, was not as automatic as originally envisioned, new concepts such as spill-back, spill-around, and encapsulation were introduced in this volume (Schmitter 1970, 844–46). In these models, one also sees for the first time some cross-fertilization and "integration" between the neofunctionalist approach of Haas and the transactionalism of Deutsch.

It is interesting to view the development of integration theory, up to this point, as a research program or paradigm.[11] Focusing only on neofunctionalism, Haas' 1958 book and 1961 *International Organization* article form the originating exemplars of the research program and define its core assumptions. This was followed by a burst of activity employing Haas' neofunctionalist model to examine the process of integration both within Europe as well as outside it. As a result of these applications, it soon became clear that many of the developments in the 1960s could not be explained by the original formulation of neofunctionalism. Following the predicted evolution of a Lakatosian research program, more complex, "revised" models began to appear in the late 1960s and early 1970s. These models did not attack the core assumptions of neofunctionalism, but rather made incremental adjustments in order to explain previously anomalous developments. Spillover remained the core dynamic of the approach, but was now augmented by explanations of why it might not always be as automatic as originally envisioned. Whether these changes represented progressive or degenerative shifts in the research program is debatable. However, as we will see shortly, the founder of neofunctionalism had written its eulogy by 1975.

We identify three factors as "contributing" to the demise of integration theory. First, though de Gaulle had disappeared from the scene, shocks from the international environment and the introduction of three new members in the early seventies seemed to have, at best, stalled the integrative process in Europe. And with integration schemes in other parts of the world disintegrating at alarming rates, some began to wonder whether they had been attempting to explain "timebound, nonrecurrent events" (Puchala 1988, 199). Second, the neofunctionalist theories that dominated the field had a very difficult time, despite the revisions mentioned, in adequately explaining either this stalling or reversal of the process. Finally, shocks such as the collapse of the Bretton Woods regime and the oil embargo also underscored the growing international interdependence of Europe. Focusing on the region may have been appropriate in the fifties and sixties as Europe attempted to rebuild after the war, but in the seventies the regional context had begun to appear strangely parochial, and academic analysts began to emphasize global interdependence.

If one were to date the end of integration theory as a distinct research pro-

Figure 2.4. *International Organization* and the Study of Integration

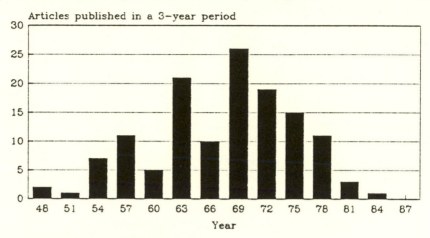

The label on the x-axis represents the
midpoint of a 3-year period, i.e.,
48 represents the years 1947–1949.

gram, 1975 would probably be the best choice. In that year there appeared two
influential essays with very similar views on the future of this approach. Both
Haas' *Obsolescence of Regional Integration Theory* and Keohane and Nye's
review article, "International Interdependence and Integration," argued that integration theory should be subsumed under the growing field of international
interdependence.[12] Keohane and Nye actually redefined integration in terms of a
condition rather than a process, with the result that it became practically synony-
mous with interdependence.[13] From the perspective of a Lakatosian research
program, this development is exactly what one would expect. Due to a "hard
core" of nonfalsifiable assumptions, it is impossible to "disprove" and thereby
reject a research program. However, one can reject a research program when
there exists a "rival research program which explains the previous success of its
rival [the original one] and supersedes it by a further display of heuristic power"
(Lakatos 1970, 155). And this is what we find in the study of interdependence, a
rival research program, which at least the dominant figures in the field felt
superseded integration theory.

To provide an illustration of the rise and fall of integration theory, we have
compiled a list of all articles published in *International Organization* that deal
broadly with regional integration. More than any other, this journal has been the
main outlet for North American and, to a lesser extent, European scholars focusing on integration studies.[14] Figure 2.4 presents a histogram of the number of
"integration" articles published in *International Organization*. Its forty-two-year

history (1947 through the end of 1988) has been divided into three-year intervals with the total number of articles focusing on regional integration within each period represented in the figure. Earlier we dated the beginning of the recent study of regional integration with the publication of works by Deutsch et al. and Haas in 1957 and 1958, respectively. However, it is clear from these journal articles that even in the early 1950s analysts were beginning to focus on integrationist stirrings in Europe. During the field's formative period there appeared two major articles by Ernst Haas in *International Organization*. In 1958 he published "The Challenge of Regionalism," which was followed in 1961 by "International Integration: The European and the Universal Process." The large spike for the 1962 to 1964 period may overrepresent work on integration because fifteen of the twenty-one articles are drawn from a single issue focused on the North Atlantic Community (vol. 17, Summer 1963). Basing one's judgment strictly on quantity, work on regional integration reached its peak between 1968 and 1970. This period culminated in the publication, in Autumn 1970, of the special issue on regional integration, edited by Lindberg and Scheingold. With both Haas' "joy and anguish" article and "revised" theories by prominent figures in the field, this issue contains some of the most imaginative and "integrative" models ever published, and yet in a way it marked the beginning of the end for regional integration theory. The declining number of articles that appeared in the early seventies also contained a significant number critical of integration theory, particularly neofunctionalism. Just as his articles in 1958 and 1961 served as stimuli to the development of a new research program, Haas' "turbulent fields" article, which appeared in 1976, brings the curtain down on regional integration theory. Though the 1977 to 1979 period still contains a significant number of articles on integration, most are case studies with a large portion of those focusing on integration schemes outside of Europe. However, it is in the 1980s when the disappearance of integration as a focus of study within international relations becomes most evident. Of the 258 articles published between 1980 and 1988, only four could be said to focus on integration, and in the last three-year period (1986–88) integration-oriented articles disappeared completely.[15]

The use of *International Organization* as an instrument for measuring the rise and fall of integration studies is certainly not perfect nor do we mean to suggest that this field of study disappeared completely in the late 1970s and early 1980s. It did continue, mainly in Europe, but the focus was most often on microlevel case studies rather than the theory-building orientation that was a large part of earlier work.[16] In 1983, Juliet Lodge concludes a review of integration theories with the following assessment: "[w]hile theorizing about European integration has become stultified, empirical studies of the processes of unification and collective decision-making continue, and regional integration generally has become reabsorbed (if temporarily) into the various strands of international relations theories" (1983, 16). Two notable exceptions to this pattern are to be found in books by Paul Taylor (1983) and Donald Puchala (1984) where they examine and reinterpret some of the earlier theoretical approaches in light of the events of the 1970s.[17]

The adoption of the Single European Act by the Council in December 1985 and the accession of Spain and Portugal at the beginning of 1986 stimulated a new perception of the process of integration—from europessimism to europhoria. And not surprisingly, this new optimism has led to a second wave of integration studies focused on the causes and consequences of these most recent changes in the EC. The focus, however, continues to remain largely on case studies and institutional developments with little, if any, attention paid to the placement of one's analysis within a broader theoretical framework.[18] So, despite the rush of new research that has appeared in the late 1980s, we stand by our basic assessment that the *research program* focused on international integration ground to a halt in the early 1970s. Work after that time, including the recent surge of interest, has been much more descriptive and policy-oriented than theoretical. It has been primarily concerned with "what is happening" rather than "why."

In concluding this section let us return to the assessments for progress made by two of the originators of this field: Karl Deutsch and Ernst Haas. In a 1979 preface to a reprinting of a 1962 article on European integration, Deutsch's tone is considerably less optimistic than in the original essay. While he still believed the process of integration was continuing, it was moving on a "time scale of decades rather than of years" (Deutsch 1979, 235). By the mid-1970s, almost twenty years after the publication of his book entitled *The Uniting of Europe*, Haas is also more pessimistic, believing it unlikely that there will be "significant international political unification during the remainder of our century."[19]

The Anomalous Disparity between "Reality" and Academic Analysis of the European Community

Why have analyses of the European Community, except for the very early years, been so uniformly negative and pessimistic, even though the Community itself has, despite some obvious problems, made such impressive overall progress economically, politically, and institutionally since 1957? One of the few works that was "optimistic" about the future of the Community to appear in the 1970s was Johan Galtung's *European Community: A Superpower in the Making* (1973).[20] In predicting a successful future for the Community, Galtung was aware that most other analyses at the time were focusing on the weaknesses of the Community. "What has been well publicized are the failures to come to some agreements," he noted, "rather than the smooth day-to-day workings of the machinery" (1973, 11). In his view, this was occurring because "journalism focuses on drama rather than on permanence" (1973, 11). Perhaps academic analysts, reliant to a large extent on journalistic sources for information on the day-to-day workings of the Community, fall prey to the journalistic tendency to regard good news as no news, and to emphasize crises, conflict, and problems.

Perhaps, also, predictions of doom are safer for academic reputations than optimistic forecasts. Those who foresee negative developments can lay an implicit claim to a superior ability to perceive accurately a complicated situation, while those who foretell "good times" give an impression of being naive, and unable to discern the whole picture, of being unable to keep their preferences from affecting unduly their predictions. According to John Kenneth Galbraith, at least, "it requires neither courage nor prescience to predict disaster. Courage is required of the man who, when things are good, says so. Historians rejoice in crucifying the false prophet of the millennium. They never dwell on the mistake of the man who wrongly predicted Armageddon" (1972, 6). Norman Angell, who predicted the end of international war in 1910, in *The Great Illusion*, will always be remembered as a notorious example of foolish, naive optimism. How many post–World War II scholars and academics who predicted that a nuclear war was a virtual certainty in the near future are equally notorious? A whole raft of scholars who predicted permanent energy shortages in the 1970s continued to make doomsday predictions in the 1980s, their reputations seemingly undamaged. Pessimism is just safer, for some reason, and perhaps this accounts to some extent for the largely pessimistic assessment of the European Community in the years since it was created.

Another reason may have to do with a serious underestimate of the significance of a certain transformation of western Europe that began after the Second World War. With the exception of a few years after the First World War, all the major powers of western Europe (i.e., at that time, the United Kingdom, Germany, France, and Italy) became "democratic" for the first time. With transitions in that direction in Greece in 1975, Portugal in 1976, and Spain in 1978, western Europe has become entirely democratic for the first time in history (Doyle 1986, 1164).

This is significant first as exemplary of, and arguably an important contribution to, a trend of possible worldwide significance. The revolutions in eastern Europe in 1989 are only the most spectacular examples of this trend. As Karen Remmer has noted recently, "since 1979, the politics of Latin America have been transformed by the largest and deepest wave of democratization in the region's history" (1990, 315). The democratization process that has had such relatively dramatic impacts in eastern Europe and Latin America has by now left visible traces in virtually every part of the world. The process was brought to a halt in Tiananmen Square in June of 1989, but elsewhere in Asia the trend has survived in Taiwan, South Korea, and the Philippines, as well as in Nepal, Mongolia, and Bangladesh. In the Middle East, Turkey and Pakistan have made recent moves in the direction of democracy, King Hussein has allowed multiparty elections to a parliament in Jordan, North and South Yemen have united into a new country based ostensibly, at least, on pluralistic principles, and Algeria has undergone reforms reminiscent of those in eastern Europe. The Persian Gulf War might inspire a powerful reaction by antiliberal, Islamic fundamentalist elements throughout the Middle East, destabilizing many governments there. But, according to Youssef Ibrahim (1991, 3) in the *New York Times*, "ever since Kuwait was invaded, the single theme on which Arab writers and commentators in the Arab media have almost unanimously agreed on has been the need for democracy." Samir al-Kalil (1990, 54) as Iraqi expatriate, also writing in the *New York Times*, has expressed a similar opinion: "The restoration of Kuwaiti sovereignty just might become the thin end of a wedge into the question of Arab democracy." Even sub-Saharan Africa, the Ivory Coast, Benin, Gabon, Zambia, Zaire, Tanzania, Kenya, as well as South Africa, show signs of being caught up in a global trend toward democracy (Beyer 1990; Yalowitz 1990).[21]

That trend in western Europe, now complete, is also significant because of its implications for relations among western European states. As demonstrated most recently, thoroughly and convincingly by Zeev Maoz and Nasrin Abdolali, "democracies . . . never fight one another in war" (1989, 3). As Jack Levy points out, "This absence of war between democracies comes as close as anything we have to an empirical law in international relations" (1988, 662). Until 1945, Europe was the site of the most frequent and bloodiest international wars in the world. Since then there have been no wars in western Europe. One might be inclined to argue that this peace is the result of the high level of wealth in that subcontinent, until one remembers that western European states have been among the richest in the world for hundreds of years, and they fought continually. The western European states also trade a lot with each other, creating interdependence that might serve as the basis for peaceful relationships. But those states have always traded heavily with each other, in between their many wars. One could also argue that the opposition of the common enemy, the Communist bloc in the East, preserved the peace in the West. But having had such a common enemy in the capitalist states did not stop the Soviets from clashing with Hungary, or Czechoslovakia, or the People's Republic of China, nor did it stop Vietnam from invading Cambodia, nor the war between China and Vietnam (Russett and Starr 1985, 416–37). Perhaps it is American hegemony that has kept the peace in western Europe since 1945, but why, then, has that hegemony not prevented the clash between Turkey and Greece over Cyprus, nor the war between Great Britain and Argentina over the Falklands, nor the war between El Salvador and Honduras in 1969? Only the explanation of peace in western Europe that focuses on the increasingly democratic nature of the region, and on the historic absence of warfare between democratic states, conforms to a clear pattern based on observations of other times and/or different places. This, we would argue, is indicative of the potential importance of the transition to democracy in western Europe for its international politics.

Maoz and Abdolali, in addition to providing evidence regarding the absence of war among democracies, also find that democracies "rarely clash with one another. . . . They are . . . less likely to engage in lower-level conflicts with one another. . . . Regardless of the level of hostility of a dispute, the likelihood of observing a democratic-democratic dyad is significantly smaller than chance alone" (1989, 3, 21). This is further evidence of the potential impact of the transition to democracy, now complete, on relations among western European states. To be more specific, democratic regimes avoid conflict, and have a correspondingly greater potential for cooperation among themselves. There is very little discussion, if any, of this factor in the theoretical literature on integration, which is almost certainly indicative of a lack of appreciation of its possible significance. This lack of appreciation may well be another factor accounting for a palpable lack of enthusiasm about the future of international integration in western Europe in almost all that literature.

But perhaps the most important reason that neofunctionalists in particular, and all other theorists in general, have underestimated the chances for success of the European Community, is a corresponding underestimate of the importance of what one of us has called the "hang together or hang separately" factor (Ray 1979, 196).[22] That is, a divided Europe will not count for much in the emerging global order, with an ascendant Japan and a more rapidly growing United States. Only together can the Europeans play a role on the world's political stage to which history has accustomed them.

Any review of integration theories will notice the relatively minor role accorded to external forces in the process of integration. In a review of Deutsch's model, Dougherty and Pfaltzgraff list nine necessary conditions for the creation of an amalgamated security community (1990, 436). What is striking is that all the conditions listed are internal to the community; no mention is made of external stimuli. As one of the major contributors to the field has noted: "the original neofunctional formulation paid insufficient attention to the role of external factors in integration processes" (Nye 1971, 73).[23] In concluding their 1981 review of integration theories, Dougherty and Pfaltzgraff note that what is needed are models "that give greater importance to the role of coercion and the impact of the international environment" (1990, 461).

Even when the impact of external forces was discussed it was usually characterized as negative, inhibiting the integrative process.[24] The perception of external forces as negative would certainly seem to be natural given the historical record of the 1960s and 1970s. For example, previous to the Single European Act of 1985, the most important proposal for further integration, a 1970 plan for European monetary union, was derailed almost immediately, and in large part, by external forces such as the collapse of a fixed-rate monetary regime and the oil embargo and price rise (Pinder 1985–86, 47). Today, however, external stimuli appear to be playing a very different role in the process of integration. In explaining the new push toward further integration, two factors, both external, seem to be most often mentioned. The first is the success of the American economy in the 1980s, specifically its ability to create jobs and control inflation. The second external stimulus is the economic threat posed by the Japanese economy. These two factors combine to create a fear in Europe that it is being left behind.[25] Unlike the 1970s when external threats, such as the oil embargo, led to national bickering and retreats from further integration, there is today a broad consensus that neither retreat nor the status quo will solve their problems. Only pressing on with the process of integration will allow Europe to maintain its position in the global political-economic order.

There are lots of signs that important Europeans understand this. Former British Prime Minister Edward Heath has asserted that "we in Europe will . . . have to face the fact that we have only got a future if we move rapidly, not only towards the economic unity I have been discussing but also towards political and military unity" (Heath 1988, 205). In an address to the European Parliament in 1984, President Mitterrand pointed out Europe's weakness in relation to the superpowers, the need for a common defense under the pressure of technological innovation by the Japanese and the Americans, and concluded that "if they did not combine their resources, the EC member-states would allow others to decide their destiny, whereas united they could 'have the necessary effect on the present and future of mankind' " (Pinder 1985–86, 49). Another European analyst has argued that "we all have at least two strong reasons for wanting further, faster European integration, particularly in economic and security policy. These are the fear that the Americans will do less (militarily) and that the Japanese will do more (economically)" (Ash 1989, 18). While the Gulf War revealed that the members of the Community are a long way from being able to formulate a common foreign or military policy, the reaction to their disarray during that war was to put the need for common policies in these areas more prominently on the agenda than it had been before the crisis. In short, together, the Europeans have the potential even to become (as Samuel Huntington suggests in the quote at the beginning of this paper) the preeminent political actor in the global system. Separately, they appear increasingly anachronistic politically, and hounded by persistent economic stagnation.

Conclusion

It is ironic that while the study of international integration was developing in the late 1960s into one of the biggest and most vital "schools" within the field of international relations, the EC was about to enter into a tumultuous, troubled decade. Just as some very complicated and "integrative" models began to appear in the early 1970s, their object of study, the process of integration, seemed to stall. While these events were interpreted by some at the time as signaling the demise of regional integration schemes, there was evidence, even during this time of turbulence, that the process of integration was continuing. In the 1970s, the Community negotiated new treaties that increased the budgetary power of the Parliament, began to coordinate voting in the UN, created the European Council, added three new members, accepted the Cassis de Dijon ruling of the Court of Justice, created the European Monetary System and the European Currency Unit, and moved to the direct election of the European Parliament. Scholarly analysis should be sensitive to current events, of course. However, it should not be so sensitive to the way the wind is blowing that it loses its sense of direction, succumbing to one fad after another.

It also should be wary of overreacting to recent dramatic events in such a way as to lose sight of important continuities, such as (we would argue) the steady development of the European Community over the last three decades. Sandholtz and Zysman, for example, insist in their otherwise useful, recent analysis that the 1992 "initiative is a disjunction, a dramatic new start, rather than the fulfillment of the original effort to construct Europe" (1989, 95). Similarly (but somewhat more accurately), Hoffmann asserts that "this new enterprise [the 1992 project] builds on the institutions and accomplishments of the earlier one, but it is not a mere continuation" (1989, 31). Surely these are arbitrary declarations, which serve to obscure the Community's continuing progress as well as to hide anomalies and miscalculations that virtually all analysts of integration in Europe need to address. "Realists" such as Hoffmann seemed vindicated by the problems the Community faced in the 1970s, but they were surprised by the turn of events in the 1980s. Were they insensitive for some reason to the "realistic" possibility that outside competition would create conditions in which progress toward integration would seem congruent with calculations based on realpolitik assumptions? Neofunctionalists lost heart in the 1970s, so they, too, have been caught by surprise by the "rebirth" of the EC. Perhaps they should have realized just how tough the economic challenges posed by the oil shocks of the 1970s were, and so been more impressed by the fact that the Community not only survived, but engaged in important institutional innovations and developments during that "dark" decade. In any case, we are quite sure that it is a mistake to pretend, or contend theoretically that history started over, in effect, for the Community in 1985 because it actually "died" in the 1970s. Sandholtz and Zysman, strong proponents of this version of the European Community "reborn," argue at one point that "in the 1950s, the European project became a matter of party and group politics. In the 1980s, the EC institutions were not the object of the debate; they were a political actor" (1989, 107). The point they are trying to make here is how different the eighties were from the fifties, but this difference between the 1950s and the 1980s was not, we would argue, so much a result of the EC starting over, or being "reborn," but of the important, continuing institutional development that occurred within the organization throughout its history, particularly in the 1970s.

We also argue that it is time to refocus attention on both the EC and integration theory. Not only may the EC become a very important actor in the international system, "Europe," in its most recent incarnation as the EC, may once again inspire widespread emulation around the globe (as it apparently did in the 1960s). All the world has already imitated the European invention of the nation-state. The EC may provide an important impetus for the worldwide trend toward democracy. Ultimately, we may see the "growing 'Common Marketization' of international relations" (Fukuyama 1989, 18). Admittedly, Third World integration schemes have experienced one failure after another to this point. But a resurgence of the EC, along with the movement toward democracy in the Third World, may yet revive such organizations among developing countries. The same might be said of eastern Europe. It is even faintly possible that after all the unrest evoked by perestroika, glasnost, and democratization and finally the dissolution of the Soviet Union, the republics of the former Soviet Union might embark on a process of reintegration. In short, economic and political integration theory may become a useful, even necessary tool for understanding much of what transpires in the global political system in the coming decades. And the process in its most advanced form will be found in the European Community.

Notes

1. As we embark on this project, we will keep in mind the warning of David Fischer to the effect that "there are two ways of manifesting intellectual subservience . . . : slavish imitation and obsessive refutation. . . . As revisionism grows more respectable, and even a prerequisite to a professional career, an increasing number . . . are delivered into the latter form of bondage" (1970, 28).

2. Data drawn from Commission of the European Communities, *European Economy* (1990, 226). Comparisons of GDP between the United States and the EC vary widely, depending on whether GDP is measured, in constant or nominal terms, as well as the form of the exchange rate used. OECD publications provide evidence that the European GDP is 7% larger than that of the United States, while the EC source noted above measures the European economy at only 85% of the American economy when a purchasing power standard, rather than the nominal exchange rate, is used. However, the basic point is that the present size of the European economy is roughly equivalent to that of the largest in the world.

3. Admittedly, indicators based on trade flows are not beyond criticism. W. E. Fisher (1969), for example, argued for a focus on political decisions and institutions rather than transactional data, a point of view with which we have some sympathy and to which we will turn shortly. Furthermore, we are aware that it is possible to modify the raw data on trade so that it reflects deviations from a null model, to establish "whether the trade between two countries [is] more or less than the amount that would be expected knowing only the share of exports and imports received by each country . . ." (Alker and Puchala 1968, 291), and that when Alker and Puchala applied this kind of measure to trade data for Europe from 1928 to 1963, they concluded that "there has been as much economic *dis*integration in Europe since 1951 as there has been integration" (1968, 315). Finally, we are aware that, as Barry Hughes (1971) has demonstrated, the choice of operational measure, even among indicators based on trade data, can make a substantial difference in the conclusions one makes about trends in integration. However, even with all those caveats, we believe that it is still useful at this preliminary stage of our revisionist view of the Community to analyze the level of intragroup trade relative to total trade.

4. "Integration effects" include: terms of trade changes, change in the propensity to import, change in exports, net EC budget payments, and labor remittances. For a complete list of Mendes' integration effects, see pp. 96–100.

5. Mendes believes that his model overestimates the negative effect for France in this early period. He suspects that a more reasonable estimate would be –25% rather than

–50% in Figure 2.1. With this change, the overall regional effect on growth goes from –2% to +5%; still very marginal, but a net positive result for "integration effects."

6. Data from *European Economy* (1990, 223). The range of unemployment across the members states varies considerably. For 1989, it ran from lows of under 2% for Luxembourg and 5.5% for Germany, through the UK (7%) and France (9.4%), to a high of 17% for Ireland and Spain. This is compared with unemployment rates of 5.3% and 2.3% for the United States and Japan, respectively.

7. All of these data are from GDP series in national currencies and so the distorting effects of exchange rates, mentioned earlier, do not affect these data.

8. Transactionalism is a term used by Donald Puchala (1988, 199) in his review of these two approaches.

9. Volume 24. This issue was later published as an edited volume, see Lindberg and Scheingold, 1971.

10. The monograph-length article by Lindberg (1970) in the same issue could actually be considered a third "revised" model. The model Nye presented in this issue became the core of his 1971 book, *Peace in Parts.*

11. In this essay we will use the term "research program," relying on the work of Imre Lakatos (1970) for its definition. One could just as well examine this tradition of research in terms of a Kuhnian research paradigm (see Kuhn 1970).

12. A version of Haas' "Obsolescence" monograph appeared in Haas (1976).

13. Haas disagrees with Keohane and Nye on this point. He believes that any definition of integration must retain its goal-oriented, teleological component. See Haas (1975, 86).

14. While *International Organization* may somewhat overrepresent the dominance of the neofunctional approach, other approaches are found in the journal. In 1963 (vol. 17, no. 3) an entire issue was devoted to an examination of political community in the North Atlantic area. Work by scholars who fall within Deutsch's transactionalist approach appear throughout the 1960s and 1970s, as well as others from less well known perspectives. See, for instance, Dahlberg (1970) or Cocks (1980).

15. There were also no integration-related articles published in 1989 or 1990, and even in the first two issues of the 1991 volume, we find only one such article (see Moravcsik 1991).

16. Two studies published in 1977 were exemplary of this trend: Wallace, Wallace, Webb (1977); and Sasse et al. (1977). The essays in the Wallace, Wallace, and Webb volume examine policy making in ten issue-areas with the intention of evaluating earlier theories against the evidence drawn from these case studies. In the second volume, Sasse and his collaborators examine decision making within the institutions of the EC.

17. Two other books, somewhat outside the mainstream of the field, which critiqued and reassessed previous theories were Holland (1980) and George (1985).

18. See, for example, Lodge (1989); Nugent (1989); Wallace (1990); Harrop (1989); and Pryce (1987).

19. Puchala, "The Integration Theorists," p. 206.

20. Actually, Galtung predicted that "a new superpower is emerging . . . the European Community is an effort to recreate a Eurocentric world, a world with its center in Europe, [and] a unicentric Europe, a Europe with its center in the West," and found the prospect depressing. Galtung has not changed his view. In *Europe in the Making* he declares that "the thesis here is that superpower status for the European Community is in the cards and has been for a long time" (1989, 22).

21. Even in the academic literature, "[t]he process of redemocratizing African politics is . . . becoming the hegemonic issue in African studies" (Fatton 1990, 455).

22. "Probably the most important factors holding Europe together are political, eco-

nomic, and military pressures from the outside world. In short, if Europeans do not hang together, they will hang separately" (Ray 1979, 196).

23. Nye (1971) addresses this weakness by including the involvement of external actors as one of eight process mechanisms in his revised neofunctionalist model.

24. Nye (1971) is again a notable exception. As one of the perceptual conditions determining integrative potential, Nye writes that "[t]he way that regional decisionmakers perceive the nature of their external situation and the manner in which they should respond to it is an important condition determining agreement on further integration."

25. This same basic argument is to be found in Sandholtz and Zysman (1989). They point to the same two changes that we have just mentioned and conclude that "Japan experienced economic growth; the United States created jobs. Europe seemed to be doing neither and feared being left behind by the U.S.-Japanese competition in high technology" (1989, 110).

References

Alker, Hayward Jr., and Donald Puchala. 1968. "Trends in Economic Partnership: The North Atlantic Area, 1928–1963." In J. David Singer, ed., *Quantitative International Politics: Insights and Evidence*. New York: The Free Press.

al-Khalil, Samir. 1990. "In the Mideast, Does Democracy Have a Chance?" *New York Times Magazine*, 14 October.

Ash, Timothy Garton. 1989. "A Two-Speed Europe: Britain vs. the Continent." *World Press Review*, January: 16–18.

Axline, W. Andrew. 1968. *European Community Law and Organizational Development*. Dobbs Ferry, NY: Oceana.

Beyer, Lisa. 1990. "Continental Shift." *Time*, 21 May, pp. 34–36.

Bressand, Albert. 1990. "Beyond Interdependence: 1992 as a Global Challenge." *International Affairs*, 66:47–65.

Cocks, Peter. 1980. "Toward a Marxist Theory of European Integration." *International Organization*, 34:1–40.

Commission of the European Communities (CEC). 1990. *European Economy* no. 46.

Commission of the European Communities (CEC). 1991. "A Community of Twelve." *European File*.

Dahlberg, Kenneth A. 1970. "Regional Integration: The Neo-Functional versus a Configurative Approach." *International Organization*, 24:122–28.

Deutsch, Karl W. 1979. *Tides Among Nations*. New York: The Free Press.

Deutsch, Karl W. et al. 1957. *Political Community in the North Atlantic Area: International Organization in the Light of Historical Experience*. Princeton, NJ: Princeton University Press.

Dougherty, James F., and Robert L. Pfaltzgraff, Jr., 1990. *Contending Theories of International Relations*. 3d ed. New York: Harper and Row.

Doyle, Michael. 1986. "Liberalism and World Politics." *American Political Science Review*, 80:1151–69.

Economist. 1989. "EEC Institutions: European Court of Justice: Where the Buck Stops," 6 May.

Fatton, Robert Jr. 1990. "Liberal Democracy in Africa." *Political Science Quarterly*, 105:455–73.

Fischer, David. 1970. *Historian's Fallacies*. New York: Harper and Row.

Fisher, W. E. 1969. "An Analysis of the Deutsch Socio-Causal Paradigm of Political Integration." *International Organization*, 23:254–90.

Fukuyama, Francis. 1989. "The End of History?" *National Interest*, 16:3–18.

Galbraith, John Kenneth. 1972. *The Great Crash of 1929*. Boston: Houghton Mifflin.

Galtung, Johan. 1973. *The European Community: A Superpower in the Making.* Oslo: Universitetsforlag.

Galtung, Johan. 1989. *Europe in the Making.* New York: Crane Russak.

George, Stephen. 1985. *Politics and Policy in the European Community.* Oxford: Clarendon Press.

Haas, Ernst B. 1958a. *The Uniting of Europe: Political, Social and Economic Forces, 1950–1957.* Stanford, CA: Stanford University Press.

Haas, Ernst B. 1958b. "The Challenge of Regionalism." *International Organization,* 12:440–58.

Haas, Ernst B. 1961. "International Integration: The European and the Universal Process." *International Organization,* 15:366–92.

Haas, Ernst B. 1970. "The Study of Regional Integration: Reflections on the Joy and Anguish of Pretheorizing." *International Organization,* 24:607–46.

Haas, Ernst B. 1975. *The Obsolescence of Regional Integration Theory.* Berkeley: University of California, Institute of International Studies.

Haas, Ernst B. 1976. "Turbulent Fields and the Theory of Regional Integration." *International Organization,* 30:173–212.

Harrop, Jeffrey. 1989. *The Political Economy of Integration in the European Community.* Aldershot, UK: Edward Elgar.

Heath, Edward. 1988. "European Unity Over the Next Ten Years: From Community to Union." *International Affairs,* 64:199–207.

Hexter, J. H. 1979. *Reappraisals in History.* 2d ed. Chicago: University of Chicago Press.

Hoffmann, Stanley. 1989. "The European Community and 1992." *Foreign Affairs,* 68:27–47.

Holland, Stuart 1980. *Uncommon Market.* New York: St. Martin's Press.

Hughes, Barry. 1971. "Transaction Analysis: The Impact of Operationalization." *International Organization,* 25:132–45.

Huntington, Samuel P. 1988–89. "The U.S.—Decline or Renewal?" *Foreign Affairs,* 67:76–96.

Ibrahim, Youssef M. 1991. "The Rulers Will Have to Face the Music." *New York Times,* 24 February.

Keohane, Robert O., and Joseph S. Nye, Jr. 1975. "International Interdependence and Integration." In Fred I. Greenstein and Nelson Polsby, eds., *Handbook of Political Science,* vol. 8. Reading, MA: Addison-Wesley.

Kuhn, Thomas S. 1970. *The Structure of Scientific Revolutions.* 2d ed., enlarged. Chicago: University of Chicago Press.

Lakatos, I. 1970. "Falsification and the Methodology of Scientific Research Programmes." In I. Lakatos and A. Musgrave, eds., *Criticism and the Growth of Knowledge.* Cambridge: Cambridge University Press.

Laurent, Pierre-Henri. 1989. "The European Community: Twelve Becoming One." In Suzanne P. Ogden, ed., *World Politics 89/90.* Guilford, CT: Dushkin.

Levy, Jack. 1988. "Domestic Politics and War." *Journal of Interdisciplinary History,* 18:653–73.

Lindberg, Leon N. 1970. "Political Integration as a Multidimensional Phenomenon Requiring Multivariate Measurement." *International Organization* 24:649–732.

Lindberg, Leon N., and Stuart A. Scheingold, eds. 1971. *Regional Integration: Theory and Research.* Cambridge, MA: Harvard University Press.

Lodge, Juliet, ed. 1983. *The European Community: Bibliographical Excursions.* London: Frances Pinter.

Lodge, Juliet, ed. 1989. *The European Community and the Challenge of the Future.* New York: St. Martin's Press.

Maoz, Zeev, and Nasrin Abdolali. 1989. "Regime Types and International Conflict, 1816–1976." *Journal of Conflict Resolution*, 33:3–35.

Marques Mendes, A. J. 1987. *Economic Integration and Growth in Europe*. London: Croom Helm.

Moravcsik, Andrew. 1991. "Negotiating the Single European Act: National Interests and Conventional Statecraft in the European Community." *International Organization*, 45:19–56.

Nugent, Neill. 1989. *The Government and Politics of the European Community*. London: Macmillan.

Nye, Joseph S. 1970. "Comparing Common Markets: A Revised Neo-Functionalist Model." *International Organization*, 24:796–835.

Nye, Joseph S. 1971. *Peace in Parts: Integration and Conflict in Regional Organization*. Boston: Little, Brown.

Osgood, Robert E. 1971. "Foreword." In Robert W. Tucker, *The Radical Left and American Foreign Policy*. Baltimore, MD: Johns Hopkins University Press, pp. v–vi.

Pinder, John. 1985–86. "European Community and Nation-State: A Case for Neo-Federalism." *International Affairs*, 62:41-54.

Pinder, John. 1989. "Economic Integration versus National Sovereignty: Differences between Eastern and Western Europe." *Government and Opposition*, 24:309–26.

Plumb, Lord. 1989. "Building a Democratic Community." *The World Today*, 45:112–17.

Pompeu de Toledo, Roberto. 1989. "The Road to 1992." *World Press Review*, January: 15–16.

Pryce, Roy. 1987. *The Dynamics of European Union*. London: Croom Helm.

Puchala, Donald. 1970. "International Transactions and Regional Integration." *International Organization*, 24:732–63.

Puchala, Donald J. 1984. *Fiscal Harmonization in the European Communities: National Politics and International Cooperation*. London: Frances Pinter.

Puchala, Donald J. 1988. "The Integration Theorists and the Study of International Relations." In Charles Kegley, Jr., and Eugene R. Wittkopf, eds., *The Global Agenda*, 2d ed. New York: Random House, pp. 199–215.

Ray, James Lee. 1979. *Global Politics*. Boston: Houghton Mifflin.

Remmer, Karen. 1990. "Democracy and Economic Crisis: The Latin American Experience." *World Politics*, 42:315–35.

Russett, Bruce, and Harvey Starr. 1985. *World Politics*. New York: Freeman.

Sandholtz, Wayne and John Zysman. 1989. "1992: Recasting the European Bargain." *World Politics*, 42:95–128.

Sasse, Christoph, Edouard Poullet, David Coombes, and Gerard Deprez. 1977. *Decision Making in the European Community*. New York: Praeger.

Sbragia, Alberta. 1990. "The European Community and Institutional Development: Politics, Money, and Law." Presented at the Brookings Institution's *Conference on European Political Institutions and Policymaking After 1992*, March 29–30.

Schmitter, Philippe C. 1970. "A Revised Theory of Regional Integration." *International Organization*, 24:836–68.

Taylor, Paul. 1983. *The Limits to European Integration*. London: Croom Helm.

Wallace, Helen, William Wallace, and Carole Webb, eds. 1977. *Policy-Making in the European Communities*. London: Wiley.

Wallace, William. 1990. *The Transformation of Western Europe*. London: Royal Institute of International Affairs.

Yalowitz, Gerson, with Eric Onstand. 1990. "The Winds of Reform in Africa: Slower, But Inevitable." *U.S. News and World Report*, 23 July, p. 45.

3

Delivering the Goods

The EC and the Evolution of
Complex Governance

Barry B. Hughes

A Third Image of Integration

The study of regional integration is diverse, but much of it falls into two general categories (see also Puchala 1988).[1] The first body of literature focuses on the development of strong central institutions and thereby essentially on state-building. We can further subdivide these works into those that adopt federalist or various functionalist perspectives. The assumption of much of this literature is that the process of integration ultimately leads to a shift in the locus of authority from contemporary states to something approximating a superstate—minimally, a federation of states. Many scholars have long warned us, however, that the outcome might be something much less, and that our focus should be on the process, not on a hypothetical outcome (Haas, 1958).

Nonetheless, the view that political union is the goal of the EC still has adherents, not least important being the many individuals involved in the process. For instance, Jacques Delors, President of the Commission in 1990, frequently urged attention to that goal and in doing so prodded former Prime Minister Margaret Thatcher to wave caution flags in the name of British statehood.[2]

A second tradition emphasizes the creation of a community among the peoples subject to integration—a nation-building process. Some authors foresee the ultimate emergence of a new nation through a proliferation of transactions (such as trade, communications, and tourism) and through attitudinal transformations.

One of the reasons for pronouncements in the mid-1970s that the study of integration had reached a dead end (Haas 1976) was discouragement with both approaches. Even today, after more than thirty years of effort in Europe, the

European Community[3] administers only about 2 percent of the GDPs of the member-states, compared with the 40 percent that the average state controls.[4] And in late 1988 only 16 percent of the citizens in the EC reported that they often think of themselves as European. Forty-four percent declared that they never so characterize themselves (*Eurobarometer* no. 30, October 1988, 7).

There has, of course, been progress on both of these dimensions. As recently as 1977 the EC's institutions controlled only 0.7 percent of combined GDP. And majorities of the population in almost all member states consistently indicate support for European institutions and their strengthening. Nonetheless, it is hardly surprising that the irregular and amorphous character of the integration process led Haas to conclude that traditional theorizing about it had three questionable properties:

> (1) the presumed predictability of the institutional outcomes of the integration process; (2) the tendency to treat the region undergoing integration as a self-contained geographical space; (3) the parallel tendency to regard that region's practices of increasing the centralization of joint tasks and concerns as an autonomous process following its own unique rules. (Haas 1976, 175)

In reaction to the limitations of the first two traditions, a third image of the integration process and its results underlies some recent thought on the subject. Daltrop suggests its nature:

> Developments in modern society are leading to the gradual acceptance of a "multi-tiered" approach to government, with functions being carried out at the lowest tier compatible with both efficiency and accessibility for those whose needs it serves. A regional grouping like that of Western Europe can form a unit large enough to act as a necessary balance between the rival superpowers, but it must give each member state benefits which it can no longer achieve on its own. It must perform only those functions of government which cannot be carried out better at lower levels, closer to the individual citizens. (Daltrop 1986, 180–81)

Along the same lines, Haas wrote of "fragmented issue linkage" and "asymmetrical overlap," attempting to convey highly complex patterns of governance in which various levels share policy-making responsibilities.

We might call this third image of European integration *complex governance*, and it might better explain a new wave of "Euro-optimism" (Smith and Ray, chapter 2 in this volume) than does traditional theory of integration. Attention to complex governance suggests that we look for further development of multiple layers of institutional structure (the EC being an important one) with shifting allocations of authority across the layers in an ongoing search for the most effective means of providing public goods to citizens.[5]

The emergence of complex governance interacts with both state-building and community-building and a search for it is largely complementary rather than competitive in providing insights into integrative *processes*—theoretical differences center instead on the nature of the *end-state*. For instance, as both federalists and functionalists argue, the strengthening of the European Community has served the peoples of Europe by increasing economic efficiency and dampening historic conflicts. At the same time, however, some public policy problems, such as environmental issues, demand a still broader scope of governance and have led to the simultaneous growth of broader European and even global structures. And a variety of European states have experienced pressures from national groups for *devolution* of power and function. To the extent that federalists and functionalists have focused on a statelike European Community as the end of the integration process, these developments fall outside their insights.

Similarly, we should expect European identities to grow in parallel with popular European institutions and policies. But we should not assume that the end product will be a replacement of French or German nationalities by an exclusively or even predominantly European nationality. Europeans have simultaneously maintained or strengthened many community identities since the signing of the Treaty of Rome: identities with traditional states, with Europe, and with ancient local communities such as Brittany or Catalonia.[6] We may need to acknowledge *complex community formation* as well as complex governance.

Complex governance is by no means a wholly new or original image of integration. Confederal and federal structures have long divided authority between central and local institutions. And in integration theory the security communities of Karl Deutsch (Deutsch et al. 1966) bind states with institutional ties of varying strength (some communities are amalgamated and some are pluralistic). The picture of complex governance, however, emphasizes not two but multiple layers, including local, state, regional, and global. In place of Putnam's (1988) analogy of a two-level game, played by state leaders, we substitute the analogy of a multiple-level game, played by individual citizens. Moreover, complexity in the overlap of multiple, regional affiliations appears to be growing: the boundaries of associations created for economic, security, environmental or other purposes are seldom identical.

Neorealists and regime theorists have drawn our attention to interstate cooperation and the complex (and overlapping) structures to which it gives rise. But those perspectives remain highly state-centric and tend to emphasize single-issue cooperation. The concept of complex interdependence takes us further in the direction we want to go here—it draws our attention to the extensiveness of interissue linkage and the considerable constraints placed on state action by a dense pattern of interactions (Keohane and Nye 1977). Moreover, complex interdependence emphasizes the existence of multiple channels among states, including extensive connections across nongovernmental elites.

Yet these neorealist or neoliberal perspectives, even complex interdependence, often remain state-centric. In contrast, the theoretical roots of complex governance are explicitly individual-centric.[7] Beginning with the assumption that all levels of government ultimately exist to serve the needs of their citizens, those citizens have in the long run the potential to shift power to, from, and among levels of government to better serve their needs.[8] In Europe societal pressure has led to strengthening of government both above and below the state level (and in many cases the simultaneous strengthening of states).

In the contemporary world, the state obviously dominates the hierarchy of governance structures, maintaining substantial ability to make or break local, regional, and global institutions. Thus, much of the subsequent discussion will focus on the actions of states and their attempts to better satisfy citizen needs. Many of those actions require, however, that states turn over authority to subsidiary or higher government levels. Ultimately, as integration theorists suggest, that could result in the state undercutting its own dominant role in human governance. Such an outcome appears an unreasonable expectation in the foreseeable future, even in Europe where the process has gone much further than it has elsewhere in the world. Short of that, however, we can expect the process to lead to substantial growth in regional and global institutions and to greater complexity of governance. This paper argues that *we should view the European Community in the context of this evolution in human governance—not as the embryo of a superstate or a supernation, but as one structure in the embryo of complex governance.*

Public Goods and Global Public Policy

In sketching some of the theoretical roots of complex governance, let us begin with the assumption that in pluralistic democracies citizens create and sustain governments of all types in order to provide themselves with goods. For the last several centuries within Europe, the state has been the primary level of governance. For a variety of reasons, to be discussed below, the state is unable to provide goods demanded by citizens as efficiently as other existing or potential structures of governance. But individuals still rely on the state heavily to satisfy needs and further rely on it to create and strengthen alternative structures to satisfy their demands. Thus the discussion below will often make it sound as if the state is our level of analysis. Again, however, we must stress that ultimately the demands of individuals underlie the argument.

Three characteristics of public goods frequently complicate the efforts of states to formulate global public policy[9] and guarantee international goods to their citizens.[10] First, *rivalry* characterizes a good when only one individual or state can benefit from a unit of the good. For instance, when a state controls a piece of territory (a good), no other state can do so. Or when one fishing fleet kills a herd of whales, no other can do so. The rivalry characteristic creates zero-sum situations.[11] In contrast, access to radio waves or television transmissions is nonrivalrous—no one's access precludes that of anyone else (rivalry does, however, characterize radio frequencies).

Second, *nonexcludability* characterizes a good when it is impossible to deny access to other individuals or states. For instance, it is impossible to fence the atmosphere—air moves across borders and anyone can use it (for breathing or for disposal of pollutants). Similarly, it is difficult or impossible to restrict access to knowledge. Even high school students have been able to compile the basic knowledge to build an atomic bomb. In contrast, it is possible to exclude countries from the world postal system or from Antarctica.

Third, *congestion* characterizes a good when the consumption of units of the good interferes with the ability of others to obtain units of it. For instance, whales already possessed the characteristics of rivalry and nonexcludability in the eighteenth century: consumption of a whale prevented consumption of it by anyone else and everyone had access to them. But at that time, there were so few who had the equipment and capability to hunt whales that there was little congestion. Currently, however, the killing of whales limits their availability to others.[12]

Categories of International Goods

Table 3.1 uses rivalry and excludability to categorize four types of international goods: private goods, coordination goods, common property resources, and pure public goods.[13] The supply of goods in each category may or may not be congested.

Private goods (in the upper left-hand cell of Table 3.1) exhibit rivalry and excludability. Territory is one of the best examples of private goods. During the expansion of empires in the nineteenth century, Britain, France, Portugal and Germany treated African territory as a private good. In the early part of the century they had limited ability to exploit that continent (in part because malaria stopped them from penetrating it) and there was no congestion with respect to claims of interior territory. By the end of the century there was a great deal of congestion and much conflict about the international good.

As this example suggests, the core problem associated with international private goods is the determination of property rights. A common solution to the problem is international agreement to privatize a good to which ownership was earlier vague or contested. The imperial powers met at the Berlin Conference of 1884–85 and resolved claims in Africa. Similarly, most countries of the world attended the Third United Nations Law of the Sea Conference between 1973 and 1982 and extended their control over ocean resources to a distance of 200 miles from their coastlines.

A second approach is to establish some form of collective control or ownership with a fairly explicit statement of privileges and obligations. For instance, the Antarctic Treaty of 1959 does not recognize previous territorial claims (or deny them) and prohibits all military activity there. Various agreements on the law of the sea guarantee free shipping on the high seas more than twelve miles

Table 3.1

A Classification of International Goods

	Rivalry	
Excludability	Yes	No
Yes	Private Goods	Coordination Goods
	Core Problem: Defining Property Rights	Core Problem: Establishing Standards
No	Common Property Resources	Pure Public Goods
	Core Problem: Overexploitation	Core Problem: Underprovision

offshore of states (and through key straits even when within twelve miles of shore) but prohibit dumping of nuclear waste. The global community has gone so far as to declare the seabed the collective property of humanity.

A third approach would potentially be to reduce congestion and thereby eliminate conflict about access to goods, even when the goods remain characterized by rivalry. For instance, some argue that agreements over colonies like that in Berlin never ultimately resolved imperial disputes—it was when countries decided that the costs of colonies were greater than the benefits that the demand fell sharply and eliminated congestion.[14]

Coordination goods lie in the upper right-hand corner of Table 3.1 and exhibit nonrivalry and excludability. For instance, all countries can benefit simultaneously from international postal service (in fact, the more states that partake of the good, the greater the benefit for other states). Yet it would be possible to exclude a country (like Albania) from any established system. International telecommunications systems have the same character.

The core problem associated with provision of these goods is the establishment of initial standards and procedures (Snidal 1985). Interstate cooperation is frequently easy to obtain on these types of goods because the benefits are great and costs are frequently low—interests are fundamentally harmonious. It is hardly an accident that the Universal Postal Union and the International Telegraph Union were among the very first modern international organizations. Yet cooperation is seldom automatic. For instance, the world now is moving toward high-definition television and there is competition among European, American, and Japanese firms to define the global specifications. The winning firm (and country) will benefit by being able to initially dominate the market for the system.

The lower left-hand corner of Table 3.1 contains international goods characterized by rivalry and nonexcludability. Because of the inability to deny access, we often call them *common property resources*. Biological resources of the high seas, like whales or tuna, illustrate these goods. Again, while rivalry is a fixed feature, excludability is partly a legal concept. Theoretically, we could brand whales in the same way that ranchers once branded cattle on the open range, thus legally excluding access to them by others, and converting them to a private good.

Similarly, geosynchronous orbital space and the spectrum of radio frequencies have the character of common property resources. While there will always be rivalry (only one satellite can efficiently use a given location), there need not always be nonexcludability. The global community could legally allocate slots and convert them into private property, even allowing purchases and sales by new owners (just as an individual can buy or sell a home).

The core problem facing states in their provision of goods in this category is overexploitation. Whaling illustrates the logic of individuals in a congested common property situation. Each whaler seeks to obtain as much of the good as possible (there is rivalry) and cannot exclude others from doing the same. This result has come to be known as the *Tragedy of the Commons* (Hardin 1968), in reference to the ancient tradition of a communal grazing area called a commons (still seen in some places).[15] As long as the population of grazing animals on the commons is small, sharing poses no problem, because the grass is an uncongested good. But as population increases and congestion develops, the individual interest comes into conflict with that of the group. Animals overgraze the commons and destroy the vegetation, to the detriment of all community members.

One approach to addressing overexploitation is collectively to regulate it. The International Whaling Commission (IWC) once set global quotas for the harvest of various whale species (in essence excluding some access). Because it did not allocate these to particular countries, it created a situation like that of access to limited goods in the Soviet Union (or many concert tickets in the United States), namely a scramble to be first—a "Whale Olympics" (Soroos 1986, 278). Since 1986 the IWC has declared a moratorium on commercial whaling.[16] Theoretically the IWC could adopt the same approach that most states use domestically with deer: sell a certain number of hunting licenses, rationing them among potential hunters (by lottery or price).

Another approach, where it is physically possible, is to redefine legal excludability and to privatize the good. Again, this is what the international community did with respect to oceans within 200 miles of coastlines. And still another approach is to attempt to reduce congestion. Those who seek to eliminate demand for products of whales (or for tusks or furs of endangered animals) wish to lessen the pressure upon the commons.

The final quadrant of Table 3.1 includes *pure public goods*, which exhibit neither rivalry nor excludability. For example, your access to radio waves (as distinct from frequencies for broadcasting) does not preclude access by anyone else—nor is there any (very effective) way of denying your access. Similarly, your use of knowledge does not interfere with the provision of that knowledge to anyone else, and it has been proven difficult selectively to deny access to knowledge.

This category of international goods is very small. For instance, it is traditional to cite air or the atmosphere as a pure public good. But in reality, your use of the oxygen in a given unit of air for breathing (or polluting) precludes my effective use of the same unit. Thus we are rivals for it. The atmosphere is actually a common property resource (which once was very abundant relative to demands upon it). As long as congestion is low, many common property resources (including whales, radio frequencies, and the atmosphere) appear much like pure public goods. But when congestion increases, the underlying element of rivalry becomes obvious.[17]

Problems of Collective Action

Each of the types of goods represented in Table 3.1 has typical problems associated with its provision and a menu of generic approaches most suited to dealing with the problems. Both pure and impure public goods frequently face still another kind of problem. Although many such goods, like whales and clean air, are at least initially "natural" and simply free for the taking, others, like global satellite communication services, exist only as a result of government action. And when "natural" goods become congested and needs for regulatory systems arise, only collective action will assure consistent access to the good. Thus the provision of large numbers of international goods requires *collective action*. The general problem that arises surrounding collective action is *underprovision*.[18] Especially when excludability is not an option (as with common property resources and pure public goods), states have little incentive to contribute to the costs of the collective action and the provision of the *collective good*.[19] Instead, they prefer to *free ride*, to partake of the good without contribution. There are even sometimes costs associated with the initial provision of a coordination good (with excludability) that states would prefer someone else paid. If all states decide to "let Denmark do it," there would obviously be no collective action. More commonly, states limit their share of the contribution and the result is underprovision.

When this problem appears within countries, the typical solution is collective coercion. For instance, travel on highways is a good that most of us would like to use without payment. If we were asked to make voluntary contributions to a national highway fund, we might kick in a few dollars, but it is unlikely that we would pay in proportion with our use. We would starve the fund for money and it would underprovide highways. Instead, we collectively agree to tax ourselves and to force everyone to pay (with gasoline taxes, payment is roughly in proportion to highway use).[20]

In the global arena, there is no central authority to administer collective coercion. And exclusion is not an option for many goods. In some *privileged groups* (Olson 1965, 49–50) one or more members has a private incentive to provide some level of the collective good to the benefit of all.[21] Returning to our highway example, if one extremely large trucking firm existed (or a small group of firms could collaborate), the firm or group might determine that its own interest lay in paying the costs of a basic national highway system and tolerating some free riding by private individuals. Although the system might still under-provide the public good, there would be some supply of it.

Privileged groups sometimes appear globally. For instance, the agreement by twenty-four countries in Montreal in 1987 to reduce CFC production and use, even in the absence of commitment by other countries, illustrates the principle. These economically advanced countries produce most of the problem, so they could assure significant provision of the collective good of CFC reduction. In fact, a somewhat smaller subgroup, the twelve countries of the European Community, subsequently decided to eliminate production totally by 2000. These leaders in the provision of the collective good do, however, worry about free riders. The production and use of CFCs in China, for example, is growing so rapidly that it could significantly offset reductions elsewhere. If so, China could become a *spoiler*, a free rider so large that it frustrates efforts by a privileged group.[22]

One of the ways in which privileged groups overcome the problem of spoilers is through side payments. *Side payments* are "exchanges among the members of a coalition to equalize any inequalities arising from their cooperation" (Luce and Raiffa 1957, 180). The richer countries could freely provide CFC-replacement technology to China as a side payment to encourage Chinese cooperation on the ozone issue.

In some cases, a single country can create a privileged group. For instance, a hegemonic world leader, like the United States today or the United Kingdom earlier, may be able (for private benefit reasons) to provide a collective good. In the security arena, the Pax Britannica of the nineteenth century or the Pax Americana of the post–World War II period, long periods of unusually peaceful inter-state relations, may illustrate the relatively beneficent functioning of a hegemon. These same hegemons have also made critical contributions to the provision of free markets that benefit other states, including those that free ride by exporting into the free markets while protecting their own. We will see that leadership in privileged groups is one important role for the European Community.

Delivering the Goods

This section looks at the EC in the context of an evolving pattern of complex governance and considers how the EC contributes to the satisfaction of demands upon government by Europeans. The discussion uses the typology of international goods from the last section to provide some insights into the problems associated with satisfying the demands of Europeans and into appropriate institutional structures for satisfying those demands. We divide citizen demands into four categories: national/ethnic autonomy, economic welfare, military security, and environmental quality. We could also have looked at demands centering on energy systems, for the development of technology, or upon infrastructure (electric grids,[23] telecommunications systems, and so on). The argument would have been much the same.

National/Ethnic Autonomy

Most so-called "nation-states" are actually ethnically heterogeneous states. A study of 132 states found only twelve to be ethnically homogeneous. In twenty-five additional states a core nationality accounted for 90 percent or more of the total population.[24] At the other extreme, the largest ethnic group in thirty-nine states constituted less than 50 percent of the population, and fifty-three states contained five or more significant ethnic groups. Under these circumstances it is surprising that scholars of world politics, after making clear and important distinctions between states and nations, continue to use the term "nation-state" synonymously with "country."

Nonetheless, the concept of nation-state conveys the desire that most, if not all, nations have to control their own destinies by way of controlling their own political institutions. Latvians did not give up on that goal, in spite of forty years of totalitarian Soviet rule. Nor have many Basques in Spain and substantial numbers of Bretons in France. Peoples want to use their own language, read and write their own literature, practice their own religion, and educate their children in their own cultural traditions. One of the most basic functions of democratic government is to facilitate their ability to do these things.

In the terms of our categories of goods (Table 3.1), control of those institutions (like schools and the media) that maintain cultural integrity is a private good for an identifiable ethnic group. There is rivalry because control of cultural institutions by one ethnic group has traditionally precluded control by others. Attempts to share control have, with a very few exceptions like Switzerland, failed (and even there it required a confederal structure with much continued autonomy). The historic tendency of dominant national groups to expel minorities and to annex national brethren outside of existing boundaries testifies to the existence of excludability.

As discussed earlier, the most common collective approach to resolving problems associated with private goods is definition of property rights. Allocating cultural autonomy to geographically concentrated peoples is in principle quite straightforward—national self-determination allows all such peoples to control their own institutions. In practice, of course, there has long been a perverse tendency of peoples to deny that option to peoples less numerous or less powerful than themselves (often because of security concerns or overlapping residence).

In the twentieth century the principle of self-determination has motivated large numbers of changes in the institutions of governance—most notably decolonization and the breakup of European empires, both those with overseas holdings and those spread across contiguous nations in Europe. No principle is likely to be more important in determining the future of governance in Europe. And in spite of limited nation-building at the European level, the reality is that older national groups are almost certain to retain the dominant loyalties of Europeans for the indefinite future.

The implications of this are clear. Although other functions of government may move to broader institutions, those that ultimately protect national identities will remain at local levels. In fact, the European Communities, as well as individual states, have increasingly supported the devolution of such governance (Burgess 1986). Belgium adopted a federal constitution in 1979 providing considerable autonomy to Flanders, Wallonia, and French-speaking Brussels (Daltrop 1986, 117; Arlett and Sallnow 1989). A Basque regional government took power in 1980. In the 1980s France granted Corsica its own assembly and Spain allowed Catalonia, Andalucia, and Galicia to redevelop regional institutions. These peoples often rally around the concept of "subsidiarity," the idea that governance should gravitate to the lowest practical level.

Some of the nationality groups of Europe have advocated an inter*national* federalist approach to European governance, in which they, rather than traditional states, would be the basic units. A Bureau of Unrepresented Nations has, in contradiction of the name, represented them in Brussels since 1977. A few European parliamentarians also represent them. Bavaria suggests that a proposed European Senate organize its representation by region (nation), not state. The German Länder are already allowed to observe the Council of Ministers and seek the right to speak.

As long as government in Brussels does not threaten, and even supports local autonomy, some further concentration of governance at the European level is completely compatible with national demands (the EC and local institutions can join forces in a challenge to the state). But any movement in the EC to centralize functions that threaten cultural autonomy would obviously engender the same intense grass-roots opposition that states have often faced and which is in many respects actually growing.

Economic Welfare

With respect to economic welfare, people place two very general primary demands on government. The first is that it facilitate their acquisition of substantial volumes of goods and services; the second is that it enforce some element of equity in distribution. People place other important demands on government, such as protection of labor against abuse by employers or assurance of employment, but we will not explore them here. Most importantly, we will ignore the role that states can play in economic bargaining with other states. If the world is moving toward competition among trade blocs, the EC will have an important mercantilist role that this chapter does not adequately discuss.

In Europe, much of the public sees a connection between acquisition of goods and improvements in the efficiency of market mechanisms. And in the pursuit of market efficiency, a key issue is the degree to which markets remain open—we therefore turn first to the relationship between trade and governance.

Trade and the Logic of International Goods

Most citizens want the good of access to extensive markets. According to western economic theory that good possesses the characteristics of nonrivalry and nonexcludability (Snidal 1985). Specifically, there is no rivalry because all countries gain by participating in free trade and no excludability because that would contradict the definition of the good.

In reality, however, excludability is very simple physically—countries impose tariffs or simply deny access to their domestic markets. Moreover, there is a common perception by states around the world that there is rivalry. Specifically, greater access by Japan to European markets may lessen American access. Thus there is tendency for states to treat trade as a private good, excluding others from international markets and preemptively capturing external markets. At the extreme this privatization strategy would result in only intrastate markets. Short of the extreme it might lead to rigid trade blocs, generally centered on one large country. In both cases, the widespread attempt to free ride on the provision of the collective good by others results in substantial underprovision of the good.

Thus an extensive free market is not a "natural" public good, with clear-cut characteristics of nonexcludability and nonrivalry. Instead it is a collective good that states must create, essentially by controlling excludability and dampening rivalry—by restricting free riding.[25] How can they do that?

A hegemon or other leadership can be useful. For instance, Great Britain and the United States have at times reduced rivalry over market access by opening their extensive markets to smaller powers. Perhaps as important, these hegemons exerted pressure on other states to maintain open markets themselves, thus increasing the supply of the public good and making its provision less zero-sum. The hegemon can, however, also selectively deny access to the good. During the cold war the United States limited access to, and in some cases completely excluded, Communist countries from its markets.[26]

A second approach is collectively to set standards as the International Monetary Fund (IMF) and the General Agreement on Tariffs and Trade (GATT) have done since the late 1940s—or the EC has done internally to an even greater degree. These international organizations again attempt to expand the supply of the good by maintaining open markets (eliminating excludability) and dampening rivalry over them. With respect to controlling excludability, they make it difficult for countries not willing to free their own markets to gain access to those of club members, while simultaneously enforcing nonexcludability within the system.[27] With respect to dampening rivalry, they exert pressure on countries that have taken too much of the good (for instance, the large surplus of Japanese exports over imports) to reduce their trade surpluses.[28]

What are the implications of this for European governance? One of the reasons for establishing the European Economic Community was to facilitate free trade in Europe. Although the EC is sufficiently large to create a formidable trading bloc, it remains too geographically restricted to satisfy contemporary demands for free trade. That has been, of course, an important reason for expanding the community over time.

One model for the future remains that of Fortress Europe, in which the expanded and strengthened EC becomes a rigid trade bloc. Conybeare (chapter 8 in this volume) explains why this is a serious danger and Oneal (chapter 9 in this volume) documents how state development agencies in the United States perceive the danger. Yet there is another model. The EC has increasingly served as a leader in a larger group of states with an interest in free trade. For example, the EC signed bilateral agreements for free trade with all European Free Trade Association (EFTA) members in 1972 and by 1984 all industrial goods moved tariff-free within the EC-EFTA area (Luif 1987; Wallace 1988). With the reintegration of eastern European countries into the world economy, it seems nearly certain that additional members will soon join the EC-EFTA free trade area. The EC also plays an active role in broader trade forums such as GATT. The current boundaries of the EC are in no sense "natural" with respect to free trade.

Deeper Economic Coordination

Delors has advanced a vision of Europe in terms of three concentric circles. The EC constitutes the innermost circle, the EC and EFTA jointly populate the second (they began talks in mid-1990 on a "European Economic Space"), and the third incorporates those countries plus eastern Europe, Turkey, Malta and Cyprus. This image has reopened a debate on the future of the EC that has often been framed in terms of "widening" versus "deepening."[29] The reality, however, as the Delors vision suggests, is likely to incorporate both processes.

Beyond the comparatively easy reduction of elimination of tariffs, further efficiency improvements in the combined economies of a set of states require even greater levels of coordination. Globally the movement toward that greater coordination can be seen in many forums (Bressard 1990). Within GATT, the Tokyo Round was the first to focus intensive discussion on nontariff barriers to trade, but the Uruguay Round has carried the topic much further—it drew attention to what traditionally were considered domestic economic policies (such as agricultural subsidies). Between the United States and Japan, the Structural Impediments Initiative pressed for alterations in the domestic structures of the

Japanese economy (theoretically also those of the United States) so as to make them more equivalent to their trading partners. Similarly, the OECD has investigated the microeconomic question of producer-subsidy equivalents across the agricultural policies of its members. And, of course, the EC has gone furthest in reconciling domestic economic policies by deciding to complete a common market by 1992. The movement toward an Economic and Monetary Union underlines again the degree to which economic coordination in the EC is far in advance of that even envisaged elsewhere (Lindberg, chapter 6 in this volume).[30]

Notwithstanding the differences in ambition and geographic scope of these efforts, they all have in common the recognition that further economic efficiency gains require both deeper and more extensive coordination of domestic economic policies. There are many reasons why such coordination might begin with a limited number of countries or go furthest within a limited set. These include the greater motivation of some countries (because of level of economic development, extensiveness of preexisting trade, or cultural compatibility) and the greater simplicity of bargaining within a smaller set of countries. But there is no reason to expect that the process should stop with the coordination of policies for 12 (EC), 18 (EC plus EFTA), 24 (OECD), 35 (CSCE), or some other fixed number of countries.[31]

Equity

Economic groupings can pursue greater equity among their members either in pursuit of strengthened community or as a calculated side payment to disadvantaged groups in order to encourage their continued participation in structures that have greater efficiency as the primary goal. The pressures for greater equity exist at many levels of political organization. Within states like France, policies target poorer areas like Brittany or Southwest France. Within the EC, the European Regional Development Fund (ERDF) has tried since 1975 to assist depressed areas; cross-national transfers have increased since the accession of Greece, Spain, and Portugal. On a broader scale, the EC assists (via trade preferences, aid and investment) an assortment (sixty-six in 1990) of African, Caribbean, and Pacific states under the Lomé Conventions. Still broader arrangements channel funds from the Development Assistance Committee (DAC) countries (most of the OECD) to countries around the world. In short, there are no obvious or natural boundaries on equity-enhancing schemes—the EC is simply one of several levels of governance with respect to them.

Military Security

Security and the Logic of International Goods

The classic realist portrayal of security (in a situation of anarchy) is that of a good exhibiting rivalry and nonexcludability. Rivalry exists because the effort of one state to increase its security can reduce that of others (the classic security dilemma).[32] Nonexcludability is the rule because no state or other actor determines who has security and who does not—it is impossible to deny access to more of it by a state determined to increase its security.

The normal realist reaction to the security dilemma has two elements. The first is to advise states that the security system is one of self-help and that they must guard their own security as if it were a private good. That approach is doomed to failures in providing security because the actions of individual states cannot change the nonexcludability characteristic. Arms races are a common result.

The second realist approach, represented by balance-of-power politics, is fundamentally an effort to control access to the good—to impose excludability and simultaneously to dampen rivalry.[33] Perhaps the most basic of the rules in a balance-of-power system is that alliances form against any actor threatening to become predominant and to use their superior power to reduce the security of other states. In essence, the rule places an upper limit on the amount of security any one state can appropriate for itself. It attempts to convert the security problem into one of coordination—a kind of standard setting with respect to security (see Table 3.1). The fundamental weakness of the strategy is that the costs of contributing to the provision of the collective good (setting upper limits on the power/security of any aggressive state) is high and many states would prefer to free ride on their alliance partners. As with most collective goods, there is underprovision of it.

Collective security is another strategy with respect to security problems that shares much of the philosophy and many of the difficulties facing balance of power. It also seeks to impose excludability and dampen rivalry, again reducing security issues to a coordination problem. Instead of *ad hoc* alliances against a potential hegemon, collective security calls for an alliance of all states against any aggressor. Again, the costs of contributing to the collective good can be very high and states will prefer to free ride.[34]

Still another security strategy turns the basic balance-of-power notion on its head. Instead of protecting the system from a hegemon, the idea is to rely upon the hegemon as a privileged actor. The hegemon has a self-interest in dampening rivalry and imposing excludability on security. Although in becoming the arbiter of security in the system it appropriates a large share for itself (one of its potential motivations also in trade systems), it can reduce conflict over security by others. A remaining problem, of course, is that a challenger will periodically arise and rivalry over security with the hegemon will become the central issue.

Still another approach to security problems draws our attention even more sharply to both rivalry and excludability characteristics. In a security community (a group of states with expectations that they will use only peaceful means to settle disputes) there is both nonrivalry and nonexcludability with respect to security. All states recognize that they can mutually increase their security by strengthening the community, and no one is excluded from the good. Security becomes in essence a pure public good (bottom right-hand corner of Table 3.1).[35]

Implications for European Governance

Historically, reliance on balances of power has dominated European efforts to assure security. Since World War II we see that strategy in the balance between NATO and the Warsaw Pact. The European Community has played a minimal role in this approach to governance in security (as a generally unequal "pillar" in the North Atlantic alliance). Members have individually and collectively relied very heavily on the United States for security guarantees (Ifestos 1988). Efforts to create a strong military pole within the EC region have historically had very limited success. In 1954 the proposal for a European Defense Community collapsed.

The decline in tension between NATO and the Warsaw Pact during the era of détente, and the more recent and dramatic dissolution of the Warsaw Pact, have fundamentally changed the modern security environment. It has become highly probable that the United States will substantially reduce its commitment to European security in the 1990s, requiring Europeans to face the issue of developing new security structures or strengthening old ones (Rudney and Reychler 1988). One early response to this was the meeting of the Ministerial Council of the Western European Union in June 1984, which set up a working group to consider the prospects for reactivating the Western European Union (WEU) (Eberle et al. 1984). So far, however, the WEU is little more than a shell.[36] And Pearson (chapter 10 in this volume) documents that although the Single European Act (SEA) intensifies some technological cooperation in security arenas, there appears little near-term probability for real strategic cooperation.

A second approach, relying on something closer to collective security (and promising ultimately a broad security community), has long vied with balance of power in its attractiveness to Europeans and helps explain the failure to pursue security cooperation within the EC. Since World War II much attention has specifically focused on controlling rivalry within the Franco-German dyad and on simultaneously expanding the geographic scope of European cooperation. The Council of Europe (now twenty-three members), established in 1949 with headquarters on the French–German border in Strasbourg and the goals of supporting European cooperation, pluralistic democracy, and human rights, symbolizes this thrust.

With the Helsinki Final Act of 1975 the Conference on Security and Cooperation in Europe (CSCE) strengthened the option of a much broader approach to European security (Bowker and Williams 1985; Seidelmann 1989). The CSCE process explicitly rejects the older bloc-to-bloc and spheres-of-influence approaches to European security (Bogdan 1989). The basket of security measures of the CSCE process initially only emphasized the inviolability of European frontiers. Subsequently the emphasis shifted to peaceful change and interaction, as in the Stockholm Conference on Confidence-Building and Security-Building Measures and Disarmament in Europe (beginning in January 1984). The thrust of agreements on Confidence- and Security-Building Measures (CSBMs) is to move military postures toward non-provocative defense and thereby control the problem at the root of the security dilemma—the fact that defensive measures by one country can appear potentially offensive to others. This process extends the effort to reduce tensions and to dampen rivalry well beyond the Franco-German dyad and the WEU, since it encompasses states from both eastern and western Europe.

If the CSCE continues to progress, then the provision of military security to Europeans may in part be served by governance with the geographic scope of the CSCE (thirty-five countries), rather than by strengthening the EC's political role. Nonetheless, the EC has a role to play even in the CSCE. Member countries have, for instance, coordinated their own positions and thereby been able to take leadership in CSCE sessions (von Groll 1982).

As Garnham (chapter 11 in this volume) points out, no single organization is likely to organize the future security environment of Europe. NATO, the EC, the CSCE, the WEU, and even the Independent European Programme Group (IEPG) are likely to share responsibility with states for pluralistic and complex governance in the security arena.

Environmental Quality

Large numbers of environmental issues are classic common property resource problems under conditions of increasing congestion. The geographic scope of the problems depends on the numbers of those who potentially have access to the common resource (such as water or air) and the scope of effective governmental arrangements will vary accordingly.

For instance, with respect to seas (both fishing and pollution issues), a wide range of institutional structures has evolved. The North East Atlantic Fisheries Convention (NEAFC) of 1954 lists membership appropriate to its area of interest (Freestone and Fleisch 1983). The Mediterranean Action Plan (Med Plan), sponsored by the United Nations Environmental Programme's (UNEP's) Regional Seas Programme, ties countries around that sea to a variety of cooperative efforts (Haas 1989). And the countries surrounding the North Sea met in 1987 and again in 1990 to hammer out agreements on reduction of dumping into that body of water (*Economist*, March 3, 1990, 55–56).

The EC has had mixed success in dealing with these problems. For instance, the Common Fisheries Policy (CFP) has been highly divisive—debates on the issue were influential in Norway's referendum to reject EC membership (Freestone and Fleisch 1983, 77). The CFP has, however, generally worked to limit the overfishing of European waters. And it gradually helped the member-states reconcile the movement by the United Nations Conference on the Law of the Sea (UNCLOS) to 200 mile Exclusive Economic Zones (EEZs) with historic fishing rights in the North Sea. There have been other successes. In 1976 the Council of Ministers agreed on a directive to control discharges of dangerous substances into EC waters (Taylor et al. 1986). The EC has adopted more than 100 legislative acts on the environment since environmental policy became an EC issue in 1972 (Johnson and Corcelle 1989, 2). These address air, water, waste management, chemicals, noise, and endangered flora and fauna. One should not underestimate the importance of an existing and strong EC institutional structure in making possible interstate cooperation.

On many air and water pollution issues, however, the EC region is inadequately broad to deal with issues that cross boundaries of European states. The United Nations Economic Commission for Europe (ECE) has more appropriate geographic representation in many cases. For instance, in 1979 it sponsored the Convention on Long-Range Transboundary Air Pollution, which twenty-seven states ratified by 1989 (Soroos 1989a). Protocols in 1985 and 1988 set specific targets for control of sulphur emissions and nitrogen oxide (French 1990). Similarly, the UNEP took the initiative within the Montreal Protocol of 1987 in restricting chemicals that deplete the stratospheric ozone layer (signed by twenty-four countries). Other problems, such as global warming, will require participation by still more countries.

The EC again has an important leadership role to play in broader environmental governance. The developed and industrial countries create a significant portion of regional and global transboundary environmental problems. And the private benefits to these states of many pollution control measures exceed private costs, even when those controls provide a broader collective good. Thus on many environmental issues groups of states are privileged. Larger players, such as the United States and the EC can play very important leadership roles.

The OECD membership list contains most developed and industrial countries and has therefore not surprisingly instituted various studies on the environment. But the OECD may be too large, and its membership too dispersed, to take active leadership on environmental issues—that appears to be a role the EC can better play. It did so by taking the lead in agreeing to completely phase out CFCs.[37] Similarly, a binding directive of the EC in 1988 commits members to reduce significantly the emissions that cause acid rain (French 1990, 32). The EC's aid program to eastern Europe will target environmental problems there, as well as economic ones, thus constituting essentially a side payment for obtaining eastern compliance with tougher western standards.

In sum, the EC does not constitute an appropriate structure of governance for most environmental issues. Its geographic scope is frequently too limited or simply inappropriate (as on pollution in the North Sea). Yet it can provide leadership to a broader Europe.

Conclusions

This brief examination of the European Community's role in satisfying demands upon governing institutions for public goods suggests a mixed conclusion with respect to the prospect for further strengthening of the EC as a level of government:

1. *The demand for national autonomy.* The EC can contribute only indirectly to the provision of national autonomy by supporting the desire of ethnic groups for their own governance. Other layers of governance beyond the traditional state also help; most notably the CSCE and the UN, with their support for self-determination. The demand is more likely, however, to lead to further devolution of government than to strengthening of EC institutions. People play the game of politics in Europe at many levels, a fact that is likely to become more rather than less obvious.

2. *The demand for economic welfare.* The EC has played an important leading role in moving much of Europe toward free trade. But it is too narrow a structure to most efficiently deliver that good (it would serve better as a trade bloc). Similarly, it can lead the way in coordinating domestic economic policies, but the movement to do so already has greater, at least OECD-wide scope.

3. *The demand for military security.* The EC continues to provide important cement for the Franco-German dyad. But the impetus for progress in supplying military security to Europeans, even those within the EC, may be shifting from narrower balance of power approaches to broader reliance upon collective security and security communities.

4. *The demand for environmental quality.* While the EC has become a leader in broader schemes to protect and improve environmental quality, and now acts more decisively than ever on issues among the twelve, the scope of common property resource problems seldom coincides well with EC membership. Increasing congestion will remain a powerful force in pushing for myriad institutional arrangements to address environmental issues throughout a broader Europe.

Overall, this review of the EC and public goods suggests that its primary long-term role may be as a seed and leader in establishing and strengthening a wide variety of governance structures with broader or at least (in the case of North Sea and Mediterranean pollution problems) alternative membership. It is not clear that the EC's current borders are "rational" for its citizens with respect to any of the issues discussed here. Often, the natural borders of European governance on economic, security, and environmental issues lie considerably beyond those of the twelve.[38] From the perspective of providing collective goods, it should not be surprising that the membership of the EC has expanded over time and that pressures to expand it further are strong.

The portrait (by Delors and others) of a Europe in concentric circles provides one image of how the movement toward alternative and more rational borders might occur. A Europe of overlapping circles might provide an even better image, however, especially when one considers the strong pressures for local control of cultural autonomy. Whereas the CSCE may be increasingly able to address North American and European security concerns, the OECD (perhaps led by the EC) seems better positioned to handle both free trade and coordination on economic issues. And environmental issues call forth their own set of over-lapping circles: some drawn around regional seas or watersheds, others over continental land masses connected by air movements, and still others encompassing the globe.

None of this discussion should in any way detract from the critical contributions the EC has made in all of these issue areas. It remains the best-developed exemplar of governance above the traditional state. There is clearly reason for further strengthening of its institutions and policy coordination. Nonetheless, there is good reason to step back and view the EC not as the core of a superstate or supernation, but as an especially well developed element in the embryonic, but rapidly evolving, global phenomenon of complex governance.

Notes

1. I want to express my appreciation for research assistance on this paper from Ritu Vij—her help was invaluable.

2. In 1988 Delors suggested that he foresaw 80 percent of key decisions being made in Brussels and only 20 percent in state capitals (Bressard 1990, 54). At the Paris summit in 1972 members agreed to create a European Union. At the Milan summit in 1985 a majority still agreed to undertake further discussions on European Union (Hinsley 1989, 1). And in the Dublin summit of July 1990, members agreed to a new conference on political union.

3. The accurate term is "European Communities," but we adopt standard usage here.

4. Daltrop 1986, 125. The total administrative staff of the commission numbers only 16,000, about that of the French ministry of culture (*Economist*, 7 April 1990, 61).

5. In an unpublished Ph.D. dissertation, Walter Yondorf foresaw a "sector integrated supranational system" (Lindberg and Scheingold 1970). See also Hanrieder (1978).

6. There has frequently been too great a tendency for scholars to argue that integration is a zero-sum process in which both identities and institutions are an either-or phenomenon. Hughes (1971) showed how this mindset has influenced transaction flow analysis.

7. Increasing emphasis on human rights and the growing network of non-governmental organizations (NGOs) that works on behalf of human rights directs our attention to the fundamental place of individual human beings in any understanding of the evolution of governance. As *The Economist* wrote in 1990, with too much idealism but with an important point, "The Community does not exist to serve the ambitions of its mandarins, nor the particular interests of its member governments, but to enhance the material and political welfare of its people" (7 July 1990, 40). Dalton and Eichenberg (chapter 4 in this volume) explore the important relationship between public opinion and European integration.

8. Governments obviously also serve the needs of particular dominant groups and therefore take on a life of their own. We can contrast a top-down "imperial" model of evolution in governance, in which protogovernments compete for resources and control, with a bottom-up or "public interest" model, in which citizens ultimately assign functions to government according to efficiency of performance (Neumann 1989). In spite of the better fit of the first model to traditional state-building (Tilly 1985), we assume here that democracy and modern pluralism (and some shift in focus of politics from military secu-

rity to issues of "low politics") have altered the process enough to make the second model increasingly apt.

9. Soroos (1986, 1987, 1988, and 1989a, b) provides useful treatments of global public policy. Whereas his approach grows primarily from the concept of commons, the one in this discussion has deeper roots in the concepts and theory of public goods.

10. For discussions of public goods and the problems of cooperation on them see Hardin (1982), Barry and Hardin (1982), and Taylor (1987).

11. The term "jointness" is sometimes used instead of nonrivalry.

12. More technically, congestion exists when the social cost of consumption is positive. Congestion interacts especially with rivalry.

13. Samuelson (1955) stated the two characteristics of pure public goods. Weimer and Vining (1989) provide an excellent discussion of rivalry, excludability, and congestion—from the perspective of domestic issues.

14. The cost–benefit analysis of colonies changed over time—for instance, costs increased with the spread of modern weaponry and benefits decreased with the growth of domestic markets.

15. Soroos (1989a) emphasizes that commons is a legal arrangement permitting use of a public resource for private gain, while common property resources are defined by their physical characteristics that permit joint use but not division or exclusion—thus, the concepts are related, but not identical.

16. Japan, Norway, and Iceland take advantage of a loophole, which allows killing for "research" purposes, to annually harvest about 500 whales (Japan killing most).

17. Another way of looking at this problem is that congestion begins to create rivalry where none existed before and moves the good to the quadrant with problems of common property resources and overexploitation.

18. Olson (1965) provides a classic elaboration of this argument. But scholars have recognized the conflict between individual and collective interests for a very long time. Rousseau explained it with a parable of five hunters collectively pursuing a stag. Should any of them break off the hunt to individually kill a rabbit and assure himself of sufficient food, the stag might elude the other hunters (reported in Waltz 1959). Russett and Starr (1989, 505) quote a statement of the problem by Aristotle: "What is common to the greatest number has the least care bestowed upon it. Everyone thinks chiefly of his own, hardly at all of the common interest."

19. Some define collective goods as public goods meeting only the nonexcludability criterion (Pearce 1983, 70). Others use collective good and public good interchangeably. Russell Hardin (1982) makes the same distinction this chapter does and provides one of the most readable treatments of the subject.

20. A second approach in this instance is to privatize highways by converting them to privately owned tollroads, facilitating exclusion of those not paying their share.

21. A group in which no subgroup has such an incentive is a "latent group."

22. Schelling (1978) discusses the size of the subgroup that can block a collective good and notes that it varies by issue. In the case of free passage through a narrow street (or narrow strait), one car (or state) can block it, so universal contribution is needed to keep it open.

23. McGowan (1990) reports on the efforts to develop an International Energy Market (IEM); it is surprising how far the electric grids of EC member states are from integration.

24. Jorgensen-Dahl (1975, 653–54). Nielsson and Jones (1988, 1) argue that "only 30 of the world's 165 states would meet the test of near congruence between the members of a nation and the inhabitants of a state."

25. Conybeare (1984) argues that the prisoner's dilemma offers a better understanding of trade issues than does the concept of public good.

26. And a hegemon may take advantage of its position not to open markets, but to appropriate them—as Britain did in Latin America and China. Hegemons need not be benevolent providers of public goods. By dictating access to trade they effectively establish a coordination good in which they unilaterally control excludability.

27. They utilize the reciprocity of the most-favored nation principle. As with a hegemon, the control these organizations exercise over excludability moves free markets toward the status of coordination goods.

28. As they also exhort deficit states to increase exports.

29. *The Economist*, 3 February 1990, 50; *Newsweek*, 12 March 1990, 38–40.

30. Yet Llewellyn (1988, 240) argues that on financial integration "the specifically European dimension is largely irrelevant and overwhelmed by a global dimension."

31. Multinational corporations actively supported the Commission in the decision to complete the single market by 1992. In 1983 they formed a Roundtable of European Industrialists, a group that reaches beyond the EC—its first chair was from Volvo (Sandholtz and Zysman 1989). For a contrary view on the inherently expansionist character of EC integration see Dosser et al. (1982, 10). They argue that the EC provides goods that exhibit excludability and rivalry (private goods) and therefore will apply "very stringent conditions" to restrict membership. But they do not elaborate that argument.

32. Congestion is important here. Rousseau posited a state of nature in which humans had little contact with each other and therefore the rivalry characteristic was less important. But he noted that as they increased in numbers and began to come into regular contact, the competition for security grew (the kind of state of nature that Hobbes posited).

33. Snidal (1985) describes the security issue in terms of nonrivalry and excludability.

34. Although globalists generally support collective security and realists attack it, the similarities with a strategy of balance of power are greater than either likes to admit. Realists might protest that balance of power calls only upon those with an immediate interest in stopping aggression to resist it—and not on those halfway around the world. But the Nazi assault on Czechoslovakia did not immediately threaten Britain and France. And in many respects the action did threaten the interests of Canada and Australia. Boundaries of interest are hard to draw.

35. In domestic environments, defense is a pure public good (Weimer and Vining 1989).

36. Turkey joined all EC members except Germany in forging a common reaction to the Iraqi invasion of Kuwait in 1990.

37. The OECD also faces pressures for expansion: both eastern European countries and Asian NICs have expressed interest in membership *(The Economist*, 3 March 1990, 66).

38. In contrast, Harrop (1989, 195) argues that expansion of the Community is essentially complete and that its current size already exceeds the "optimal." He argues in terms of the difficulties of agreement among a larger number of more heterogeneous members.

References

Arlett, Sarah, and John Sallnow. 1989. "European Centres of Dissent." *Geographical Magazine*, September, 6–12.

Barry, Brian, and Russell Hardin, eds. 1982. *Rational Man and Irrational Society?* Beverly Hills, CA: Sage.

Bogdan, Corneliu. 1989. "Crossing the European Divide." *Foreign Policy*, 75: 56–75.

Bowker, Mike, and Phil Williams. 1985. "Helsinki and West European Security." *International Affairs*, 61: 607–18.

Bressard, Albert. 1990. "Beyond Interdependence: 1992 as a Global Challenge." *International Affairs*, 66: 47–65.

Burgess, Michael, ed. 1986. *Federalism and Federation in Western Europe.* London: Croom Helm.

Conybeare, John A. C. 1984. "Public Goods, Prisoner's Dilemmas and the International Political Economy," *International Studies Quarterly,* 28: 5–22.

Daltrop, Anne. 1986. *Political Realities: Politics and the European Community.* 2d ed. London: Longman.

Deutsch, Karl W., et al. 1966. "Political Community and the North Atlantic Area." In *International Political Communities.* Garden City, NY: Anchor Books, pp. 1–92.

Dosser, Douglas, David Gowland, and Keith Hartley. 1982. *The Collaboration of Nations: A Study of European Economic Policy.* New York: St. Martin's Press.

Eberle, James, John Roper, William Wallace, and Phil Williams. 1984. "European Security Cooperation and British Interests." *International Affairs,* 60: 545–60.

Freestone, David, and Anna Fleisch. 1983. "The Common Fisheries Policy." In Juliet Lodge, ed., *Institutions and Policies of the European Community.* New York: St. Martin's Press, pp. 77–84.

French, Hilary F. 1990. *Cleaning the Air: A Global Agenda.* Worldwatch Paper 94 (January). Washington, DC: Worldwatch Institute.

Haas, Ernst B. 1958. "Persistent Themes in Atlantic and European Unity." *World Politics* 10: 614–29.

Haas, Ernst B. 1976. "Turbulent Fields and the Theory of Regional Integration." *International Organization,* 30: 173–212.

Haas, Peter M. 1989. "Do Regimes Matter? Epistemic Communities and Mediterranean Pollution Control." *International Organization,* 43: 377–403.

Hanrieder, Wolfram F. 1978. "Dissolving International Politics: Reflections on the Nation-State." *American Political Science Review,* 72: 1276–87.

Hardin, Garrett. 1968. "The Tragedy of the Commons." *Science,* 162: 1243–48.

Hardin, Russell. 1982. *Collective Action.* Baltimore, MD: Johns Hopkins University.

Harrop, Jeffrey. 1989. *The Political Economy of Integration in the European Community.* Aldershot, England: Edward Elgar.

Hinsley, Sir Henry. 1989. "The European Community: A Body-Politic or an Association of States?" *The World Today,* 45: 1–3.

Hughes, Barry B. 1971. "Transaction Analysis: The Impact of Operationalization." *International Organization,* 25: 132–45.

Ifestos, Panayiotis. 1988. *Nuclear Strategy and European Security Dilemmas.* Brookfield, VT: Gower.

Johnson, Stanley P., and Guy Corcelle. 1989. *The Environmental Policy of the European Communities.* London: Graham and Trotman.

Jorgensen-Dahl, Arnfinn. 1975. "Forces of Fragmentation in the International System: The Case of Ethno-Nationalism." *Orbis,* 19: 652–74.

Keohane, Robert O., and Joseph S. Nye. 1977. *Power and Interdependence: World Politics in Transition.* Boston: Little, Brown.

Lindberg, Leon N., and Stuart A. Scheingold. 1970. *Europe's Would-be Polity: Patterns of Change in the European Community.* Englewood Cliffs, NJ: Prentice Hall.

Llewellyn, David T. 1988. "Financial Intermediation and Systems: Global Integration." In D.E. Fair and C. de Boissieu, eds., *International Monetary and Financial Integration—the European Dimension.* Boston: Kluwer Academic Publishers, pp. 239–60.

Luce, R.D., and Howard Raiffa. 1957. *Games and Decisions.* New York: Wiley.

Luif, Paul. 1987. "The European Neutrals and Economic Integration in Western Europe." *European Yearbook,* 35: 1–23.

McGowan, Francis. 1990. "Towards a European Electricity Market." *The World Today,* 46: 15–19.

Neumann, Manfred J. M. 1989. "Contribution to a Roundtable on 'The Appropriate Level of Regulation in Europe: Local, National or Community-wide?' " *Economic Policy*, October, 467–70.

Nielsson, Gunnar, and Ralph Jones. 1988. "From Ethnic Category to Nation: Patterns of Political Mobilization." Paper presented at the 1988 meeting of the International Studies Association, St. Louis, Missouri.

Olson, Mancur. 1965. *The Logic of Collective Action*. Cambridge: Harvard University Press.

Pearce, David W., ed. 1983. *The Dictionary of Modern Economics*. London: Macmillan.

Puchala, Donald J. 1988. "The Integration Theorists and the Study of International Relations." In Charles W. Kegley, Jr., and Eugene R. Wittkopf, eds., *The Global Agenda*. New York: Random House, pp. 198–215.

Putnam, Robert D. 1988. "Diplomacy and Domestic Politics: The Logic of Two-level Games." *International Organization*, 42: 427–60.

Rudney, Robert, and Luc Reychler, eds. 1988. *European Security Beyond the Year 2000*. New York: Praeger.

Russett, Bruce, and Harvey Starr. 1989. *World Politics*. New York: W. H. Freeman.

Samuelson, Paul A. 1955. "Diagrammatic Exposition of a Theory of Public Expenditure." *Review of Economics and Statistics*, 37: 350–56.

Sandholtz, Wayne, and John Zysman. 1989. "1992: Recasting the European Bargain." *World Politics*, 42: 95–128.

Schelling, Thomas C. 1978. *Micromotives and Macrobehavior*. New York: W. W. Norton.

Seidelmann, Reidmund. 1989. "The CSCE Process: A Way to European Peace in Security." In Graeme P. Auton, ed., *Arms Control and European Security*. New York: Praeger, pp. 111–20.

Snidal, Duncan. 1985. "Coordination versus Prisoner's Dilemma: Implications for International Cooperation and Regimes." *American Political Science Review*, 74: 923–42.

Soroos, Marvin S. 1986. *Beyond Sovereignty: The Challenge of Global Policy*. Columbia: University of South Carolina Press.

Soroos, Marvin S. 1987. "Global Commons, Telecommunications, and International Space Policy." In Daniel S. Papp and John R. McIntyre, eds., *International Space Policy*. New York: Quorum Books, pp. 139–56.

Soroos, Marvin S. 1988. "The Tragedy of the Commons in Global Perspective." In Charles W. Kegley, Jr., and Eugene R. Wittkopf, eds., *The Global Agenda: Issues and Perspectives*. 2d ed. New York: Random House, pp. 345–57.

Soroos, Marvin S. 1989a. "Conflict in the Use and Management of International Commons." Paper presented at the Tampere Peace Research Institute, Orivesi, Finland.

Soroos, Marvin S. 1989b. "Climate Change as a Problem of Managing a Global Common Property Resource." Paper prepared for a seminar on Contemporary Global Problems, University of Maria Curie-Sklodowska, Lublin, Poland, December 5–9, 1989.

Taylor, D., G. Diprose, and M. Duffy. 1986. "EC Environmental Policy and the Control of Water Pollution: The Implementation of Directive 76/464 in Perspective." *Journal of Common Market Studies*, 24: 225–46.

Taylor, Michael. 1987. *The Possibility of Cooperation*. Cambridge, England: Cambridge University Press.

Tilly, Charles. 1985. "War Making and State Making as Organized Crime." In Peter B. Evans, Dietrich Rueschemeyer, and Theda Skocpol, eds., *Bringing the State Back In*. Cambridge: Cambridge University Press, pp. 169–91.

von Groll, Götz. 1982. "The Nine at the Conference on Security and Cooperation in Europe." In David Allen, Reinhardt Rummel, and Wolfgang Wessels, eds., *European Political Cooperation*. Boston: Butterworth Scientific, pp. 60–68.

Wallace, Helen. 1988. "The European Community and EFTA: One Family or Two." *The World Today*, 44: 177–79.

Waltz, Kenneth. 1959. *Man, the State, and War*. New York: Columbia University Press.

Weimer, David L., and Aidan R. Vining. 1989. *Policy Analysis: Concepts and Practice*. Englewood Cliffs, NJ: Prentice Hall.

PART II

THE CONSEQUENCES
OF THE 1992 PROJECT

4

A People's Europe

Citizen Support for
the 1992 Project and Beyond

Russell J. Dalton and Richard C. Eichenberg

Europe stands at a historic threshold as the process of European integration moves toward the ambitious goals of the "1992 Project." After a decade of rancorous stagnancy, the European Community is taking dramatic steps to create a single market and to restructure the institutions of the Community. The Single European Act (SEA) of 1985 sets out a program of economic liberalization and the removal of trade barriers that will create a truly common market for the European economy. Equally important, it will also expand the EC's role into new policy areas such as the environment and social policy. The SEA includes procedural reforms that broaden the scope of majoritarian decision making and extend the powers of the European Parliament. Moreover, the changing international environment is propelling the Community toward a central institutional role in the post–cold war world. The December 1991 Maastricht Summit further laid the groundwork for a European monetary union and a new role for the Community in foreign and security policy. The developments are involving the EC in a deeper and broader array of policy concerns.

One correlate of the Community's expanding activities is the increasing importance of public opinion in the integration process. Early steps in the building of the Community were generally examples of "negative" integration, that is, the removal of obstacles to free exchange between the member states (Shepard 1975; Pinder 1989). Since there were few real costs and major benefits from cooperation, active public support was not essential. At most, the public provided elites with a "permissive consensus" for actions they undertook in the name of unification (Lindberg and Scheingold 1970).

With the steady growth in the Community's political authority, and with the advent of new policy areas incorporated within the 1992 Project, it is claimed that the Community has entered a stage of "positive" integration that involves more active efforts to create new European policies and spur the process of integration. Such positive actions create the potential for public opinion to play a greater role in facilitating or discouraging new policy initiatives or the transfer of new political authority from national governments to European supranational institutions. The extent of popular support for the single market concept, for example, will be an important influence on whether there will be a truly free exchange of workers and goods between nations. If the European Community wants to deal forcefully and effectively with issues such as monetary union, social equalization, and constitutional reform, it will require more than just the permissive consensus that previously characterized public attitudes toward Europe.

Not only is the nature of the public's deliberations about Europe changing, but it is also apparent that public sentiments are exercising a growing weight on national policy makers and on the institutions of the Community itself. Referendums on Community expansion were held in Ireland, Denmark, Norway and France in the early 1970s, marking the public's first direct participation in Community affairs. This involvement continued with the 1975 British referendum on Community membership, the referendums on the Single European Act (SEA) in Denmark (1986) and the Republic of Ireland (1987), and the 1989 European Constituent Referendum in Italy, and future referendums are being discussed to ratify national decisions on monetary reform and structural change of EC institutions. The direct elections of the European Parliament (EP) that began in 1979 have institutionalized this development, and the advent of a directly elected Parliament gives public opinion a voice in the governance of the Community. With direct elections has come increased legitimacy for the European Parliament, and consequently increased powers through the SEA. Moreover, even with these developments, there are frequently expressed concerns about the "democracy deficit" within the Community, with corresponding calls to increase the representation of the public through further institutional reforms. Slowly but steadily, the Community is moving toward its proclaimed objective of a people's Europe. In the EC of the future, Europeans will decide their own fate.

We would not argue that public opinion is the single driving force of the integration process because the Community's course on the SEA has been primarily determined by decisions taken at the elite level (Sandholtz and Zysman 1989; Moravcsik 1989). Nonetheless, although elites may have directed the passage of the SEA, its *implementation* will cause economic and social dislocations, so that public consensus on the overall goals of the SEA as well as on specific policy initiatives will be crucial to the future of the program. Popular support for deciding certain policies at the European level can facilitate the expansion of Community authority to these areas, just as resistance to supranational decision making can strengthen national forces that oppose a transfer of political sovereignty. Certainly policy makers may choose to ignore public preferences, but the contours of public opinion still provide useful guidance on which paths toward the goal of European union might be easily followed and which paths offer substantial political obstacles.

The growing political relevance of public attitudes toward the European Community makes these sentiments a useful starting point for the detailed policy analyses contained in this volume. This chapter maps the contours of public support for the basic elements of the SEA reforms and also describes popular sentiments toward expanding the Community's authority into new policy areas—including those covered in the 1992 Project and beyond. These analyses are based on the rich series of public opinion surveys conducted by the Commission of the European Communities, the *Eurobarometer* studies.[1]

The 1992 Project and Beyond

Public support for the general principles and goals of European integration varies across both time and space (Inglehart 1971, 1977; Shepard 1975; Dalton and Duval 1986; Hewstone 1986; Dalton and Eichenberg 1990; ZEUS 1990). Among the six founding members of the Community, support for Europe reached a high plateau of about 60 percent positive by the late 1950s, and generally remained at this level for most of the next three decades. Support for the European ideal has been more ambivalent among the subsequent expansion nations—British, Danish and Greek politicians tend to be the most vocal critics of the Community, and this is often mirrored in the opinions of their respective publics. But even in the expansion nations, the base of support broadened in the later half of the 1980s.

Although most people endorse the general principle of European integration, the ambitious objectives of current integration efforts are putting this support to a test. Called upon in the past to express abstract support for the Community, citizens are now challenged by basic changes in the very structure of the European marketplace. Other proposals call for a expanding the Community's policy-making authority into new issue areas. The mobilization of public support for these proposals thus represents a rigorous test of the depth of the public's true commitment to the European ideal.

The Provisions of the Single Common Market

Jacques Delors has described the single market as "an invaluable asset which can help restore our firms to economic health and a strong competitive position. It is one of the main driving forces that will take us on to European Union." The Community is asking European citizens to share in this challenge. The Single European Act asks Europeans to open their borders to the free flow of labor and capital, to open their markets to competing products, and to further integrate their economies. These changes require not just abstract support for the concept of European integration or symbolic commitments, such as acceptance of a European passport or a European flag; they demand change in the structure of European economies and the power of national governments.

The implementation of the SEA provisions by the member-states has generated extensive discussion of the potential consequences of a single market (Cecchini 1988; Emerson et al. 1988). The public has learned that the free flow of labor and capital may create new areas of economic growth, but also new areas of economic decline. Unions in Germany, France and Italy have expressed their concern about potential increases in unemployment; economic analysts point out that some businesses will be less competitive in a European market; consumer groups have raised questions about product safety if national regulations are removed; and other interest groups and politicians have joined the debate about the consequences of the SEA (Sbragia 1992).

How do Europeans react to such debates about the consequences of the single market concept? The depth of integrationist sentiment among Europeans is strikingly displayed in their support for the provisions of the Single European Market. In recent years the *Eurobarometer* surveys have asked Europeans whether they thought ten key provisions of the single market represent more of an advantage or a disadvantage for them (Table 4.1). By overwhelming margins, citizens think that the advantages of the SEA reforms outweigh the disadvantages. For example, labor unions in several nations have expressed concern with the free flow of workers because of the potential impact on labor markets, and conservative politicians have openly worried that unrestricted migration may undermine national cultures. Yet averaged across all twelve nations, about three-quarters of all Europeans see unrestricted labor migration as a net advantage. Similarly, the potential problems of open borders have been widely discussed in the popular press—shopkeepers fret about competition from low-tax products from neighboring countries, Germans worry about the influx of drugs from Holland, and the French are anxious about the influx of Germans—but two-thirds of the public favor the elimination of customs controls at intra-EC borders. The lowest level of support concerns public works projects, though a majority are still positive toward single market provisions in this area.

We should be cautious about interpreting these figures as informed and solid judgments about the cost/benefits of a single market, but these survey results do represent the climate of popular opinion toward the concept of the single market. And in this sense, our findings are striking. In every area included on this list of policy initiatives, a clear majority sees the advantages of the reform as outweighing the disadvantages. Moreover, averaged across the Community as a whole for all these provisions, evaluations of the relative advantages of the single market appear relatively unaffected by the shifting political debates that have accompanied SEA legislation. The 1989 evaluations of these SEA proposals almost exactly mirror these same opinions just after the SEA was adopted.

Underlying the European patterns in the rating of these various proposals are

Table 4.1

European Perceptions of the 1992 Single Market Provisions

	Oct. 1987	April 1988	Oct. 1988	April 1989
Percentage saying each item is an advantage:				
Opportunity to live in another EC nation	79	77	80	80
Ability to make easy payments within whole EC	80	79	80	82
Removal of currency restrictions on intra-EC travel	79	79	79	81
Possibility to buy products of any nation within EC	81	77	79	81
Opportunity to work in another EC nation	80	76	77	78
Possibility to open bank account in other EC nation	70	70	73	74
Possibility to buy land throughout EC	69	68	72	71
Bringing VAT rates closer together	69	66	65	69
Eliminating border controls between EC countries	67	64	64	66
Contracting of public works to companies from other countries EC	54	52	55	56
Average	73	71	72	74

Source: Eurobarometer, issues 27–31. Percentages are based on the Communitywide sample, Eurobarometer, issues weighted by size of national population aged 15 and over.

Question text: "The coming into being of the Single Common European Market in 1992 will mean the free circulation of persons, goods and property within the European Community countries. Some people think this will be mostly an advantage, others think it will be a disadvantage. Can you tell me, for each aspect of this Single Common European Market which I am going to mention, whether you personally think it will be an advantage or disadvantage?"

some systematic differences in how specific nations view the relative strengths and weakness of the SEA package (Table 4.2). Citizens in the poorer, peripheral nations of the Community—Ireland, Italy, Portugal, Spain, and Greece—are more likely to rank freedom of movement (for residence and work) as among the most positive advantages of the single market. Residents of the more affluent and heavily industrialized nations—such as Germany, France, and Britain—see greater advantages in the relaxation of currency restrictions and the increase in consumer choice. Similarly, where some nations see the standardization of the value-added tax (VAT) as a significant advance, those nations that benefit from low VAT levels are less likely to see VAT standardization as an advantage.

Although there are some national differences in how the SEA is perceived, the other lesson of Table 4.2 is the general breadth of support for these proposals. National differences across policy domains are actually somewhat weaker than

Table 4.2

Perceptions of the 1992 Single Market Provisions

	France	Belg.	Holland	Germ.	Italy	Luxem.	Den-mark	UK	Ireland	Greece	Spain	Port.	EC Avg.
Percentage saying each item is an advantage:													
Opportunity to live in another EC nation	84	81	73	76	89	81	60	70	93	83	86	86	80
Ability to make easy payments within whole EC	87	79	82	81	86	86	69	80	85	74	81	76	82
Remove currency restrictions on intra-EC travel	87	78	74	84	80	87	66	80	82	79	79	77	81
Possibility to buy products of any nation within EC	83	79	76	83	85	87	59	76	83	79	86	73	81
Opportunity to work in another EC nation	82	77	72	61	91	66	60	79	93	78	85	85	78
Possibility to open bank account in another nation	74	74	64	73	75	74	49	77	79	68	80	76	74
Possibility to buy land throughout EC	71	72	64	72	75	70	31	69	69	63	79	73	71
Bringing VAT rates closer together	85	69	79	58	77	22	76	61	88	66	65	65	69
Eliminating customs controls at intra-EC borders	68	75	60	74	65	62	52	45	78	78	74	82	66
Contracting of public works to companies from other EC countries	60	51	57	50	57	35	41	50	60	62	67	71	56
Country Average	78	74	70	71	78	67	65	68	81	73	78	76	73

Source: Eurobarometer 31 (June 1989).

issue-by-issue variation in support for these proposals. Nations vary in the range of their support and the ranking of issues, but in very few instances is support for these proposals actually withheld. For instance, the highest overall support for the ten reforms is found in the three newest members of the Community and the lowest support is found in the nations that joined the EC in 1973—but the range between these extremes is fairly small (76 percent supportive versus 67 percent).

Even if most Europeans have not read the Cecchini report (1988), they clearly share its optimistic estimates of the consequences of a single market. The concept of a single European market is not something that has to be sold to the average citizen of the Community; most individuals view the SEA reforms as offering greater benefits than costs. A variety of other questions available from the *Eurobarometer* surveys document this same point.[2] The breadth of this support may be due to two factors. First, much like the dynamics that shaped the Treaty of Rome, the compromises that created the SEA include benefits for everyone in the package, even if the relative value of these benefits varies across nations. Southern Europeans look forward to the opening of labor markets in the north, while northern Europeans look forward to EC-wide economies of scale and to the opening of product markets in the south. If the perceived advantages outweigh the disadvantages in overall terms, and if the proposals are presented as a single package, this generates support for the entire program of reform. Second, even though the SEA might mark a dramatic new step in the process of European integration, the content of these reforms still largely involves examples of negative integration—removing existing impediments to the flow of labor and goods within the Community. In this sense, the SEA does not push the Community into new areas. Indeed, the Community has claimed to represent a "Common Market" for over two decades; the SEA merely implements the vision of the Treaty of Rome, a vision that European citizens have long supported.

National versus Community Decision Making

If the 1992 Project is to move Europe significantly toward its goal of political and economic union, the real test will lie in the expansion of Community decision making into new policy areas that follow from the reforms of the 1992 Project and in creating new institutional arrangements to develop and implement these policies. The economic emphasis of the SEA reforms has led some member states to press for equal attention to social and cultural issues. The Greek and Spanish governments, for example, have called on the Community to create a "Common European Social Space" to parallel its economic progress; the Commission has debated the promulgation of a Social Charter to guarantee fundamental social rights; environmentalists have pressed the Community to take a more active role in setting Europewide pollution standards; others have proposed a "Technological Community" to keep Europe competitive in new scientific developments; and the 1988 "Delors package" stressed the need to expand the

Community's role in social policy if economic reforms are to succeed. Such reforms would mark important new steps in the integration process, often involving the Community in new areas of political authority.

From the standpoint of public opinion, support for extending the policy-making powers of the Community would represent a more rigorous test of public commitment to Europe than support for the abstract concept of integration or even the examples of "negative" integration embedded in the Single European Act. Indeed, although political conflicts within the Community sometimes address the general principles underlying the integration process, more often they focus on specific policy issues: the provisions of the Common Agricultural Program, disagreements over the standardization of national social policies, dissension about a European monetary union, conflicts over the allocation of budget and taxing policy within the EC, and debate about the EC's role in foreign and security policy. A public endorsement of Community-level action in these other areas could provide popular legitimacy for EC legislation and could facilitate the expansion of Community responsibility, just as citizen opposition to European action could retard the integration process.

Both before and after the creation of the 1992 Project, the Commission of the European Community has been asking Europeans what type of Europe they would prefer. Paralleling the public's general support for the principle of European integration, previous public opinion surveys have routinely found widespread support for European policy making in several domains. In the 1960s, two-thirds or more of the European public favored common policy making on free market provisions that closely mirror the SEA (elimination of tariffs and the free circulation of workers and firms), a common agricultural policy, a common program of scientific research, equalizing social benefits across member-states, and even a common foreign policy (Lindberg and Scheingold 1970, 57). Europeans were ready for Community action before the Community was. Research from the 1970s found continuing strong public commitment to Community decision making (Dalton 1978). A majority of Europeans were willing to transfer political responsibility from the nation-state to the Community for a wide range of policy areas: environmental protection, modernizing agriculture, energy supplies, regional development, fighting inflation, and relations with the superpowers. In fact, in several areas the public displayed greater support for European policy making than for the abstract principle of integration.

When these questions were repeated in the 1980s in a slightly different format, the European public remained supportive of expanding Community decision making into new areas, although there are also many policy activities that they wish to remain in the purview of national governments (Table 4.3).[3] Large majorities of the European public are willing to see the Community expand its activities into at least three new policy domains. First, the internationalization of environmental problems—from oil spills, to acid rain, to Chernobyl—has sensitized people to the need to develop and enforce environmental protection mea-

Table 4.3

Support for Community Decision Making by Policy Area (by percent)

	1985	1987	1988	1989	1990	1991
Scientific and technological research	70	60	63	77	75	78
Cooperation with developing countries	77	42	51	76	74	79
Protection of the environment	69	61	68	67	66	72
Foreign policy toward countries outside the EC	—	44	50	66	64	71
Reduce regional differences in EC	63	—	—	—	—	—
Fight unemploymennt	59	—	—	—	—	—
Fight terrorism and crime	58	—	—	—	—	—
Currency	—	43	48	57	51	59
Fight rising prices	52	—	—	—	—	—
Rates of value-added tax	—	—	—	51	48	52
Security and defense	58	60	57	48	47	51
Protect consumer against false advertising	58	—	—	—	—	—
Basic rules for broadcasting and the press	—	—	—	47	45	49
Protection of personal information on computer files	—	—	—	39	39	42
Health and social welfare	—	—	—	38	39	42
Codetermination	—	—	—	36	37	41
Education	—	—	—	34	38	41

Source: Eurobarometer, issues 24, 27, 29, 31, 33, and 35. Results are based on the combined European sample, weighted by the size of the national population aged 15 and over. Question text in 1989 and after: "Some people believe that certain areas of policy should be decided by [national] government, while other areas should be decided jointly with the European Community. Which of the following areas of policy do you think should be decided by the [national] government? And which do you think should be decided jointly within the European Community?" Table entries are the percentage replying that each policy area should be decided jointly within the Community rather than by the respective national governments.

sures at an international level. In data extending back to the 1970s (Dalton 1978), about two-thirds of Europeans prefer environmental policy to be made at the EC level. In 1990, European-level environmental action is preferred over national policy making in every member-state (see Table 4.4, page 85); even in Denmark, a country that has repeatedly criticized the EC for its environmental inaction and had its own progressive environmental legislation challenged by the Community, a majority of the electorate (55 percent) prefers the EC-level decision making over policy making by their national government. The Single European Act of 1986 finally added environmental policy to the responsibilities of the Community, and these data indicate that the popular mandate already exists for the Community to exercise this new authority.

Even before recent political events had stimulated debate on the Community's role in the changing international system, foreign policy constituted a second area where Europeans are willing for the Community to expand its authority. Nearly three-quarters of the public favor Community-level action on policies of (economic) cooperation with Third World nations, an endorsement for political action that extends back to the 1970s at least. Similarly, recent surveys find that nearly two-thirds of the EC public think the Community should exercise the primary role in foreign relations with non-EC nations. In part, people may simply be responding to the growth of the Community's existing role in foreign policy (Ginsberg 1989). In addition to the more institutionalized aspects of Community foreign policy, or European Political Cooperation (EPC), such as the Lome Conventions, the EC has acted in concert during the past decade by enacting sanctions against Rhodesia, Argentina, Israel, Iran, Poland, the Soviet Union and Iraq. Perhaps more important in explaining the recent trend of public opinion, the Community has played a prominent role in preparing responses to the dramatic upheavals in Eastern Europe during 1989 and 1990, and to the Persian Gulf crisis. At the same time, however, the Community struggled in developing its reaction to Yugoslavia. In any case, the clear import of these data is that the plurality of the public in every EC member-state is willing to see past European political cooperation among national governments develop into a more active role for the Community in the setting and implementation of Europe's external political relations. The policy decisions of the Maastricht Summit to expand the foreign policy role of the Community thus mirror the long-standing sentiments of the European public.

An even stiffer test of citizen support for the Community as an international actor involves opinions toward defense. The effort to create a European Defense Community (EDC) in the 1950s was a major failure of the integration process, and this has led to the belief that the sensitive national interests included within this area make it more resistant to unification efforts (Hoffmann 1966). This view gained strength with several decades of subsequent foreign policy experiences—nuclear weapons, the Soviet Union, and various NATO policy initiatives—that illustrated the difficulties Europeans had in forming a European alternative to the North Atlantic security community.

Even before elite discussion of a common European defense, a large number of Europeans are willing to see security and defense decisions determined at the Community level. Table 4.3 indicates that roughly half of the European public in 1989 and 1990 think that security policy should be decidedly jointly within the Community (this is down slightly from 1987–88, but this comparison is affected by a change in question format, see footnote 3). Even more telling, a recent survey finds that more Europeans favor the EC over NATO as a vehicle for making decisions about the future security of western Europe (*Eurobarometer* 32, October 1989). The question read, "In your opinion, should NATO continue to be the most important forum for making decisions about the security of Western Europe in the future, or should the European Community make these decisions, or should some other organization make these decisions?" The EC was named by 36 percent of all Europeans, NATO by 30 percent, 8 percent mentioned other organizations (such as the WEU), 7 percent spontaneously said that each nation should make its own decision, and 19 percent expressed no opinion. In fact, this 1989 survey is the first in many years to show a plurality of Europeans favoring the EC over NATO. In the past, despite an abstract affinity for a European security policy, Europeans have generally opted for NATO when forced to choose between the European and the Atlantic connection, presumably because the security threat from the Soviet Union made NATO indispensable (Eichenberg 1989, 128–131). Coming as it did after the implementation of Gorbachev's perestroika and new thinking in security policy, *Eurobarometer* 32 suggests that the decline in cold war tensions has attenuated the bonds that made NATO an indispensable option in the past.[4] And a Europeanist sentiment in the security field has also grown in the wake of the uncertainties raised by the Iraqi invasion of Kuwait; a full 59 percent of the EC public say that a common defense organization for the Community is now necessary, and only 31 percent say it is not necessary (*Eurobarometer* 34, October 1990). These figures approach historical highs of "Europeanist" sentiment on this sort of question. To be sure, we might expect that this general endorsement of EC authority in the making of foreign policy and defense policy would weaken if essential (and possibly conflicting) national interests are at stake. And in fact, there are numerous examples of the Community failing to take a common stance because of the conflicting interests of its member-states. Still, the potential for the Community to exercise a broader role in foreign affairs discussed by Pearson and Granham in chapters 10 and 11 of this book is more than just an abstract ideal. It is a political option now favored by many Europeans.

The greatest support for an expansion of Community authority exists for a third area of scientific and technological research. The vast majority of Europeans see scientific and development policy as something that is best handled at the European level. This endorsement of Community action probably reflects a combination of factors. On the one hand, the Community has a track record of past performance in this area, ranging from Euratom to the Eureka project (Sandholtz 1992). On the other hand, the growing popular awareness of the technological progress being made in Japan and the United States undoubtedly contributes to a belief that Europe must pool its resources if it wishes to remain competitive in the development of new products and the utilization of new technologies (Hoffmann 1984; Sandholtz and Zysman 1989).

Popular support for EC decision making is lowest for a diverse mix of policies. Barely a third of Europeans favor EC action on matters of education policy, even though the Community has been fairly effective in developing Europewide training standards and the recognition of technical training within the Community. Similarly, only a minority of the public is willing to see health and social welfare policies addressed at the European level. Broadly speaking, it appears that the public is hesitant to see the Community become involved in matters of the welfare state, perhaps because many individuals are heavily dependent on welfare state provisions and are hesitant to see these entitlements open to revision. Ironically, they are more willing to have the EC decide on essential economic matters, such as dealing with unemployment and inflation, than with health and welfare benefits.

The broad contours of citizen support for EC decision making sometimes vary, often in interesting ways, across the EC member states. Table 4.4 presents the national patterns in the *net difference* between the percentage preferring Community action minus those favoring national-level decision making. Comparing across nations, the greatest net support for European-level action is found among the six founding nations, with most policy areas showing a plurality of support for EC action. The Germans, however, fall noticeably below the other founding states; Germans are less enthusiastic than their neighbors about the seemingly consensual issues for European action—science and technology, foreign aid, and environmental protection—and are hesitant to yield national autonomy on matters such as currency reform and VAT rates. While Germans, and their government, voice strong support for the European ideal, they are now more cautious in actually transferring authority to Brussels. This skepticism is generally shared by the expansion nations, with the Danes being the least supportive of shifting policy authority to the Community.

Policies that evoke general support (or opposition) to Community action are not likely to be a source of political contention, but policy areas that evoke opposing reactions from various nationalities hold the potential for becoming issues of disagreement within the Community. For example, security and defense policy is an area where nations differ sharply in their willingness to transfer authority to the Community. The public in five of the EC founder states (excluding France) lean toward EC decision making, while the plurality of the electorates in the remaining nations prefer national policy making on security and defense issues.[5] In other areas, the opinions of the public lag behind policy makers; in a third of the member-states a plurality of the public still favors national action on monetary and currency union (Britain, Germany, Spain, and Portugal). In some instances, publics appear to favor European action to replace their own struggling programs; for instance, the Italian and Greek electorates are more positive toward European action on social programs, while national decision making is preferred by other nationalities. The potential for further integration is probably limited in these areas of disagreement, because conflicting national priorities would make it difficult for the Community to assume a broader policy role even if a plurality of Europeans favor such action.

European Publics and the Lessons for European Integration

As Smith and Ray point out in their introductory chapter, the process of European integration appeared to slow in the 1970s and early 1980s, at least to analysts of the Community. But no one told this to the European public. Our

Table 4.4

Net Support for Community versus National Decision Making by Nation

	France	Belg.	Holland	Germ.	Italy	Luxem.	Den-mark	UK	Ireland	Greece	Spain	Port.	EC Avg.
Percentage saying each item is an advantage:													
Scientific and technological research	61	67	65	39	67	67	46	54	59	54	58	37	56
Cooperation with developing countries	57	56	52	43	73	65	32	65	51	33	62	32	57
Protection of the environment	29	38	65	39	41	33	12	45	6	19	34	3	37
Foreign policy toward countries outside the EC	40	51	42	28	59	42	2	36	36	0	48	17	39
Currency	33	44	8	–6	42	22	9	–9	20	11	–9	–16	11
Rates of VAT	43	49	42	–9	14	–36	3	–17	22	–3	8	–9	9
Security and defense	–10	14	39	6	26	48	–13	–13	–47	–28	–13	–29	0
Basic rules for broadcasting and the press	10	6	18	2	7	18	–53	–19	–6	4	–6	–9	–1
Protection of personal information on computers	–16	–8	–2	0	3	–8	–64	–19	–20	0	3	–29	–7
Health and social welfare	–34	–15	–7	–26	17	–13	–68	–25	–28	14	–14	–6	–16
Codetermination	–5	–18	–19	–22	0	–5	–58	–5	–1	–6	–17	–19	–12
Education	–9	–35	–25	–28	10	–8	–53	–40	–41	8	–16	–21	–19
Country Average	17	21	23	6	30	19	–17	4	4	8	12	–4	13

Source: Eurobarometer 33 (May 1990). Table entries are the percentage replying that each policy area should be decided jointly within the Community *minus* those who believe the area should be decided by the respective national governments.

findings here, and those in other work (Dalton and Eichenberg 1990), describe a European public that is broadly and fairly consistently supportive of the European ideal. Moreover, this support encompasses many of the new reforms of the 1992 Project and even an expansion of policy responsibilities beyond the 1992 goals. Even the ambitious policy goals of the 1991 Maastricht Summit—a common currency, a common foreign policy, and a common defense policy—were endorsed by a majority of the European public before Community elites took action. These findings mean that European elites can continue to draw upon a reservoir of popular support for the EC, and a more assertive public might actually increase the pressure for further progress.

But in addition to these substantive findings, our research also has something to say about the process of European integration. Citizen attitudes toward European integration represent the aggregation of thousands of calculations about the advantages and disadvantages of European union; moreover, public sentiments represent preferences for how the process should proceed, and thus may provide a unique perspective on the underlying processes that guide the integration process but are difficult to see by focusing on specific policy outcomes. In other words, our findings provide an opportunity to evaluate contending theories of the integration process as these theories are translated into popular attitudes toward the Community.

The classic *functionalist model* of integration maintains that intrinsic qualities of a policy domain define its susceptibility to harmonization and the spillover effects of the integration process (Sewell 1966; Haas 1958). It was expected that success in the most fertile policy areas would "spill over" into other policy domains as the interdependence resulting from international cooperation became apparent. In this respect, functionalist theories of interdependence are very similar to more recent theories of global interdependence and cooperation (Keohane and Nye 1989). From this perspective, the Community was able to harmonize the postwar agricultural system because of the obvious need for agricultural reform in the 1950s in a setting of a developing world agricultural trade market. The Community's growing involvement in environmental issues, such as acid rain and pollution of international waterways, might be another example of this functionalist logic.

Hoffmann (1966; see also: Moravcsik 1989) has offered an alternative classification of issue domains based upon considerations of *national sovereignty*. Hoffmann argues that the greatest support for Community decision making exists for what he terms "low politics" issues, matters that do not touch essential national interests. In these cases, national elites (and the general public) are more willing to grant decision-making authority to a supranational body over which they will obviously have less control. Correspondingly, Hoffmann maintains that national governments (and publics) will resist yielding control of "high politics" issues that touch essential national interests. Thus, efforts to establish a customs union or a common foreign aid program might succeed, but attempts to develop a single European Army would fail. Hoffmann's definition of high and low politics issues is somewhat fuzzy, but the former include such issues as national security, control of the domestic economy, and general rights of national sovereignty. Low politics issues encompass such matters as welfare policies, tariff policies, and other lower priority policies. Hoffmann's categorization of issue domains has the further benefit of offering an explanation of why European integration stagnated in the late 1960s as the concerns of the Community shifted from the easy progress of "low politics" or negative integration issues to the more contestive high politics issues.

Finally, other analysts suggest that the integration process moves forward at the greatest speed in *newly emerging policy areas* where established interest groups and government bureaucracies are not yet established at the national level. All else being equal, the lack of an entrenched network of issue interests makes it easier for the Community to assume policy responsibility in these emerging areas. The best illustration of this theory is the development of Euratom in the 1950s and Eureka in the 1980s. Rabier and Inglehart (1981) utilize this rationale in suggesting that political elites are more likely to favor Europe-level action for the new postindustrial issues facing European societies.

Certainly no single explanation is sufficient for describing the actual course of European integration, and indeed the history of the Community is dotted with examples that undercut the validity of each theory. For instance, the functionalist argument is at odds with the basic pattern of Community history; instead of spillover flowing from one policy domain to the next, the Community actually experienced a very uneven pattern of development (and regression). And of course, as experience with monetary policy has shown, interdependence can create divisive conflict as well as pressure for cooperation. Moreover, the basic flaw of the functionalist argument is that it is difficult to predict which areas are most susceptible to collective action and which are not; this appears to be a trial-and-error process rather than an easily predictable entity. Hoffmann's emphasis on national interest might be useful in explaining some Community actions, such as the defeat of the European Defense Force in 1954. But the very origins of the Community involved coordination of the steel and coal industries *because* they were vital components of national economic power that would be needed to develop a warmaking capacity. The recency thesis has similar weaknesses. The core of the Community's present activities are comprised of long-standing areas of concern to modern governments—agricultural policy, trade policy, the coal and steel community, and customs policy—and not new policy issues. In fact, the Community is commonly criticized for being slow to take up such new causes as environmental protection and women's rights.

Our analyses of European public opinion suggest that both the Hoffmann "realist" perspective and the functionalist "interdependence" perspective have some explanatory power, and some limitations in explaining public attitudes. Clearly, there are some core "high politics" interests that dilute the enthusiasm of citizens for supranational integration. As we noted above, the national security field is one that has divided policy makers in the past, and although opinion on an EC role in security is higher than realist theorists would predict, the public remains evenly divided on this matter. Although a majority have recently expressed support for an EC security policy, citizen opinions seem sensitive to changes in the security environment. In addition, this is a policy area in which national differences in opinion are clearly visible. Significantly, public opinion in countries with the most extensive international security involvements are relatively unenthusiastic about security integration (France, Germany and Britain). At the same time, however, if security policy is the sharpest example of a high politics issue, it is surprising that half of the European public seems willing to grant the EC greater authority in this area of vital national interests. In terms of the expectations derived by realist theories, the popular support we find for European decision making in the security area is surprisingly high.

Rather than national security, Europeans appear more sensitive to policies of personal social security that regulate domestic income distribution, labor relations, and social mobility (education). As we saw in Table 4.3, Community-level action in these policy domains is less popular among European publics. But even here, our findings lead to a recalibration and redefinition of the meaning of "high politics" issues, because social policy epitomized low politics issues in Hoffmann's original typology. Indeed, our findings suggest that citizens may define "high politics" issues from the perspective of their own individual interests, and less from assessments of a separate, abstract national interest.[6]

Even when the public displays a hesitancy to transfer authority to a European level, this does not mean that domestic support for further integration in these fields is impossible. Rather, we would hypothesize that because external security and social security touch on matters of national and personal interest, they are more sensitive to the nature of the external and internal political environments. Unlike functionalist theories, then, this perspective does not predict a slow, gradual growth of supportive political groups or interdependencies that "push" or "spill over" the process of integration. Rather, it is the confluence of international change (in the military balance of power) and internal change (in economic variables that sensitize domestic groups to distributional issues) that influences public opinion toward European supranationalism. Applying the arguments of both Putnam (1988) and Sandholtz and Zysman (1989), it appears that domestic support for European integration flows from the complicated connections between domestic and international bargains, and their results.

Yet, the opinion data also suggest that the functionalist, interdependence logic does hold in some areas. The obvious example is the environment, where the logic of interdependence seems to have taken a powerful hold on public opinion. The same might be said for the broader market regulations of the Treaty of Rome and the SEA itself, for the logic of market expansion and liberalization is to create positive economies of scale that result from a single market. This logic certainly holds for the growth of business support for 1992, which students have ascribed to businesses' recognition that a broader, integrated market was necessary to allow for effective European competition in a global economy. And market liberalization will certainly create spillover, as the promulgation of Commission regulations clearly illustrates.

In short, like the integration process itself, public opinion seems to reflect a tug of war between the logic of national interests and sovereignty versus the logic of interdependence and cooperation. But even with these contending concerns, Europeans remain generally positive about the Community and the prospects for further European action. In one sense, therefore, the 1992 Project represents the transformation of existing popular support for the European ideal into a political reality.

Notes

1. The data utilized in this chapter were made available by Karlheinz Reif of the Directorate General for Information, Communication and Culture of the European Communities and by the Inter-university Consortium for Political and Social Research at the University of Michigan. Neither the original collectors of these data nor the Consortium bear any responsibility for the analyses and interpretation presented here.

2. An October 1988 survey (*Eurobarometer* 30) shows that Europeans were more likely to approach the Single Market with a feeling of hope (67 percent) than with fear (22 percent). Another question finds that the number of Europeans who think completion of the Single Market will be a "good thing" outweighs those who think it will be a "bad thing" by about a 5-to-1 ratio.

3. In 1987 and 1988 this question was asked only of the roughly half of the sample who first expressed approval for the general idea of a European government. We would expect, therefore, that this format should inflate support for EC policy making in these surveys.

4. This reasoning matches our finding in a study of aggregate support for European unification, which is negatively related to the state of East/West conflict. That is, support for Europe in the past two decades has tended to rise as East/West tensions decline (Dalton and Eichenberg 1990).

5. However, when given the choice between NATO or the EC as a forum for international security, the public in Mediterranean Europe favors the EC.

6. It also appears that calculations of national interest are more important for European political elites than for the European public-at-large (see Rabier and Inglehart 1981).

References

Cecchini, Paolo. 1988. *The European Challenge 1992: The Benefits of a Single Market.* Aldershot, England: Gower.

Dalton, Russell. 1978. "The Uncertain Future of European Integration." Paper presented at the annual meetings of the American Political Science Association, New York.

Dalton, Russell, and Robert Duval. 1986. "The Political Environment and Foreign Policy Opinions: British Attitudes toward European Integration, 1972–1979." *British Journal of Political Science*, 16:113–34.

Dalton, Russell, and Richard Eichenberg. 1990. "Europeans and the European Community: The Dynamics of Public Support for European Integration." Paper presented at the annual meetings of the American Political Science Association, San Francisco.

Eichenberg, Richard. 1989. *Public Opinion and National Security in Western Europe*. Ithaca, NY: Cornell University Press.

Emerson, Michael, et al. 1988. *The Economics of 1992: The EC Commission's Assessment of the Economic Effects of Completing the Internal Market*. New York: Oxford University Press.

Feld, Werner, and John Wildgen. 1976. *Domestic Political Realities and European Unification*. Boulder, CO: Westview Press.

Ginsberg, Roy. 1989. *The Foreign Policy Actions of the European Community*. Boulder, CO: Lynne Rienner.

Haas, Ernest. 1958. *The Uniting of Europe*. Stanford: Stanford University Press.

Hewstone, Miles. 1986. *Understanding Attitudes toward the European Community*. Cambridge: Cambridge University Press.

Hoffmann, Stanley. 1984. "Cries and Whimpers: Thoughts on West European Relations in the 1980s," *Daedalus*, 113: 221–52.

Hoffmann, Stanley. 1966. "Obstinate or Obsolete: The Fate of the Nation-state and the Case of Western Europe." *Daedalus*, 95: 862–915.

Inglehart, Ronald. 1971. "Public Opinion and Regional Integration." In Leon Lindberg and Stuart Sheingold, eds., *Regional Integration*. Cambridge, MA: Harvard University Press.

Inglehart, Ronald. 1977. *The Silent Revolution*. Princeton, NJ: Princeton University Press.

Keohane, Robert, and Joseph Nye. 1989. *Power and Interdependence*. 2d ed. Boston: Scott, Foresman.

Lindberg, Leon, and S. Scheingold. 1970. *Europe's Would-be Polity*. Englewood Cliffs, NJ: Prentice Hall.

Moravcsik, Andrew. 1989. "Negotiating the Single Act." Working Paper Series of the Center for International Affairs, no. 31. Harvard University.

Pinder, John. 1989. "The Single Market." In Juliet Lodge, ed. *The European Community and the Challenge of the Future*. London: Pinter.

Putnam, Robert. 1988. "Diplomacy and Domestic Politics." *International Organization*, 42:427–60.

Rabier, Jacques-Rene, and Ronald Inglehart. 1981. "What Kind of Europe: Support for National Independence, Cooperation and Integration in the European Parliament." *Government and Opposition*, 16:185–99.

Sandholtz, Wayne. 1992. *High-Tech Europe*. Berkeley: University of California Press.

Sandholtz, Wayne, and John Zysman. 1989. "1992: Recasting the European Bargain." *World Politics*, 42:1–30.

Sbragia, Alberta, ed. 1992. *Euro-Politics*. Washington, DC: Brookings Institution.

Sewell, James. 1966. *Functionalism and World Politics*. Princeton, NJ: Princeton University Press.

Shepard, Robert. 1975. *Public Opinion and European Integration*. Lexington, MA: Lexington Books.

Taylor, Paul. 1989. "New Dynamics of EC Integration in the 1980s." In Juliet Lodge, ed., *The European Community and the Challenge of the Future*. London: Pinter.

ZEUS. 1990. "Structure in European Attitudes." Mannheim: Zentrum für Europaische Umfrageanalysen und Studien.

5

Asymmetrical Integration in the European Community
The Single European Act and Institutional Development

Alberta M. Sbragia

The "1992 Project" has both an economic and a political significance. The European Community is not only creating a single integrated market but also transforming the way it governs itself. It is that double impact that makes it such a watershed in the history of European integration. The 1992 program involves both markets and governance.

Economically, the project to create a single integrated market by the end of 1992 is designed to create, within the territorial confines of the European Community, the world's most important market. Not since the American single market was painstakingly stitched together in the nineteenth century has an economic effort of this magnitude and complexity been seen.[1] Furthermore, the timetable established by its protagonists is so compressed that the creation of the single integrated market within the European Community may rank as a unique effort in economic history.

The objective is so noteworthy that most analysts have focused on the economic implications of "1992" (Hufbauer 1990). The far-reaching political significance of its legislative parent, the Single European Act, has received less attention. Yet, the Act had constitutional significance. It expanded the Community's jurisdiction and changed the nature of many of the "games" involving the Euro-

Note: This is a revised version of a paper given at the Brookings Institution's Conference on "European Political Institutions and Policymaking after 1992" in March 1990. I am grateful to Peter Hall, Helen Wallace, and Joseph Weiler for very helpful comments on the original version of the paper. I am also deeply indebted to Helen Wallace and Joseph Weiler for their general assistance on the project from which this paper is drawn.

pean Community's institutions and those of national governments.

Creation and maintenance of an integrated market typically require the exercise of concentrated government power.[2] The Single European Act (SEA) in fact establishes the institutional conditions necessary to begin thinking of closer *political* union in a serious way. By establishing new decision-rules designed to allow Community policy making to be less constrained by any single member-state, the Act represents a major step in the construction of a European Community that goes far beyond a "common market." It increased the degree to which member-states were willing to pool their sovereignty. Further, it extended the policy competence of the Community into new policy areas. In particular, the Community's new powers in environmental policy make it more than an economic actor. In brief, the "relaunching" of Europe that took place with the signing of the Single European Act in February 1986, reinforced by the decisions taken during summits subsequent to the signing, has made the Community both an economic and a (albeit limited) political force to be reckoned with.[3]

The Community's institutional development has not yet reached a plateau. As Leon Lindberg (chapter 6) points out, economic and monetary union is very much on the agenda. During the Strasbourg Summit in December 1989, the European Council decided that an Intergovernmental Conference (a code for a meeting of constitutional significance) would consider changing the treaties so as to proceed further toward economic and monetary union. Such union could eventually lead to a common central bank, a "Eurofed" (Woolley 1991). At the Dublin Summit of June 1990, the European Council decided that an Intergovernmental Conference on Political Union would be held parallel with the Conference on Economic and Monetary Union. Those two conferences culminated in the Maastricht Summit in December 1991.

The SEA represented a significant step in the institutional development of the Community because it transformed (albeit selectively) decision making within the Council of Ministers. Nonetheless, it is important not to assume that the structure of decision making within the Council of Ministers is the only one that matters. The Council of Ministers, in fact, exists within a fairly complex institutional landscape.

The institutional development of the Community will be understated if other key institutions are not included in an overview of institutional development within the Community. The Single European Act's significance will likewise be only partially appreciated if its integrative thrust is not situated within its larger institutional context. This chapter, therefore, offers a sketch of both the significance of the Single European Act for the Council of Ministers as well as of the other decision-making institutions of importance to the Community.

The European Community as a Policy Actor

Although the Single European Act represents a significant step in the history of the European Community, it is important not to assume that before the Act, there was nothing. It is certainly true that the Community had reached a *political* stalemate during the 1970s that continued into the 1980s. The need for unanimity on all decisions taken by the Council of Ministers had led to political paralysis in the Council. Time after time, policy initiatives were blocked because of the opposition of a few member governments.

Yet it is also true that by the early 1980s, the Community was an important policy actor in certain sectors and was therefore involved in extremely complex relations with its member governments. Carole Webb, writing in 1982, described this duality of political paralysis and selected policy vitality:

> On the surface much of the political activity—-elaborate European Council meetings and persistently unproductive Council of Ministers' sessions—yields no result. . . . Yet there is another side. To the lawyer, trader, consumer, or farmer, the EC is a complex political and economic organization through which demands are channelled, resources claimed and power and influence sought. Community politics take on substance and reality in spite of the political flux and posturing on the surface. (Webb 1983, 1)

The Community's policy presence and weight varied depending on the policy area being considered. In fact, each policy sector had its own distinctive policy-making process (Wallace 1983, 52). In a few areas, the Community was clearly the dominant actor—agricultural policy and external trade agreements being examples. In others it played a regulatory role, in still others it contributed money, which was more important to the poorer members (regional policy), and in still others (education) it was very marginal (Wallace 1983, 50–53)

It is important to note that Community "dominance" in policy making does not imply that Community policies were formulated at a distance from national interests. It does mean that final decisions were made through the policy-making process at the Community rather than national level. The making of such policy at the Community level, in a dynamic characteristic of nation-states in which territorial representation plays a significant policy-making role, allowed member-states to assert and protect their national interests.

The assertive role played by member-states in representing their national interest during the formulation of a "common" policy was at odds with the general view that a "common" policy would be one in which national interests would be subordinated. Thus, in the area of agricultural policy, Joan Pearce concluded that

> Policy-making consists not of furthering the interests of Community agriculture as a unit but of satisfying a collection of national agricultural interests. . . .
> In negotiations the combination of central institutions and diverse national interests results in concessions being mutually traded and applied, often expensively and wastefully, to all members to maintain the appearance of a single policy. . . . (Pearce 1983, 171)

Analysts of the Community often seemed either surprised at or critical of the role of territorial representation. Neofunctionalist theory did not address theories of federalism. It therefore did not sufficiently acknowledge the key role that territorial representation plays in many polities (such as the Federal Republic of Germany) and that it would inevitably play in a Community composed of member-states with deeply institutionalized political, administrative, and economic structures. Neofunctionalists consequently postulated a transfer of loyalty to Community institutions that would seem unrealistic to those familiar with the workings of federal systems.

Neofunctionalists, as Scharpf points out, emphasized "the perspectives and actions of a plurality of political elites, rather than . . . the institutional self-interests of national governments" (1988, 266). They did not view the effective representation of territorial interests in the decision-making process as integral, indeed essential, to the successful evolution of political integration. They tended to identify integration with the strength of the center, that is the Commission. Policy making in the unitary state seemed to be, even if implicitly, the major analytic referent. Perhaps for that reason, vigorous territorial representation was viewed as essentially inimical to the integrative process rather than as a necessary ingredient in the long process of achieving balance between central and noncentral power.[4]

If analysts had approached the process of integration using federalist policy-making dynamics and theory as the referent, the role of territorial representation might have been evaluated quite differently. It certainly would have been expected. For example, Daniel Elazar, one of the foremost students of federalism, approaches the study of political integration quite differently from those who view the success of integration as measured by the strength of central institutions. In his words, "The measure of political integration is not the strength of the center as opposed to the peripheries; rather the strength of the framework. Thus both the whole and the parts can gain in strength simultaneously and, indeed, must do so on an interdependent basis" (Elazar 1979, 1). Students of federalism, in fact, would be predisposed to view integration as successful to the extent it led to a measured balance of power between central and noncentral institutions.[5] Vigorous territorial representation, in this view, is a *sine qua non* of successful integration.

While territorial representation does not necessarily lead to decision-making paralysis, it is likely to if such representation is combined with the need to use unanimous voting.[6] The continuation of the unanimity rule was imposed by de Gaulle to forestall movement toward qualified majority voting. (It is for that reason that the Single European Act's introduction of qualified majority voting is so important, as I shall argue later in the chapter). And in fact, the Council of Ministers was unable to agree on major new policy initiatives. The combination of national interests vigorously pursued, the Community's uneven and restricted policy presence, and the inability of the Council of Ministers to arrive at agreement because of the requirement of unanimity in voting understandably led many analysts to conclude the Community was stagnating.

The picture, however, was more complex than the image of "stagnation" and "stalemate" would suggest. As I argue in the next section, the Community was composed of more than the Commission and the Council of Ministers, and thus blockage in the Council did not necessarily mean all integrative processes were forestalled.

Asymmetrical Integration

The Community was of interest to those sectors of society mentioned by Carole Webb (1983) because it had developed a policy capacity in three key policy sectors. Even before the Single European Act, anyone interested in European food, money, or law could not escape the Community's influence. Ironically, the general popular image of the (pre-1992) Community as "gray" and unexciting had to do with the fact that none of those three areas excited the popular imagination. Sugar beets, the European Monetary System, and the European Court of Justice are not subjects of popular interest. They are nonetheless the very stuff of governance.

The pivotal role played by food, money, and law, in fact, illustrated the asymmetrical integration that occurred in the Community after its founding. Legal integration had proceeded quite rapidly, so that national judicial elites began to orient themselves to an EC institution more quickly and with more commitment than other types of national elites.[7] Monetary integration also showed progress, although within a more limited scope than in the judicial area. The integration that occurred in these arenas provides an important antidote to the "stagnant" picture of the Community portrayed by those who focused solely on the paralytic effect of unanimous voting on the Council of Ministers.

Agriculture

Integration in the decision-making processes controlled by the Council of Ministers, in fact, had been frozen by de Gaulle's insistence on unanimity in voting. As late as 1988, therefore, agriculture (or at least the Common Agricultural Policy, CAP) was the only policy area "in which the European Community is approaching the full powers of a federal government" (Scharpf 1988, 251). The Council of Ministers had simply been unable to agree on any other policies of the magnitude of the CAP.

The Council managed to be important in the agricultural sector because agriculture has been a central policy area since the founding of the Community. The objectives of agricultural policy were actually set out in the Treaty of Rome. The Community developed its initial institutional capacity, especially its first regulatory apparatus, in this policy arena. In that sense, agriculture was a "constitutive" element in the founding of the Community.

Although the 1970s saw continual squabbling over the content of the Common Agricultural Policy, the policy machinery was in place and delivering policy outcomes (however controversial). Paralysis in the Council could block *change* in the CAP, but since agricultural policy as such became a Community concern at the birth of the Community itself, the CAP kept functioning regardless of the disputes within the Council. Although the member-states were far more important in formulating CAP policy than those analysts who favor a preeminent role for the Commission would have liked, Joan Pearce concludes that "the development of the CAP has led to the establishment of a highly intricate—and within its own limited terms an effective—process for managing the agricultural market of the Community" (1983, 171).

It is important to note that in all three areas—food, money, and law—the paralysis in the Council of Ministers was neutralized in one fashion or another. Thus, although *decision making* did not become "federalized" due to the requirement of unanimous voting, the Community was able to deepen its institutional capacity in those policy areas that were not dependent on decisions made by the Council. It is important to note the asymmetry between areas needing Council initiative and approval and those that did not, especially since political scientists tend to focus on the former while neglecting the latter. A great deal of governance can go on at a fair distance from so-called "political" processes and institutions, as analysts of American politics well know, and the phenomenon of policy being made at arm's length from both the Commission and the Council of Ministers characterized the European Community during the 1970s.

Money

Money has been a key policy area for the Community, but its history differs strikingly from that of agriculture. While agriculture was negotiated in the treaty-making process, monetary policy was at best only a marginal concern of the framers of the Treaty of Rome. While the regulatory machinery of the Common Agricultural Policy developed within the confines of the Commission, the apparatus for regulating monetary policy did not develop under the aegis of either the Commission or the Council of Ministers. The regulation of monetary policy, exchange rate policy in particular, therefore, represents an example of a policy area with definite links to the Community but not subject to the Community's decision-making procedures. While paralysis characterized decision making within the Council of Ministers, Community building was going on elsewhere.

Exchange rate policy came to be regulated through the European Monetary System (EMS). In December 1978, the European Council (which itself was an institutional innovation that bypassed the Council of Ministers) established the System, but each member-state was allowed to decide whether to participate in the System's Exchange Rate Mechanism, which in turn was the critical control mechanism. The original six founding members of the Community (France, Italy, the Federal Republic of Germany, and the BENELUX countries) all agreed to join the ERM, but the newer members joined only later. In fact, the United Kingdom did not join until October 1990. Although launched by the European Council, the operations of the ERM are controlled by the participating member's central banks rather than by the Council of Ministers. Until the Single European Act specifically brought the EMS into the treaties governing the Community, the ERM represented extratreaty collective action by some of the Community's member-states' central banks (Glaesner 1987, 298–99). The SEA, however, did not increase the Community's powers in the field of monetary policy and did not dilute the powers of the member-states' central banks.

The EMS has formulated exchange rate policy for its member-states with the objective of minimizing exchange rate fluctuations. In the words of Helmut Schmidt, one of its founding fathers, the purpose of the EMS was "to maintain exchange rates between the currencies as stable as possible in order to foster monetary and price stability as well as intra-European trade and thereby also economic integration within the boundaries of the European Community" (Schmidt 1985, 87). In fact, much to the surprise of most analysts who had been very skeptical of the System's significance, the EMS now has to be viewed as one of the major achievements linked to the Community (see, for example, McDonald and Zis 1989). It was certainly an important step toward Economic and Monetary Union (EMU).

The goals of Economic and Monetary Union had been accepted at the Hague Summit of December 1969, but a variety of factors killed it. For one, the "monetarists" and "economists" could not agree. The French, with their emphasis on monetary policy (exchange rate policy in particular), and the Germans, with their emphasis on coordinating economic policy in the medium term, did not agree on the strategy to pursue. Furthermore, the entire structure of the international financial system was in turmoil: the Bretton Woods system of fixed exchange rates collapsed in the period when EMU was being seriously considered. The oil shock affected the various member-states differently and inflation rates diverged widely. Finally, the French were not willing to give up any national authority to a supranational body.

However, the end of EMU did not mean the end of the effort by Community members to act collectively in the regulation of exchange rates. It did mean proceeding more modestly, more slowly, and allowing networks, contacts, and experience to build up. In 1972 a "snake" was tried, and although sterling, the franc, and the lira withdrew, it kept existing as a "minisnake." In turn, that meant that the BENELUX countries and Denmark accepted linking their currency to the Deutchemark. Again, the minisnake can be seen as a temporizing measure. As Tsoukalis argues, "the survival of the snake, even with limited membership, in the difficult period following the first oil shock of 1973–4 meant that there would be something there to build on as soon as economic conditions became more favorable" (1983, 125).

And in fact, in October 1977, the new president of the Commission, Roy

Jenkins, proposed trying again. To general surprise, the Germans responded favorably and then were followed by the French. The political leadership shown by Schmidt and Giscard was critical, for creating the EMS was a difficult political decision. Schmidt especially had to overcome strong resistance to his plan from the Bundesbank (Tsoukalis 1983, 136).

The EMS in many ways was similar to the 1992 program. It was shaped by historical experience, contemporary problems, a fear of stagnation leading to disintegration, and the leadership of a few key Community and national leaders. On the basis of experience, member countries wanted neither fixed exchange rates nor completely floating rates. The Germans were worried by their constantly rising D-mark. While the French have always favored fixed exchange rates, they had begun acknowledging the inflationary consequences of devaluation. Furthermore, the Community seemed to be under severe stress and fears of disintegration were fairly widespread. Thus, Jenkins and Schmidt, and then Schmidt and Giscard, put together a bold plan designed both to promote integration and to deal with the policy dilemma of volatile exchange rates. Belonging to the Exchange Rate Mechanism of the EMS is not cost-free for participants.[8] France for one, and French socialism in particular, has felt those costs. In Claude Imbert's words,

> . . . without admitting it, on the day in March 1983 that French socialism decided not to leave the European Monetary System in order to pursue a more traditionally leftist economic policy it was making the same radical switch that had pushed West Germany's Social Democrats to reject Marxism at their 1959 Bad Godesberg congress. (Imbert 1989, 50)

Jacques Delors led the battle within the French government to maintain French participation in the EMS. It is undoubtedly one of the reasons why the Germans supported his candidacy for presidency of the Commission.

It gradually became clear that the EMS was allowing the Bundesbank, with its strong anti-inflationary policy, to dominate the monetary policy of all ERM members. France and Italy in particular were allowing the Bundesbank to carry out anti-inflationary policy, which their national governments found difficult to do through the mechanisms available through domestic politics. By the late 1980s, the role of the Bundesbank had become widely discussed within the EC, and steps toward EMU were analyzed with the Bundesbank as the referent. Many analysts have expressed surprise that France and Italy would accept such subordination. Here it is important to recognize that national monetary authorities may well have institutional interests which differ from those of other central government actors. In fact, the compatibility of interests among EC central bank officials provides a good example of what Keohane and Nye term trans-governmental relations (Keohane and Nye 1989, 33ff). In a similar vein, Katseli argues that monetary officials were willing to constrain the autonomy of domestic monetary policy and follow the Bundesbank "rather than face the erosion of their political autonomy by international commercial banks, by national governments or by other domestic actors" (Katseli 1989, 48).

The surprising success of the EMS is now accepted as a given. In fact, British membership in the ERM is viewed by most analysts as completing the Community's first step toward eventual Economic and Monetary Union. Few observers, writing at the time of its founding, would have predicted that the EMS would become so significant as a policy arm of the Community that membership would be made mandatory.

Law

EC law is implemented by national courts that have accepted the supremacy of Community law over national law.[9] That fact is central to any analysis of the role of law in the Community. The existence of "a unitary system of judicial decision making" has a pervasive, albeit often unrecognized, effect on Community politics (Weiler 1982a, 55).[10] In contrast, public international law is notoriously weak. International courts do not have the means of implementation, and member governments are very selective about accepting their judgments.

In the EC, national courts typically accept the preliminary rulings handed down by the Court of Justice and render verdicts in accordance with such preliminary rulings. In that fashion, the Court is able to rule on the compatibility of national law with Community law and yet have the national court render the actual verdict. Dehousse and Weiler conclude that "the final decision on compatibility will, therefore, be rendered by a *national* court, and it will enjoy all the authority a legal system attaches to its own decisions—including the ultimate power of coercion" (Dehousse and Weiler 1990, 255).

The legal integration of the Community has proceeded so far that legal scholars now argue that the Community has "a constitutional framework for a federal type structure in Europe" (Stein 1981, 1). The judicial activism of the European Court of Justice has been such that the European Community is a "legal" Community to a greater degree than it is an "economic" community or a "political" community. Clearly, legal integration has proceeded further than either financial or decisional integration.[11]

The de Gaulle–inspired Luxembourg Compromise, which accepted the rule of unanimity rather than qualified majority voting in the Council of Ministers, meant that "decisionally, the Community [was] closer to the United Nations than . . . to the United States" (Cappelletti et al. 1986, 29). The requirement of unanimity slowed decision making, and the enlargement of the Community combined with that requirement led to political stalemate in the Council of Ministers.

The European Court of Justice, however, was not included in the Luxembourg Compromise. The Court continued functioning by majority vote and continued as well its policy of secrecy concerning both the number of votes in the majority and minority and how each judge had voted. No dissenting opinions are made public.[12] During the 1960s and 1970s the Court created a "European Community judicial system" in a series of landmark cases that applied the doctrines of direct effect, supremacy, and preemption.[13] Once all the national courts had accepted the supremacy of Community Law as interpreted by the Court, the Court had successfully managed to establish the right of judicial review. Qualified majority voting was not the only way to construct the European Community.

Whereas traditionally one of the criteria used in interpreting international treaties is that of protecting the sovereignty of the treaty's signatories, the Court "constitutionalized" the Treaty of Rome. The Court, in effect, "took crucial, even revolutionary, strides" (Weiler 1982b, 270). It clearly viewed itself as an institution whose mission it was to advance the integration of the Community. In effect, it made Community law binding.

The Single European Act

It is within the institutional context of asymmetrical integration that the Single European Act was passed. By 1986, it was clear that treaty provisions and Council of Minister decisions were backed by a truly powerful, albeit flexible, judicial system. It was also clear that the EMS had achieved a stature in the management of exchange rate fluctuations that few had expected. Coexisting with impressive legal and monetary integration, however, was the problem of decision making within the Council of Ministers—and the lack of a truly single integrated market.

The Single European Act addressed both the question of paralysis in decision making and the creation of a single integrated market.[14] (For varying perspectives on why the SEA was passed, see: Sandholtz and Zysman 1989; Moravcsik 1991; Cameron 1992.) The two were viewed by many as inextricably linked; that is, that it would be impossible to create a truly single market without reforming the decision-making procedure. The Single European Act began raising the level of integration in the "political" sphere toward that found in the other three areas. The asymmetry began to be narrowed.

Such narrowing was not, however, immediately apparent. The Act did not push integration in the decision-making process as far as many "integrationists" would have liked, and it was therefore widely viewed as a rather modest change.[15] Further, it was not clear that qualified majority voting would have the impact it subsequently did have. In general, the Act was not viewed as necessarily a watershed in the Community's history of governance.[16]

It has gradually become clear that the permissibility of qualified majority voting lies at the core of the institutional changes wrought by the SEA. Such voting applies to most of those areas linked to the creation of the internal market; two-thirds of the proposals suggested by the Commission's White Paper on the Internal Market are eligible for such voting (Dehousse 1988, 319).[17] Either the

Commission or a member-state can ask for a vote, and only a majority vote in the Council of Ministers is required in order to proceed to a qualified majority vote.

The politics of qualified majority voting are very different from the politics of unanimity. Rather than relying on the veto to defend its interest or needing to worry about another's veto, each member-state needs to search for allies whether it favors or opposes a proposal from the Commission. This is as true for the big as for the small countries, the wealthy as well as the poor member-states.

From a total of seventy-six votes, fifty-four are required for a Commission proposal to be adopted by qualified majority voting. Twenty-three votes, thus, are needed to block approval. The distribution of votes is such that potentially likely voting blocs will be unable to exercise a veto or impose their own views.[18] For example, Spain, Portugal, and Greece (the poor Mediterranean members as well as the most recent members) with eighteen votes between them will be unable to veto; similarly the original six with forty-two votes cannot impose their views. The five biggest countries—Italy, France, the United Kingdom, the Federal Republic of Germany, and Spain—with forty-eight votes need some smaller countries as allies as well. Similarly, the four poorest countries—Greece, Spain, Portugal, and Ireland—cannot in concert veto proposals as they have only twenty-one votes between them.

Above all, the use of qualified majority voting has changed the dynamics of decision making. Wallace finds that "The language of the negotiations is now the language of voting. Officials and even occasionally ministers are prepared to use the vocabulary of majorities and minorities" (Wallace 1989b, 37). Even though the Commission prefers to obtain a consensus in the Council of Ministers, the *option* of resorting to qualified majority voting has increased the power of the Commission and encouraged member-states to accept compromise. Member-states have an incentive to "stay in the game" so that they can have an impact on the formulation of the Commission's proposal as well as on the bargaining in the Council of Ministers. Isolation now can lead to simply being out-voted, so that the pressures toward compromise are far greater than they were under unanimity voting. Dehousse and Weiler conclude that

> . . . in order to assess the real impact of the shift to majority voting rendered possible by the Single Act, one should have regard not only to actual instances of a vote, but also to the time needed to achieve a consensus when no vote has been taken; in many fields where, for years, no decision had been possible, a compromise has now been reached within months. (Dehousse and Weiler 1990, 248)

The option of resorting to qualified majority voting has, in fact, resulted in much speedier passage of new legislation. Proposals that had been blocked for over a decade have been passed by the Council of Ministers, so that the march toward the legislative creation—at least at the Community level—of the internal market by the end of 1992 is not terribly far behind schedule. (On the other hand, the member-states are falling behind in incorporating the Community's directives into their own legal systems). The option of qualified majority voting is also becoming less problematic for the states, and as many expected, the Maastricht Treaty extends this decision-making procedure into several new areas.

The impact of qualified majority voting versus unanimity can be seen most dramatically in the area of environmental policy.[19] Although the Community had developed environmental programs since 1973, such programs were not based on Treaty provisions and had not intruded on (typically weak) national responses to environmental problems. The Single European Act explicitly gave the Community authority in environmental affairs and stated that environmental concerns must be an important aspect of economic policy making. The "1992 Project," as embodied in the Single European Act, includes environmental issues as well as those of market integration (Kramer and Kromarek 1990; Kramer 1987).

In the section of the SEA dealing explicitly with environmental protection, provision is made for unanimous voting. Further, qualified majority voting can be used in deciding on implementing decisions only if the member-states unanimously agree to use such a procedure. Thus if a directive is proposed by the Commission under Article 130 of the Treaty, unanimity prevails, even at the implementation stage if the member-states so wish.

However, if an environmental directive is proposed as necessary to the creation of the internal market, the procedure for qualified majority voting applies. If the Commission uses Article 100A as the legal basis for the directive, therefore, the dynamics of decision making are very different from those found if Article 130 is used. The legal basis chosen by the Commission for a proposed directive becomes very important as different articles are associated with different decisional rules.

The relevance of this seemingly arcane distinction becomes clear if we examine the politics of two issue areas within environmental policy. In the early drafts of a 1990 proposal on landfilling, the Commission adopted restrictions on the landfilling of both liquid and hazardous waste that were viewed as too stringent and too standardized by the United Kingdom. However, using Article 100A as its legal justification for the proposed directive, the Commission needed only a qualified majority vote to obtain approval. The *Ends Report* concluded that the UK's

> . . . line of argument would clash fairly directly with the Commission's approach, but there must be some doubt whether the UK will succeed in having the basic thrust of the proposal amended. The current draft is based on Article 100A of the EEC Treaty, and as such would be open to adoption by a qualified majority vote in the Environment Council. (*Ends Report*, April 1990, 31)

In a similar vein, the Commission was considering, in mid-1990, proposing a "carbon tax" to reduce carbon emissions that would be subject only to qualified majority voting for approval. Not surprisingly, strong member-state opposition to the use of qualified majority voting was expected (*Ends Report,* June 1990, 30).

The option of using qualified majority voting, thus, changes the calculus of both the national governments and the Commission. The policy process—and the policy outcome—are likely to differ rather sharply depending on whether unanimity or qualified majority voting is imposed as the decisional rule. It is to be expected that, for both national governments and the Commission, the desired policy outcome is intimately related to the desired decision rule.

The Dilemma of Future Institutional Development

The use of qualified majority voting has rendered the problem of the "democratic deficit" more insistent. Linkages between voters and the actual policy-making institutions of the Community are very tenuous, while, by contrast, the institutions of the Community have acquired more power over national policies. None of the institutions mentioned thus far are directly elected by a "European" constituency. The judges for the European Court of Justice are appointed by member governments as are the Central Bank Governors who control the European Monetary System. The Commission is appointed by member governments, and the Council of Ministers is composed of members of the executive branch of the member-states' parliaments.

A directly elected legislature, whether national or European, is conspicuous by its absence from this analysis. Although the European Parliament's powers were increased marginally by the SEA, it is still a weak institution very dependent on the Commission for the exercise of the power it does have. And national parliaments, many of which are weak policy actors within their respective national political systems but which do hold the executive accountable, are completely unrepresented at the Community level.

In the recent Intergovernmental Conference on Political Union, both the role of national parliaments and that of the European Parliament were considered. Given the new importance of qualified majority voting, increasing the role of one institution as opposed to the other has profound implications. Increasing the role of the European Parliament substantially (for example, by giving it the power of codecision with the Council of Ministers) would begin to define, if only embryonically, a constituency oriented toward European institutions. Even if the elections to the Parliament continued to be viewed as reflections of national partisan conflicts, the potential would exist for that dynamic to change over time. Especially as the provisions for the Single European Market and those for environmental protection begin to be felt by firms, subnational governments, and individuals, the relevance of the European Parliament would grow.

The implications for the decision-making process within the Community would depend to a great extent on the partisan makeup of the Parliament, on whether the political parties could continue to organize themselves trans-nationally within the Parliament if they actually became important, and on the relationships that developed between the national parliamentary and the European parliamentary wing of each party. It is likely that a newly empowered European Parliament would try to act, in policy-making terms, more like the German Bundestag than the British House of Commons or the French National Assembly. The problems such an effort might encounter *vis-à-vis* the Council of Ministers (especially if the latter differed in its partisan composition from the Parliament and was not accountable to it) as well as with the national parliamentary parties cannot be disentangled here, but it is clear that simply giving the European Parliament more formal powers will not necessarily make it an effective force in Community decision making. The "democratic deficit" will not be solved simply by increasing the powers of the European Parliament.

Increasing the role of the national parliaments does not begin cultivating the development of a "European" constituency. Rather, it broadens the scope of territorial representation. As it stands, national executives represent the member-state governments within the Community. The Council of Ministers is made up of those who form the executive within their national parliamentary bodies. "Backbenchers" are not represented. If national parliaments are represented in some fashion and/or integrated into the policy-making process, the territorial dimension of the Community would be strengthened and in fact given more legitimacy because of its broader scope.

The introduction of qualified majority voting in the SEA was a step toward creating a Community decision-making process which, while safeguarding the role of territorial representation within the Community, gave it a different cast. The member-states as a collectivity are still central to the decision-making process, but not all states will necessarily be central all the time. The veto made each one central, while the use of majorities changes the focus to coalitions and away from states acting individually.

The integration of national parliaments into this new process would continue the process of representing existing governments, that is, of emphasizing territorial politics rather than state–society relations. By contrast, strengthening the European Parliament would emphasize the representation of electoral constituencies, of voters rather than of governments.

The Maastricht Summit, which produced incremental increases in the power of the European Parliament, did not resolve this tension between societal and territorial representation. The "democratic deficit" was not fundamentally altered, and the tension within the Community between the representation of governmental institutions and that of electoral constituencies is likely to persist.

Notes

1. For analyses of the creation of a single market in the United States, see Shapiro 1986; Fine 1956; Sunstein 1988.

2. For a seminal theoretical treatment of the relationship between public authority and the creation and maintenance of markets, see Polanyi 1944.

3. In particular, the Brussels Summit of February 1988 increased the financial security of the Community, constrained agricultural spending, and allocated significant new funds for the poorer countries. At the Madrid Summit in June 1989, the commitment to economic and monetary union was reinforced when Mrs. Thatcher agreed that the United Kingdom would join the Exchange Rate Mechanism of the European Monetary System. (In fact, the United Kingdom joined the System in October 1990).

4. That is not to say that territorial representation leads to "efficient" or even "effective" policy making. As Fritz Scharpf has pointed out, federal structures can lead to suboptimal policy outcomes. Federal systems, or at least ones structured in the way the German system is, are more concerned with representing territorial claims than with efficiency in decision making (Scharpf 1988).

5. Having said that, Jacque and Weiler point out that

> [T]he student of comparative federalism discovers a constant feature in practically all federative experiences: a tendency, which differs only in degree, towards controversial concentration of legislative and executive power in the centre/general power at the expense of constituent units. (Jacque and Weiler 1990, 13)

6. In the German case, territorial representation when combined with unanimous voting does not lead to paralysis—although it does lead to inefficiency, inflexibility, unnecessary programs, and a lack of democracy. However, the lack of paralysis may be due to the fact that the German federal government has resources at its disposal which the Commission does not have:

> While decisions of the European Community are completely determined by the outcome of negotiations among member governments, the German federal government has a political identity, resources and strategic and tactical capabilities of its own. It cannot adopt and implement effective public policy without *Lander* agreement, but it can design and pursue bargaining strategies against the *Bundesrat* which the European Commission cannot similarly pursue against the Council of Ministers or the European Council. (Scharpf 1988, 255)

7. For a description of the "legal elite" linked to the European Court of Justice in the framework of a European judicial process, see Stein 1981, 1–3.

8. As Sandholtz and Zysman point out, the EMS is "a constraint on domestic politics that pushes toward more restrictive macroeconomic policies than would otherwise have been adopted" (Sandholtz and Zysman 1989, 112).

9. In the EC judicial system, national courts are "courts of coordinate jurisdiction" rather than inferior courts as they would be in a full-fledged federation (Jacobs and Karst 1986, 234).

10. For a discussion of the possible effect of such a binding system of law on decision-making dynamics within the Council of Ministers, see Weiler's seminal article (1982b). I have drawn very heavily on Weiler's published work as well as on his comments on an earlier draft of this chapter.

11. Weiler sets out the distinction between "normative and decisional supranationalism." In this view, supranationalism has two facets, each of which can progress at very different speeds. Normative supranationalism refers to "the relationships and hierarchy which exist between Community policies and legal measures on the one hand and competing policies and legal measures of the Member states on the other." Decisional supra-

nationalism refers to the way policies are "initiated, debated and formulated, then promulgated and finally executed" (Weiler 1982b, 269; 1982a).

12. Such a rule shields judges from pressures from their respective governments. By contrast, judges on the International Court of Justice at the Hague vote publicly and "are continually reluctant to vote against their own states" (Freestone 1983, 44).

13. This legal system of course applies only in those policy areas where the Treaty of Rome (and subsequent modifications) gives the Community competence.

The doctrine of direct effect was declared in 1963 in *Van Gend en Loos,* a case in which the Court ruled that EC law had direct effect. The doctrine of supremacy was asserted in *Costa* v. *ENEL* in which the Court ruled that EC law was superior to the law of the member-states, even if the latter were constitutional law. In the area of preemption, the Court has made claims but its position is still fluid (Freestone 1983; Simon 1974).

14. The Single European Act defined the "internal market" more narrowly than the EEC Treaty defines the "common market." (See van Themaat 1988, 109–111.)

15. The *Economist,* for example, headlined its story on the SEA "Europe's Smiling Mouse." Its account of the Luxembourg Summit of December 1985, which produced the Act, concluded by saying "But the Community has produced something. Squeak, squeak" ("Europe's Smiling Mouse," *Economist,* 7 December 1985, p. 48).

16. The reasons for skepticism were well stated by Helen Wallace shortly after the ratification of the Act:

> Many Treaty articles remain which preserve unanimity rules and there was no statement of intent about activating existing majority rules. The Luxembourg compromise was neither withdrawn nor clarified. The hard reality is that it will persist as a resort available to governments. . . . As regards majority decision rules, only time will tell how far these will actually be introduced for the internal market and with what effect. Experience . . . suggests that their activation will not be easy in the absence of pressures from unavoidable timetables. (Wallace 1989a, 200)

Furthermore, already prior to the Single European Act, qualified majority voting had regularly applied in the formulation of the EC's budget and sporadically in the cases of agriculture and external trade. In fact, qualified majority voting procedures were used to make over 100 decisions in 1986 (Wallace 1989a, 196, 200; Nugent 1989, 105).

17. The official citation for the White Paper is *Completing the Internal Market: White Paper from the Commission to the European Council,* Luxembourg, June 1985, COM (85). For a discussion of the White Paper, see Emerson 1988.

18. The votes are distributed as follows: Germany, France, the United Kingdom, and Italy have ten votes each, Spain eight, Portugal, Belgium, the Netherlands, and Greece five each, Denmark and Ireland three each, and Luxembourg has two.

19. The impact of qualified majority voting is also beginning to show up in the Commission's proposals for an "Internal Energy Market." Because the Commission thought that the energy sector would present particularly difficult political and technical problems, the White Paper skirted around the energy sector. However, at least partially because of the use of the qualified majority voting procedure, the Commission is now determined to make progress in creating an Internal Energy Market, particularly in the area of electricity. (See McGowan 1990, 16.)

References

Cameron, David R. 1992. "The 1992 Initiative: Causes and Consequences." In Alberta M. Sbragia, ed., *Euro-Politics: Institutions and Policymaking in the "New" European Community.* Washington, DC: Brookings Institution.

Cappelletti, Mauro, Monica Seccombe, and Joseph H. H. Weiler. 1986. "Integration Through Law: Europe and the American Federal Experience, A General Introduction." In Mauro Cappelletti, Monica Seccombe, and Joseph Weiler, eds., *Integration Through Law: Europe and the American Federal Experience*, Vol. 1: *Methods, Tools and Institutions*, Book 1: *A Political, Legal, and Economic Overview*. Berlin: Walter de Gruyter.

Dehousse, Renaud. 1988. "Completing the Internal Market: Institutional Constraints and Challenges." In Roland Bieber, Renaud Dehousse, John Pinder, and Joseph H. H. Weiler, eds., *1991: One European Market? A Critical Analysis of the Commission's Internal Market Strategy*. Baden-Baden: Nomos.

Dehousse, Renaud, and Joseph H. H. Weiler. 1990. "The Legal Dimension." In William Wallace, ed., *The Dynamics of European Integration*. London: Pinter.

Economist. 1985. "Europe's Smiling Mouse,"7 December, p. 48.

Ends Report. 1990. "Early Draft of EEC Landfill Directive Would Have Major Impact on UK Practices." No. 183, April, p. 31.

Ends Report. 1990. "EEC Summit Pushes Eco-Taxes, National Environment Plans." No. 185, June, p. 30.

Elazar, Daniel. 1979. "Introduction: Why Federalism?" In Daniel Elazar, ed., *Federalism and Political Integration*. Ramat Gan, Israel: Turtledove.

Emerson, Michael. 1988. "1992 and After: The Bicycle Theory Rides Again." *Political Quarterly*, 59:289–99.

Fine, Sidney. 1956. *Laissez Faire and the General-Welfare State: A Study of Conflict in American Thought, 1865–1901*. Ann Arbor: University of Michigan Press.

Freestone, David. 1983. "The European Court of Justice." In Juliet Lodge, ed., *Institutions and Policies of the European Community*. New York: St. Martin's Press.

Glaesner, H. G. 1987. "The Single European Act." *Yearbook of European Law 1986*. Oxford: Clarendon Press.

Hufbauer, Gary Clyde, ed. 1990. *Europe 1992: An American Perspective*. Washington, DC: Brookings Institution.

Imbert, Claude. 1989. "The End of French Exceptionalism." *Foreign Affairs*, 68:48–60.

Jacobs, Francis G., and Kenneth L. Karst. 1986. "The 'Federal' Legal Order: The U.S.A. and Europe Compared, A Juridical Perspective." In Mauro Cappelletti, Monica Seccombe, and Joseph Weiler, eds., *Integration Through Law: Europe and the American Federal Experience*, vol. 1: *Methods, Tools and Institutions*, Book 1: *A Political, Legal and Economic Overview*. Berlin: Walter de Gruyter.

Jacque, Jean Paul, and Joseph H. H. Weiler. 1990. *On the Road to European Union—A New Judicial Architecture: An Agenda for the Intergovernmental Conference*. Unpublished.

Katseli, Louka T. 1989. "The Political Economy of Macroeconomic Policy in Europe." In Paolo Guerrieri and Pier Carlo Padoan, eds., *The Political Economy of European Integration: States, Markets and Institutions*. New York: Harvester Wheatsheaf.

Keohane, Robert and Joseph Nye. 1989. *Power and Interdependence*. 2d ed. Glenview, IL: Scott, Foresman.

Kramer, Ludwig. 1987. "The Single European Act and Environment Protection: Reflections on Several New Provisions in Community Law." *Common Market Law Review*, 24: 659–88.

Kramer, Ludwig, and Pascale Kromarek. 1990. "Le Droit communautaire de l'environnement: mai 1988–decembre 1989." *Revue Juridique de L'Environnement*, 81–105.

McDonald, Frank, and George Zis. 1989. "The European Monetary System: Towards 1992 and Beyond." *Journal of Common Market Studies*, 27:183–202.

McGowan, Francis. 1990. "Towards a European Electricity Market." *The World Today*, 46:15–19.

Moravcsik, Andrew. 1991. "Negotiating the Single Act: National Interests and Conventional Statecraft in the European Community." *International Organization*, vol. 45, no. 1 (Winter 1991): 19–56.

Nugent, Neill. 1989. *The Government and Politics of the European Community*. Durham, NC: Duke University Press.

Pearce, Joan. 1983. "The Common Agricultural Policy: The Accumulation of Special Interests." In Helen Wallace, William Wallace, and Carole Webb, eds., *Policymaking in the European Community*, 2d ed. Chichester: Wiley.

Polanyi, Karl. 1944. *The Great Transformation*. New York: Farrar & Rinehart.

Sandholtz, Wayne, and John Zysman. 1989. "1992: Recasting the European Bargain." *World Politics*, 42:95–128.

Scharpf, Fritz W. 1988. "The Joint Decision Trap: Lessons from German Federalism and European Integration." *Public Administration*, 66:239–78.

Schmidt, Helmut. 1985. "The European Monetary System: Proposals for Further Progress." *The World Today*, 41:85–91.

Shapiro, Martin. 1986. "The Supreme Court's 'Return' to Economic Regulation." In *Studies in American Political Development, An Annual*, volume 1.

Simon, Manfred. 1974. "Enforcement by French Courts of European Community Law." *The Law Quarterly Review*, 90:467–85.

Stein, Eric. 1981. "Lawyers, Judges, and the Making of a Transnational Constitution." *American Journal of International Law*, 75:1–27.

Sunstein, Cass R. 1988. "Protectionism, the American Supreme Court, and Integrated Markets." In Roland Bieber, Renaud Dehousse, John Pinder, and Joseph H. H. Weiler, eds., *1992: One European Market? A Critical Analysis of the Commission's Internal Market Strategy*. Baden-Baden: Nomos.

Tsoukalis, Louis. 1983. "Money and the Process of Integration." In Helen Wallace, William Wallace, and Carole Webb, eds., *Policymaking in the European Community*, 2d ed. Chichester:Wiley

van Themaat, Pieter Verloren. 1988. "The Contributions to the Establishment of the Internal Market by the Case-Law of the Court of Justice of the European Communities." In Roland Bieber, Renaud Dehouse, John Pinder, and Joseph H. H. Weiler, eds., *1992: One European Market? A Critical Analysis of the Commission's Internal Market Strategy*. Baden-Baden: Nomos.

Wallace, Helen. 1983. "Negotiation, Conflict, and Compromise: The Elusive Pursuit of Common Policies." In Helen Wallace, William Wallace, and Carole Webb, eds., *Policymaking in the European Community*, 2d ed. Chichester: Wiley.

Wallace, Helen. 1989a. "The Best is the Enemy of the 'Could': Bargaining in the European Community." In Secondo Tarditi, Kenneth J. Thompson, Pierpaolo Pierani, and Elisabetta Croci-Angelini, eds., *Agricultural Trade Liberalization and the European Community*. Oxford: Clarendon Press.

Wallace, Helen. 1989b. "Dealing in Multiple Currencies: Negotiations in the European Community." Unpublished paper.

Webb, Carole. 1983. "Theoretical Perspectives and Problems." In Helen Wallace, William Wallace, and Carole Webb, eds., *Policymaking in the European Community*, 2d ed. Chichester: Wiley.

Weiler, Joseph. 1982a. "Community, Member States and European Integration: Is the Law Relevant?" *Journal of Common Market Studies*, 21: 39–55.

Weiler, Joseph. 1982b. "The Community System: The Dual Character of Supranationalism." *Yearbook of European Law 1981*. Oxford: Oxford University Press.

Woolley, John. 1991. "1992, Capital, and the EMS: Policy Credibility and Political Institutions." In Alberta Sbragia, ed., *Euro-politics: Politics and Policymaking in the "New" European Community*. Washington DC: Brookings Institution.

6

Financial Deregulation, Monetary Policy Coordination, and Economic and Monetary Union

Leon N. Lindberg

The Single European Act's provisions for financial deregulation (liberalization of capital movements and financial services industries) have propelled the member-states of the European Community toward important reforms of the European Monetary System (as of July 1990) and have helped ignite a debate on the formation of an Economic and Monetary Union (i.e., European-level reregulation of monetary and fiscal policy). The EMU issue—to the surprise of most observers—acquired in the late 1980s an almost irresistible political momentum of its own. Financial deregulation, extensive European-level coordination of national monetary policies, and monetary union are radical and ambitious tasks with potentially momentous implications for the conduct of macroeconomic policy, for power relations among economic agents and political actors within each country, for the relationships among national governments, and collective intergovernmental, national, and "supranational" institutions, and for the "style of capitalism" that may come to characterize a resurgent European political economy.

Of course, capital movements and monetary and macroeconomic issues have been on the EC agenda for a long time and until recently the policy record has been one of persistent failure, except for the modest success of the European

Editors' Note: This chapter was completed before the Maastricht Summit, and so does not reflect the 1991 EMU Treaty that calls for the Community to move toward full economic and monetary union before the end of the decade. The focus of the chapter is the presentation of a framework through which to analyze not only the processes and negotiations that led up to this historic treaty, but also the debates, disagreements, and delays that will undoubtedly erupt throughout the 1990s as the Community moves toward its implementation.

Monetary System (EMS). Most serious economic and political analysts were skeptical that the prospects would improve in the foreseeable future. Nor is it clear that the chief obstacles to financial and monetary integration identified in the past have been significantly attenuated. On the other hand, one can identify a number of new contextual factors both internal to the EC and to its members, and external, and shifting patterns of private and public interest perceptions and preferences that suggest that this time the outcomes might be different.

This chapter will provide a preliminary overview of these new contextual factors, interest perceptions, and patterns of private and public preferences as they influence the bargaining behavior of states and the institutional dynamics of national, intergovernmental, and supranational systems. The issues of financial deregulation, monetary and fiscal coordination, and economic and monetary union are exceedingly complex. Economic and political factors drive each other in unexpected ways, and many types of conflict and cooperation "games" will be played at different levels and in different arenas. Most studies we have had in the past and are likely to get in the next several years as these events unfold are narrowly focused on one or another aspect, or they are constrained by restrictive economic assumptions and theoretical concerns, or are limited by beguiling historical analogies. This chapter is part of a larger effort to develop a theoretically informed synthetic political economy framework that will focus on the institutional politics of EC financial and monetary integration and its broad structural and political economy implications. In particular, I want to develop a methodology for discerning the medium-to-long-term institutional outcomes (i.e., what kind of European polity?) that are implied by the strategic choices with respect to financial and monetary issues made by governmental and nongovernmental actors in the critical transition years that lie ahead.

Hopefully, such an analytical framework will enable us to draw together specialized studies and to integrate them with a careful multilevel analysis of the bargaining behavior of state and societal actors in four interrelated arenas between the late 1980s and early 1990s: the regulation or governance of financial industries at a national and an EC-level, the politics of the recently strengthened EMS structure for monetary coordination that entered into operation in July 1990, the progress toward EMU, and selected national-level debates and political struggles that drive and are driven by continued monetary integration. Future research will focus on the intersection of these arenas and the interplay among different levels of bargaining as private agents, state actors, and intergovernmental and supranational institutional actors pursue their diverse objectives.

Financial and Monetary Integration

Financial service industries (commercial and investment banking, securities, insurance, etc.) and financial markets are of special political and economic significance to states. Efforts to liberalize, coordinate, or integrate in these areas are unusually salient both politically and economically. Struggles over the regulation, deregulation, and reregulation of these industries have occupied an important place in national politics and in the evolution of distinctive national forms of capitalism in western Europe as elsewhere (Moran 1984; Cox 1986; Lash and Urry 1987). The particular forms of state–finance industry relations that emerged historically have had distinctive consequences for long-term financial stability, for economic performance, and for economic structures (Hall 1986; Zysman 1983; Ellsworth 1985). Furthermore, national macroeconomic stabilization strategies with respect to GNP, employment, price stability, and balance of payments, depend on deploying instruments of monetary regulation and money supply control, all of which depend for their efficacy on the shifting relationships among public monetary authorities and diverse private financial agents. These national-level relationships have been in flux as forces pushing the globalization of finance have gained momentum in recent years.

In Europe, government-initiated transformations in the governance of finance began with Britain's "Big Bang" (1983–86), followed closely by the liberalization of financial markets in France between 1984 and 1989, and in Spain beginning in 1987. Germany's heavily regulated and bank-mediated system has resisted change for a variety of reasons. Other EC member countries occupy various positions along a continuum from market-mediated to bank- and state-mediated financial systems. All EC countries are experiencing mounting pressures—internal, European, global—for financial change. The freeing of capital movements and the liberalization of financial products, services, and intermediaries called for in the 1992 Project represent one significant policy response to these pressures. So does the renewed search for joint or collective European-level monetary policy-making and -implementing institutions symbolized by Economic and Monetary Union (EMU).

Propelled by the Single European Act and the 1992 Project's stipulations with respect to freeing capital flows and liberalizing financial service industries, western European finance has been plunged into what the *Economist* (1989) has termed "an orgy of competition." This is taking place at three levels. First, competition is increasingly vigorous among financial firms within the expanded EC market; domestic mergers, cross-border mergers, declining profits, increased risk-taking by financial intermediaries are all accelerating. Second, competition among financial centers is in the offing; Paris, Amsterdam, and Frankfurt are eyeing London's business. Third, there is heightening competition between different traditions of capitalism, "between the Anglo-Saxon preference for markets as a source of finance and outlet for investment" and the continental European preference "for banks."

> Both models are changing, converging as they compete, and the evolution of a new European style of capitalism may be the single most interesting outcome of the forging of a single European financial market. (*Economist* 1989, 9)

Echoing the distinctions drawn by Zysman, Cox, and Hall, the *Economist* noted the existence in the EC of three broad types of financial systems.

> The Anglo-Saxon tradition relies on equity capital, strong shareholders, relatively open capital markets, a range of different sorts of institutions active in them, and arms-length relations between banks and industry. . . . West Germans, at the opposite pole, lean on loan finance, as well as strong links between banks and industry. German banks are members of the underdeveloped equity markets; savers prefer fixed-income assets; and what securities they do own they probably bought through their banks. . . . Somewhere in between are countries which share France's Napoleonic stock-market tradition, including Italy, Belgium, Spain and Portugal. Banks there have been excluded from stock exchange membership but nonetheless dominate finance for industry and personal investment. (1989, 7)

The literature on comparative financial systems suggests that these different structural relationships between industry and finance, on the one hand, and between finance and the state, on the other, are strongly related to a propensity for short- as against long-term investment strategies, to a preference for government-mediated financial stability as against more market-driven financial flows, and to a greater or lesser industrial policy capacity. Perhaps the research agenda sketched in this chapter will help us draw some preliminary assessment of the extent to which EC financial and monetary integration might produce a convergence around one or another of these models, or toward something new. We can expect that this will have important implications for investment behavior, financial stability, and industrial policies at a national or EC level.

For these reasons it can be argued that the most significant new substantive commitments called for in the Single European Act and The European Community Commission's White Paper were to free capital movements by mid-1990 for the most advanced countries and by the end of 1992 for all but Greece and Portugal, and to liberalize financial services by the end of 1992. If fulfilled, these commitments would propel the European Community from a "customs-union-plus" to a "pure common market"—from Stage 6 to Stage 8 of "Market Integration From Above" according to Pelkmans. Pelkmans argues further that this stage will confront the EC with the daunting issues of "macroeconomic integration."

> The pure CM [Common Market] is a union without public economic frontiers (except for macroeconomic policy that is now severely constrained). Although the pure common market may be theoretically envisaged, it would constrain the operation of domestic stabilization and redistribution policies so much that its realization seems to be entirely dependent on developments in macroeconomic integration. . . . autonomous money supply or interest rate policies would be impossible as money and short-term financial assets would flow in or out as soon as the interest differentials with neighboring economies become

smaller or larger than the risk premium for expected exchange rates. . . . autonomous budgetary deficits are possible but will lead immediately . . . to exchange rate or interest rate reactions, more or less neutralizing the desired expansionary effects. . . . Exchange rate policy becomes next to impossible. (Pelkmans 1985, 341)

The clear implication is that a real commitment to financial market integration involves much more than the "negative integration" of liberalizing capital movements and financial services. The viability of these measures depends on subsequent progress in coordinating, approximating, or integrating monetary and fiscal policies.

Although formal provision for extended European-level monetary policy making was explicitly excluded from the SEA, it was quickly taken up again by the French and West German governments and especially by the Delors Committee, and was pushed with such vigor at the Madrid Summit (June 1989) and at the Strasbourg Summit (December 1989) that even the long skeptical *Economist* (1989) judges that the monetary union objective had acquired a "momentum of its own that will be very difficult to check," and that the debate was now "over the preferred vision of a monetary union."

The proposed liberalization of financial markets does indeed present a most serious threat to the stability of the existing monetary rules and practices of the European Monetary System. The EMS was created in 1979, and provides for the creation of an embryonic European currency unit—the ECU—and for an Exchange Rate Mechanism (ERM) through which governments agree to keep cross-rates of their currencies within relatively narrow fluctuation margins of central rates, which can be adjusted only by mutual consent. Central banks are required to intervene when exchange rates reach fluctuation margins and to grant each other unlimited short-term credit for that purpose. The EMS is widely considered an unexpected success: "a set of unwritten rules" has emerged and has become progressively tighter; realignments have occurred "because the EMS doesn't aim at fixed, nominal rates but at stable, real rates reflecting economic developments in each country"; all of this is supervised by the EC Monetary Committee, "a kind of (intergovernmental) college engaged in the common pursuit of stability" (Holm, forthcoming).

What was agreed at the December 1989 meeting of the European Council at Strasbourg was to initiate major parts of Stage One of the Delors Committee's proposal (the Delors Committee was made up of the heads of the twelve EC central banks, two members of the Commission, and three independent experts) for an EMU by July 1990 and to convene an intergovernmental conference in December of 1990 to discuss further stages whose enactment would require major treaty changes. Stage One will last at least until a new EMU Treaty takes effect. In the intervening period, the existing Committee of Central Bank Governors will build up a staff of its own and take on new advisory and monitoring functions with respect to how national Central Banks should conduct monetary policy, foreign exchange intervention, and banking and securities supervision. In addition, a new system for coordinating macroeconomic policy is to be set up including twice yearly reviews of the general economic situation in each member-state and the EC as a whole by the ECOFIN Council. Also called for are the publication of regular country studies including recommendations on current account and budget deficit matters. During the course of Stage One it was envisaged that the four countries whose currencies do not yet participate in the Exchange Rate Mechanism would join. (All but Greece and Portugal have now joined.)

Past Failures in the Monetary Field

These recent successes must be seen in the context of the EC's past failures in the monetary field. Exchange rate stability, an asset to be used in settling debts, a European stabilization fund, a common currency, monetary policy coordination, and monetary union have long been on the EC agenda. Many ambitious proposals have been tabled by the Commission and some have been enacted by the Council but never implemented. It is indeed striking to note the similarities in Commission reports and proposals of the 1960s and 1970s and those recently advanced by the Commission under Delors' presidency. The consensus of the literature is that very little has been accomplished in the area, with the exception of the modest success of the EMS, because of incompatible policy stances, divergent national economic conditions, exogenous shocks and global economic or financial trends, or the sheer political salience of monetary policy as the final repository (with defense) of national sovereignty (Tsoukalis 1977, 1983; Pelkmans 1985; Kindleberger 1984).

Pelkmans argued as recently as 1985 that the EC was likely to remain "encapsulated" at the level of a "customs-union-plus" because of its repeated failures over the years to incorporate financial market integration or to make significant progress toward the coordination or integration of monetary (and fiscal) policies. He argued that policy and performance divergences among the member-states were too great and "integrationist loyalties" too weak to support broader ambitions. Similarly, Tsoukalis noted in 1983 that although these issues would always be on the EC agenda, repeated failures suggested there was little likelihood that ambitious monetary policy efforts would be revived "in the foreseeable future." Hans Schmitt, writing in 1968, observed that it is precisely at the point of monetary integration and the creation of a common currency that the "urge to draw back will be the strongest."

Cohen (1989) argues that financial integration is a public good that has been constantly undersupplied in the EC. According to Cohen, conventional economic analysis tells us that substantial gains in economic welfare can be expected to accrue to a group of countries from the creation of a single financial market. This occurs because opportunities for more efficient financial intermediation will be thereby enhanced with important consequences for the allocation of investible funds among competing claims and the aggregate volume of savings and investment.

This public good is undersupplied for two reasons. First are the burdens and losses associated with the *transitional period*: "in any given actor's rational calculation of the attractiveness of a single market for banking services, the burden of adjustment is bound to figure prominently" (Cohen 1989, 150). Thus it follows that actors will use quite a high discount rate "when estimating the present value of future gains to be compared with losses in the short term." The second reason has to do with the divergence between collective incentives and individual incentives that arise from "differences in the gains and losses that can be anticipated by each actor separately" (p. 151).

Kindleberger (1984) finds the obstacles to EC financial integration even more daunting. He argues that "there will be no achievement of [European] financial integration without the strong leadership of the sort that Prussia provided for German political unification . . . and that Piedmont. . . furnished for Italian political and monetary unification. . . ." Accordingly, "Europe's best chance would be one in which German leadership achieved political integration followed by German provision of the public goods of European money, a European central bank, and European institutions necessary to harmonize economic policy" (p. 463).

Schmitt (1968) offers a societal variant of this general position, arguing that moving in the direction of monetary union implies the preexistence of a "dominant business community." According to Schmitt the political significance of monetary union lies in the fact that a disciplined surrender of command over its resource base is required of each member-state if the monetary authority's currency issues are to have unchallenged purchasing power in the territory of all. This a not an issue, he argues, inside nation-states because national Central Banks are rooted in a single business community, which serve its interests and are backed by its resources. Within national boundaries money derives its character as a generally accepted means of payment from being a claim not on any individual debtor alone but on a business community collectively. "By requiring its collective resources for its backing, the establishment of a single currency may in fact be looked upon as the constitutive act whereby such a business community formally comes into existence" (Schmitt 1968, 230).

New Contexts, Interest Perceptions, and Public and Private Preferences: A Framework for Analysis

Considering the political stakes and policy implications of financial deregulation, and monetary policy coordination and monetary union, and considering the policy record of relentless disappointment in the past, how shall we explain the extensive and unexpected new commitments thus far made by member-states in all three areas and the very real momentum that these processes seem to have achieved? While we should not underestimate the complexities and difficulties that lie ahead, nor the very real possibility that the current momentum will be dissipated as more sober assessments are made, there do seem to be grounds for thinking that the situation in the late 1980s and early 1990s is sufficiently different from the past to warrant a new look. The outcomes might be different this time because it appears that important internal and external contexts of public and private action have changed with important implications for interest perceptions and patterns of preferences and therefore for bargaining behavior. This suggests a somewhat more complex and dynamic set of *political* benefit/cost calculations than are conventionally considered. It might also imply that "getting the politics right" may take precedence over "getting the economics right" (Woolley 1990). We can understand this by conceiving of financial and monetary integration as an interrelated multilevel set of conflict and cooperation "games" (Cohen 1989). Six levels or games seem to be involved, each involving its distinctive set of actors and each implying distinctive accounts of the behavior of those actors, as well as distributional stakes and outcomes.

Financial Markets and the Restructuring of Financial Industries

Most fundamentally, financial deregulation involves competition, national and transnational mergers, joint ventures and other cooperative agreements among commercial banks, investment banks and securities firms, insurance companies, stock exchanges in reaction to and in anticipation of an EC-wide market for financial services. Bankers, securities analysts, and many economists argue that EC financial integration is only a belated response to the inevitable technology and market-driven globalization of finance. The initiative here is seen to lie mainly in the hands of financial agents seeking to increase their freedom of action and pursue higher profits and market shares, with governments merely reacting (Pauly 1987).

An Emergent Pan-European Financial-Business Elite

As we have seen, Schmitt suggested in 1968 that European monetary integration might come about as "the constitutive act whereby . . . a (European) business community formally comes into existence." From the perspective of such a class or group financial services liberalization, a Euro-Fed and EMU closely modeled on (or linked to) the German Bundesbank would provide a European stage from which European finance could play global games. To assure such a platform, guarantees must be sought for price stability, exchange rate stability, and a political environment in which governments could not interfere in the activities of financial markets in pursuit of their "parochial" national political concerns.

Domestic Political and Policy Games

It is clear that governments frequently set out to deliberately restructure markets and the institutional arrangements that govern them for *reasons of their own* (ideological, political, international competition, war-preparation, and war-fighting). Alternatively, structural change may be precipitated by *intrastate* or *state–society policy stalemates* that produce escalating economic performance problems (inflation, balance of payments deficits, budget deficits, misallocation of investment, and so forth).

It has been argued (Emerson 1988; Woolley 1990) that the real significance of the SEA and the 1992 Project is that governments and EC institutions have set out to change the information sets, future expectations, and thereby the behaviors of economic agents and national political actors. The strategy was deliberately adopted to make *irreversible precommitments to new consitutional rules of decision making* such as majority voting, the norm of mutual recognition, the substantive commitment to financial deregulation and monetary policy coordination. These commitments would be enforced by automatic market penalties. By making such precommitments, government's and EC institutions' economic policy objectives became credible in the eyes of private agents as well as in the eyes of political actors in domestic political games (for example, in struggles over relative power in national financial policy networks).

We can hypothesize a variety of reasons why EC governments facing increased international competition might pursue financial and monetary integration:

• To try to accelerate the pace of domestic change in financial service regulatory institutions and policy networks (because of power concentrations in the historical role of banks, notaries, stock exchanges, etc.). Examples are Italy and Spain.

• To overcome persistent budget deficits because of political alignments or institutional stalemates (Italy) or constitutional arrangements (Portugal?) by tying the hands of governments in favor of European commitments.

• To help control domestic inflationary forces by embracing the discipline of a Bundesbank-dominated European monetary policy—Britain in the 1990s, France since 1983, Italy since 1979.

Important in this regard is the gradual evolution of the EMS from a loose cooperative arrangement that was initially written off by most observers (e.g., Kindleberger) into an increasingly constraining set of institutions and norms through which governments could demonstrate the credibility of their commitment to exchange rate stability and to reducing both rates of inflation and national differences in inflation rates (Holm, forthcoming; Thiel 1989; DeCecco and Giovannini 1989).

National Interest Games: Hegemons and "K-groups"

Which member-states are likely to promote EC financial and monetary integration for fundamental national-interest reasons? Students of financial history take it as nearly axiomatic that financial integration is a nuclear process in which hegemonic states or center or core economies necessarily take the lead.

But in Europe, the only potential candidate—Germany—has been a very reluctant hegemon indeed (Ludlow 1982; Kindleberger 1984; Tsoukalis 1983). Nevertheless, it is possible that German unification will change the balance of forces within Germany on this issue as well as make German financial and monetary leadership more acceptable to other member-states. The political triumph of Kohl's strategy for German unification may set the stage for a more assertive German position with respect to EMU.

An interesting variant in the hegemony theme has been suggested by Schmitt (1968) and may well prove to be the most powerful dynamic pushing member-states toward some kind of EMU. Schmitt observed that the alternative to accepting the leadership of the center would be for all countries to relinquish to supranational bodies the measure of financial sovereignty they intend the core not to exercise on its own! Indeed, apprehensions about continued *de facto* Bundesbank domination—especially of EC exchange rate policies and unilateralism in interest rate decisions that have damaged the interests of other countries—are widely discussed as motives for the growing support for EMU within previously skeptical governments, notably in Denmark, the Netherlands, and even the United Kingdom.

Another variant on the hegemony theme is to be found in the literature explicitly criticizing the theory of hegemonic stability as espoused by Kindleberger and others. Hardin (1982) and Snidal (1985) have argued that cooperation is possible in groups that lack a single member willing and able to bear the costs of hegemony. They have developed the concept of the "K-group"—the smallest subgroup among a larger group of potential cooperators that is capable of providing a public good without cooperation from others. In the European financial and monetary setting the prime candidates as K-group members appear to be France and Germany. France and Germany are each other's most important trading partners and together account for between 40 and 50 percent of total EC GNP and inter-EC imports and exports. As their cooperation in setting up the EMS shows, they share interests in controlling EC monetary instability—both external from the dollar, and internal from divergent inflation rates.

Europe and the World Economy

As Holm (forthcoming), Ludlow (1982), and others have pointed out, the EMS and EMU represent much more than a project for central bank cooperation in order to induce domestic financial restructuring and monetary stability. From its origin, the EMS was to some extent an expression of German and French political frustration with the Carter Administration and with U.S. economic and monetary policies and a *geopolitical* expression of European aspirations to assert greater policy independence from the United States. And in the background is the aspiration of some Europeans for the Ecu to become a global key currency that might allow Europeans to counterbalance U.S. monetary and fiscal mismanagement and to acquire some of the "special privileges" or "seignorage" that goes along with the role of a global key currency, for example, in terms of freedom of maneuver for both foreign and domestic policies.

Chief among the advantages of a prospective EC seignorage would be the ability to pursue domestic and foreign policy objectives without short-term balance of payments constraints, and liberation from being held hostage to America's chronic monetary and fiscal disequilibria and the negative effects on western European liquidity of high U.S. interest rates (Puchala 1989). Creating such a key currency would then be an act of "high politics." Having one "is comparable to having one's own language used as world language" (Holm, citing Kindleberger).

The Supranational Level: The Commission and Other EC Institutions

Neofunctionalist integration theory of the 1950s and 1960s focused on the sources of group and national preferences, on the dynamic potential of supranational and intergovernmental institutions in shaping political choices, and on the processes whereby preferences, interest perceptions, and institutions change. Integration theory stressed learning and the emergence of new collective understandings. In this perspective, learning is the adoption by sociopolitical actors and by government policy makers of new interpretations of reality, new "rates of time preference" and new perceptions of interest as these arise out of the transactions and interactions of actors in new regional institutional settings.

The Commission of the EC, after having been written off in the 1970s and early 1980s as an agent of integration, has reemerged after 1985 under President Delors as a key actor, particularly with respect to financial integration and economic and monetary union. The Commission's policy initiatives, Delors' tireless espousal of EMU and its broadly federalist institutions, the role of the Commission as interlocutor with European business and financial interests, with the French and German governments and with the European Council, the ECOFIN Council, the Monetary Committee, and the Community of Central Bank Governors attest to the central position played by supranational institutions committed to Euro-federalist institutional outcomes.

Neofunctionalists were clear that the positions and interests of national governments will set the limits within which financial integration, monetary policy cooperation, and EMU will or will not take place. But national positions and interest perceptions can be and have been altered in the context of supranational and intergovernmental bargaining. Furthermore, it is the Commission that is strategically positioned to play the role of catalyst and honest broker and constructor of complex package deals once governments decide they want to reach agreements (Lindberg and Scheingold 1970).

A Research Agenda for the 1990s

We now have a framework for analyzing the complex sets of motivations that might lead the twelve EC member-states to continue to pursue financial and monetary integration. We can add this to the formidable list of economic and political obstacles so ably analyzed by Tsoukalis, Ludlow, Kindleberger, Cohen, and many others. How will these overlapping and competing motivations play out at both private and public, national and EC levels in the years of intense scrambling and bargaining to come?

Research should analyze the intersections of these different levels or games in four specific bargaining arenas. How will "plays" and outcomes at one level or game relate to plays and outcomes in others? How will new actors, interest preferences and time perspectives suggested by changing internal and external contexts relate to well-known obstacles that have frustrated financial and monetary integration in the past? Will long-term political advantages and economic gains balance off short-term losses and distributional disequilibria?

The bargaining arenas to be monitored are described in the following sections.

The Regulation or Governance of Financial Industries in National and European Financial Policy Networks

In each nation there are established policy networks that govern the commercial banking, securities, and insurance industries. An important part of this research agenda will be to monitor and analyze the changes that are taking place in these networks in anticipation of or as a result of financial integration. Change should be anticipated in all these policy networks because of the opportunities capital market and financial services liberalization will create for economic agents seeking to increase their freedom of action and pursue higher profits and larger market shares. Financial innovation, mergers, and other opportunistic strategies will create new problems for national regulators. It is also clear that national-level adjustment will interact with EC-level activity. We can expect to see increased efforts at EC-wide coordination, cooperation, and oversight and mutual monitoring by governmental regulators, for example in the EC's Banking Advisory Committee of national banking supervisors, or in bilateral governmental forums such as the Anglo-German negotiations about the liberalization of the insurance industry (see *Financial Times*, 31 March, 1990). And we can expect to see competition *and* cooperation at the level of private financial institutions, for example, among national stock exchanges.

The Coordination of Monetary Policies in the Strengthened EMS Structure That Entered into Operation July 1, 1990

The first stage of the EMU proposed in the original Delors Committee Report entered into force on July 1, 1990, and involves expanded roles and responsibilities for the Committee of Central Bank Governors and the Monetary Committee. What is involved is an elaboration of the EMS and, if anything, an increase in the *de facto* power of the Bundesbank in EC monetary and exchange rate policies. The Commission considers such a system to be unacceptable in the long run for both political and economic reasons. Nevertheless, how these institutions operate over the next couple of years will surely offer important clues to the actual policy and power alignments that exist or will emerge beneath the surface rhetoric of the EMU as a "great political leap forward" for the EC.

It remains to be seen whether there will be convergence or divergence in national inflation rates, budget deficits, tax policies, interregional capital transfers, etc. This will be a crucial arena in which to monitor the domestic politics of monetary and budget policy making as the initial effects of financial deregulation manifest themselves and as governments and political coalitions react (Persson and Tabellini 1990).

Negotiating the EMU Treaty

One of the most dramatic developments in recent years has been the growing political momentum behind the proposal for an EMU. The negotiations which will lead to a treaty offer us an opportunity to assess the nature and strength of the perceived *political* advantages different national actors see in rapidly moving toward an EMU agreement. They will be forced to deal with the considerable perceived economic uncertainties and disadvantages that would counsel a more gradualist approach. How will the different benefit/cost calculations and time preferences of politicians, economic policy makers, and economic agents play off against each other? What role will the Commission succeed in playing as it advances its own agenda and "European vision"? How will national and EC-level games interact? What transnational coalitions or groups will emerge and what roles will they play in pursuit of what agendas?

National Political Struggles over Structural and Institutional Implications of EMS and EMU

We may also anticipate a process whereby EC-level institutional struggles and policy games will play out at the national level, for example, in pressures to strengthen central banks in their relationships to Minister of Finance and Cabinet politicians. (See *Economist*, 10 February, 1989, "Liberating Central Banks" for an interesting discussion of the issues involved and the variations that exist among EC countries in central bank "independence.") It is clear that in some countries, for example Italy, EMU is seen as a way of liberating the Bank of Italy and its conduct of monetary policy from "irresponsible" political interference, whereas in other countries, EMU is feared as a threat to national and political "sovereignty" over monetary policy.

We should also monitor the positions and roles taken by labor unions and Social Democratic and other leftist parties as they come to more clearly understand the "neoliberal," "anti-interventionist," and potentially deflationary implications of the EMS and EMU arrangements (for a further discussion see Kurzer in chapter 7 of this volume). Some on the Left may argue that there can be no European role for labor or for Social Democracy in a Europe that *lacks* an internal and external monetary and economic policy capability. (Only in a Europe with a global key currency can reflationary policies be pursued.) Whether such a long-term vision can overcome short-term threats and losses seems dubious. But can labor and Social Democracy block financial and monetary integration? Are there better options available at a national level?

Institutional Outcomes and Development Paths

The 1992 Project is predominantly an exercise in deregulation and deinstitutionalization. This is clearly the case as far as capital movement and financial services liberalization are concerned. But monetary and budgetary policy coordination in the strengthened EMS and the development of some kind of EMU imply a degree of EC-level reregulation and institution building. Thus it must be a key goal of research to develop a methodology for discerning pathways of institutional development toward alternative European polity outcomes. How this can be done is not yet clear.

Economists like Gros (1989) distinguish different degrees of *monetary union* or monetary integration: *ex post macro* (fixed exchange rates plus full capital mobility but with escape clauses), *ex ante macro* (credibly irrevocable fixed exchange rates), and *micro MU* (an area that behaves as if there were only one money, or where there is a supranational parallel currency). But these "stages" are not associated with clearly articulated institutional arrangements, and it is not clear how or if one necessarily leads into another in a continuous process. Cobham (1989) and Vaubel (1978) contrast *alternative strategies* for monetary integration: *Coordination strategies* ("snakes," harmonization of national monetary policy, or a combination of fixing exchange rates and agreeing monetary targets) stress gradualism and can be seen as ways to create commitment, but run the risk of national defections. *Centralization strategies* ("big leap approach" of establishing a full monetary union, free currency competition, and creating a parallel currency) stress automaticity and are best seen as ways of implementing an existing commitment by locking the parties into "a predictable and unstoppable" process. Which strategy or strategies are selected clearly has implications for the discretion and autonomy of national policy makers, for the intergovernmental rules and decision styles that may emerge over time, and for the roles that can be assumed by such new quasi-federal institutions as the proposed independent Euro-fed or European Central Bank System.

We must try to combine insights drawn from the economic literature (e.g., Giavazzi et al. 1988; Franz 1989) with political theories of integration that postulated types of institutional outcomes (Haas 1975, 1976) and decision analysis (e.g., Scharpf 1988) that theorizes about the capacities of different decision systems to reach agreement on collective political choices.

References

Cobham, David. 1989. "Strategies for Monetary Integration Revisited." *Journal of Common Market Studies* 27:203–18.

Cohen, Benjamin. 1989. "European Financial Integration and National Banking Interests." In Paolo Guerrieri, and Pier Carlo Padoan, eds., *The Political Economy of European Integration: States, Markets and Institutions*. New York: Harvester Wheatsheaf.

Committee for the Study of Economic and Monetary Union (Delors Committee). 1989. Report on Economic and Monetary Union in the European Community.

Cox, Andrew, ed. 1986. *State, Finance and Industry*. Brighton: Wheatsheaf Books.

DeCecco, Marcello, and Alberto Giovannini, eds. 1989. *A European Central Bank? Perspectives on Monetary Unification after Ten Years of the EMS*. Cambridge: Cambridge University Press.

Economist. 1989. "A Survey of Europe's Capital Markets." 16 December.

Ellsworth, Richard R. 1985. "Capital Markets and Competitive Decline." *Harvard Business Review* (September–October):171–83.

Emerson, Michael. 1988. "1992 as Economic News." Manuscript.

Franz, Otmar, ed. 1989. *European Currency in the Making*. Sindelfingen: Libertas.

Giavazzi, Francesco, Stefano Micossi, and Marcus Miller, eds. 1988. *The European Monetary System*. Cambridge: Cambridge University Press.

Gros, Daniel. 1989. "Paradigms for the Monetary Union of Europe." *Journal of Common Market Studies*, 27:219–30.

Haas, Ernst B. 1975. *The Obsolescence of Regional Integration Theory*. Institute of International Studies, University of California.

Haas, Ernst B. 1976. "Turbulent Fields and the Theory of Regional Integration." *International Organization*, 30:173–212.

Hall, Peter. 1986. *Governing the Economy*. Cambridge: Polity Press.

Hardin, R. 1982. *Collective Action*. Baltimore, MD: Johns Hopkins University Press.

Holm, Erik. Forthcoming. "The Politics of Europe's Money." In B. Crawford and P. Schulze, eds., *European Self-Assertion: A New Role for Europe in International Affairs*.

Kindleberger, Charles. 1984. *A Financial History of Western Europe*. London: Allen and Unwin.

Lash, Scott, and John Urry. 1987. *The End of Organized Capitalism*. Madison: University of Wisconsin Press.

Lindberg, Leon, and Stuart Scheingold. 1970. *Europe's Would-Be Polity*. Englewood Cliffs, NJ: Prentice Hall.

Ludlow, Peter. 1982. *The Making of the European Monetary System.* London: Butterworth.

Moran, Michael. 1984. "Politics, Banks and Markets: An Anglo-American Comparison." *Political Studies*, 32:173–89.

Pauly, Louis. 1987. *Opening Financial Markets: Banking Politics on the Pacific Rim.* Ithaca: Cornell University Press.

Pelkmans, Jacques. 1985. "The Institutional Economics of European Integration," in M. Cappalletti et al., *Integration Through Law*, vol. 1, Book 1. Berlin: De Gruyter.

Persson, Torsten, and Guido Tabellini. 1990. "The Politics of 1992: Fiscal Policy and European Integration." Manuscript.

Puchala, Donald J. 1989. "The Pangs of Atlantic Interdependence." In H. M. Belien, *The United States and The European Community: Convergence or Conflict.* The Hague: Universitaire Pers Rotterdam.

Scharpf, Fritz W. 1988. "The Joint-Decision Trap: Lessons from German Federalism and European Integration." *Public Administration*, 66:239–78.

Schmitt, Hans. 1968. "Capital Markets and the Unification of Europe." *World Politics*, 20:228–44.

Snidal, Duncan. 1985. "The Limits of Hegemonic Stability Theory." *International Organization*, 39:579–614.

Thiel, Elke. 1989. "Global Monetary Interdependence and Patterns of West European Monetary Integration." Manuscript.

Tsoukalis, Loukas. 1983. "Money and the Process of Integration." In H. Wallace, W. Wallace, and C. Webb, *Policy-Making in the European Community.* Chichester: Wiley.

Tsoukalis, Loukas. 1977. *The Politics and Economics of European Monetary Integration.* London: Allen and Unwin.

Vaubel, L. 1978. *Strategies for Currency Unification.* Tübingen: Mohr.

Woolley, John. 1990. "1992, Capital, and the EMS: Political Institutions and Monetary Union." Manuscript.

Zysman, John. 1983. *Governments, Markets, and Growth: Financial Systems and the Politics of Industrial Change.* Ithaca, NY: Cornell University Press.

7

The European Community and the Postwar Settlement

The Effect of Monetary Integration on Corporatist Arrangements

Paulette Kurzer

Introduction

Regardless of whether the European Central Bank and European Monetary Union will be in place by January 1993, the tenor of the Single Market project is, above all, to stress price stability, monetary policy constraints, and market liberalization (Sandholtz and Zysman 1989; Grahl and Teague 1989). This chapter looks back to the earlier period of the European Monetary System (EMS), the predecessor of the European Monetary Union, to estimate what we can expect from the Community's new plan for full monetary and economic union. Unless the unity program is permanently shelved, everything seems to suggest a further strengthening of Germany's dominant position in Community developments (Kurzer and Allen 1992). The evidence for this comes from the events that have taken place in Belgium, Denmark, and the Netherlands. Gradually, they have adopted an economic policy agenda that has undeniable German parentage. This chapter asks why these countries not only have tolerated a loss of policy autonomy but have in fact positively replicated the neoliberal German model. Not too long ago, each of the three countries was considered a prototypical corporatist society with generous and universalistic social welfare entitlements (Esping-Andersen 1990).

Though union density and Labor party participation in government cabinets was not that high in Holland, hundreds of tripartite bodies, councils, and agen-

---

Note: The author wishes to thank John Conybeare for his comments on an earlier draft.

cies ensured stable labor representation in public policy. Similarly, employers and unions in Belgium agreed to set up a social system whereby workers obtained political recognition and full employment guarantees in return for no-strike promises. Denmark, too, followed this route and changed the balance of power in the industrial and political marketplaces. Yet as Germany has increasingly defined the boundaries of economic policy choices through its leading role in the EMS, governments and domestic interest groups in small countries surrendered an ever larger portion of their national sovereignty. Governments in welfare state societies embraced a monetary regime, which was basically hostile to a continuation of fiscal spending and social legislation, because a powerful minority wanted to see greater monetary restrictiveness and an end to social concertation or budgetary intervention on behalf of ailing firms and labor markets. In other words, national government delegates in the EC negotiations had two audiences—the European Community and influential domestic economic actors—and their respective demands were sufficiently flexible to enable national leaders to join the EMS without having to fear a domestic backlash. Which powerful minority advocated membership in the EMS to advance European unity and discipline domestic spending patterns and priorities? Primarily, central bankers, big business, and liberal ideologues, coalescing around a casual coalition of groups who were united in their hostility toward the postwar accords and applauded the loss of domestic autonomy in return for participation in the EMS. To some extent, this mirrors the two-level game metaphor in that a new political leadership of center-right governments reaches across influential economic actors in an effort to augment its power *vis-à-vis* organized labor and in the process enables its new allies to force through budget cuts, pay freezes, and decentralized wage negotiations (Putnam 1988).

Before describing how the consolidation of German-type institutional frameworks through the EMS displaced previous pro-labor arrangements, the next section explains the workings of the EMS and its record. Following this description, the second part explores why the small countries did not raise greater objections to the loss of policy autonomy and the third part concludes with a brief discussion on the future European Monetary Union (EMU) (for a more in-depth discussion, see Lindberg, chapter 6 in this volume).

The EMS

Many studies stress the "disciplinary" character of the EMS,[1] but what is meant by that? and who disciplines whom? The key to understanding the restrictive effects of the EMS on fiscal and budgetary policies is the dominance of the German mark in the system. Because of the size and strength of the German economy, the D-mark determines the external value of the EMS grid of bilateral rates and is also the key intervention currency (Ungerer et al. 1986; Wood 1988).

When the founders designed the arrangement, the strength of the DM was seen in a positive light because it would help with the fight against inflation. Preferring slow growth to inflation or full employment, German governments purposefully deflated the domestic economy in the early 1980s. German business and labor, however, had the means to withstand an explicit deflationary climate but countries with a weaker industrial structure and less resilient export sector required extra stimuli to restore business confidence and labor market equilibrium. Because of the EMS framework, however, they could not inflate unilaterally their own economy (de Grauwe 1987; Mastropasqua et al. 1988, 283). If they grew faster than Germany, the current account would start to record deficits. These external deficits would then put pressure on the exchange rate, require central bank intervention, and provoke speculative currency transactions. If the exchange rate intervention fails to stabilize the currency within the bilateral margins, which is likely, the participating central banks and finance ministries meet to decide on an exchange rate realignment.

The EMS entered into a more stable period after the relative uncertainties of the inflationary period of 1979–83 because economic policies did indeed increasingly converge. Before, divergent inflation rates and different economic programs necessitated frequent central bank interventions and occasional exchange rate realignments. The other reason, however, for the decline in exchange rate adjustments was precisely the requirement to seek prior consultations. Only after the approval of the entire Monetary Committee or the Committee of Ministers of Finance and Economics are member governments allowed to proceed with the exchange rates realignment. Changes in exchange rates affect the export competitiveness of the country's trading partners. An EMS member must, therefore, demonstrate that other remedies have been exhausted and that the devaluation will not be used as a makeshift measure but will be accompanied by appropriate economic changes. Economic reforms include budget cuts, mandatory pay freezes, and the abolishing of cost-of-living indexation (Artis and Taylor 1988; McDonald and Zis 1989).

By and large, the outcome of the negotiations inside the EMS structure is predetermined. German representatives hold the key to a successful realignment since no devaluation can succeed without their active consent. The bilateral grid of exchange rates is stabilized through extensive intervention by the central banks of the participating currencies. Monetary officials, however, cannot sell or purchase large quantities of another country's currency without the approval of the issuing central bank. This always means that since the German Bundesbank issues the most important intervention currency, it has considerable influence over the final outcome. As a rule, the Germans prefer a stable alignment with ample intramarginal intervention but few exchange rate adjustments. It should also be noted that German monetary officials are suspicious of governments that lack the internal will to control their spending habits. Hence, they insist that governments first utilize budgetary instruments to lower consumption and reduce import demand before an exchange rate realignment is negotiated. Knowledge-

Table 7.1

Economic Performance of Small European States: EMS Member-States[a] and Nonmembers[b] 1980–85

	Real Growth	Unemployment	GFCF[1]
EC	1.4	9	–0.6
Small EMS	1.0	10.8	–0.9
Small non-EMS	2.5	2.5	2.6

Source: OECD, Economic Outlook Historical Statistics 1960–85.
[a]Belgium, Denmark, Ireland, Netherlands.
[b]Austria, Finland, Norway, Sweden, Switzerland.
[1]Gross Fixed Capital Formation.

able insiders report that weak currencies have not been allowed to devalue without the appropriate economic adjustment packages (Padoa-Schioppa 1984).

To be fair, not only German representatives but other national representatives as well prefer to see domestic to external adjustments. Thus, the rationale of the EMS is to undercut monetary autonomy in exchange for intra-European stability. Competitive devaluations or constant exchange rate realignments weaken the credibility of the EMS and central banks. Nevertheless, some studies (Giavazzi and Giovannini 1989, 66–82) show that central banks other than the Bundesbank assumed the burden of intervention by adjusting their exchange rates. And a comparison of the economic performance of the small EMS members also shows that theirs deteriorated more acutely than that of the EC area and the small countries outside the EMS (Table 7.1). Harmonization imposed asymmetric costs as the weaker economies had to bring down inflation through coercive incomes policies and fiscal spending retrenchments while the leading country did not provide the others with a growth stimulus.

It might be argued that the EMS members made sacrifices in the early eighties to be on a stronger footing in the closing years of that decade. To some extent this is indeed the case. Growth rates have picked up tremendously and unemployment has dropped. However, the current spurt in growth is, among other things, a function of the lack of growth in previous years and the economic improvements have not accompanied a basic industrial or economic transformation to overcome structural imbalances or an unfavorable export position. Similarly, unemployment is still comparatively high.

Why would governments in Belgium, Denmark, and the Netherlands have agreed to subordinate their national interests to that of a monetary arrangement? Besides my own interpretation, several counterarguments need to be considered.

In all likelihood, it would have been inconceivable for Belgian and Dutch officials not to participate in a major EC initiative. Both countries are founding members of the European Community and have been enthusiastic proponents of European integration. They were also supportive of supranational rather than intergovernmental frameworks because the former would protect them against the hegemonic aspirations of the larger countries (Woyke 1985). Though the EMS is so far an intergovernmental arrangement, it was supposed to evolve into something more substantial with strong supranational features (Ungerer et al. 1986; Padoa-Schioppa 1984).

Second, intra-European trade accounts for a considerable share of total exports and GDP of the three countries. The promise of a stable exchange rate environment is attractive to open and small economies with substantial foreign trade sectors. Third, a majority of the small European countries have opted for a link with a strong currency like the German mark. Motives for pegging the national currency to that of a large trading partner sprang from the urge to sterilize speculative expectations and fluctuations of their currency in foreign exchange markets.

Economic considerations alone seem to provide a perfectly adequate explanation for why these countries voted for monetary integration. What this ignores, however, is that it took a while before the operating rules of the EMS were in place and that the execution of its objectives was left to the discretionary power of the participating countries (Mastropasqua et al. 1988; Woolley, forthcoming). Following the examples of France and Italy, the smaller countries could have asked for special treatment in light of their structural problems and weak labor market performance. Like so many other European initiatives, the EMS was less than what the originators had envisioned. At least, some national governments entered the EMS agreement with the provision that they need not remove capital or exchange controls. Stability in exchange rates has been facilitated by the existence of widespread capital controls to discourage sudden outflows and disturbances.[2] Financial liberalization, as pursued by the three countries, is incompatible with discretionary budget decisions. Divergent fiscal policies are often the main cause for an exchange rate crisis unless the domestic market is artificially detached from international influences (Grilli 1989). Moreover, Denmark could have pointed out that since a significant portion of its trade was with Britain and the Nordic countries, a weighted basket of currencies that included those of its other trading partners would be justified.

The successful continuation of the EMS depended on the internal political commitment of the participants because it had no mechanism to bind government officials. The sources of that determination rested with the central bank, monetary authorities in general, and politicians. Had central bankers perceived deep contradictions between external obligations and domestic economic management, governments would have demanded the sort of safeguards granted to the larger countries. Calculating the costs of the various trade-offs, they must have come to the conclusion that the costs were more than offset by future gains. These gains included the elimination of a system of wage indexation, the suspension of consensual centralized bargaining and coupling of private- to public-sector pay. Submission to the discipline of the EMS would arrest further growth in social expenditures, a goal that had eluded the anti-Keynesian/welfare state coalition so far.

But why did the "game" of central banks to hitch a ride on the back of German monetary conservatism not provoke wider public criticism and cheating? One reason for the absence of objections is that such an action would have been very costly. The arrival of the EMS was accompanied by the deregulation and liberalization of financial markets and capital flows. In the absence of unambiguous commitment to stable parities, the financial community would probably have fled the country. This would cause enormous economic disruptions and psychological damage so that the monetary arrangement could quickly deteriorate into an unprecedented disaster. It would require rounds of consultation with Frankfurt and the Monetary Committee in Brussels to settle things at home and affected governments would be asked to bring whatever provoked the waves of speculation and capital flight in the first place under control. With that, politicians would find themselves at exactly the sort of impasse they had tried to avoid earlier. Their cheating was driven by the pressure to escape the collective decision-making rules of the EMS and its constraints on policy autonomy. Financial instability would necessitate even more drastic cures and probably incite voter retaliation. All in all, once inside the EMS and a full participant, not much is left to the imagination of the elected policy official. This means that the first step in accepting the transfer of national decision-making autonomy to collective deliberations has critical importance for holding on to a small margin of action to defend the "national interest" later (Rey 1988, 138; Woolley, forthcoming).

The small countries discussed in this chapter—Belgium, Denmark, and the Netherlands—did not think twice about the consequence of being fair players. They disallowed themselves this halfway option to balance competing demands from domestic forces and international obligations. This is because powerful groups in the policy process wanted to see an end to pro-labor arrangements. A core feature of the German model is the increased autonomy of the central bank *vis-à-vis* the government. Participation in the EMS enhances the autonomy of the central bank to conduct policies independent from the government. This is not to suggest that the Germans conspired to take over the economic affairs of their smaller neighbors. Rather, a convergence of interests arose among central bank personnel, Liberal parties, and business circles in the high public spending countries and the German leadership. They wished to achieve a redesigned policy process in favor of balanced budgets, low interest rates, and price stability. Monetary integration became a convenient pretext for rolling back the advances of the welfare state and for placing a moratorium on public-sector growth and social spending.

More likely than not, EMS participation would induce a real reduction in public expenditures, bring an end to a system of wage bargaining that yielded wage compensations above national productivity increases, and limit consumer spending. In theory, every consumer and producer stands to gain from low inflation and stable exchange rates. In reality, financial agents assign much greater value to price stability and central banks are quicker to trade economic growth and employment for low inflation (Burdekin and Laney 1988; Schor 1985; Willett and Banaian 1988; Woolley 1985). Paradoxically, central banks transferred their constitutional powers to an intergovernmental institution in order to enlarge their domestic influence over the direction of economic policy. The EMS appeared at a convenient moment because central banks in these three countries had lost their institutional capacity, not so much to control inflation as to curb wage growth and social spending.

The Economic Recession and the New Monetary Discipline

Of the three central banks, the Danish and Belgian central banks are less independent than the Netherlands Bank. In 1936, the Central Bank Act of Denmark established formal parliamentary supervision over money and credit. However, the Act was a product of a tortuous compromise in which the social democratic bloc granted the greatest concessions. While the Bank Supervisors are recruited from Parliament, various ministries, labor, and business, the actual leadership is in the hands of the Board of Management. Members of the Board of Management are elected by the Bank Supervisors or appointed by the Crown (government). None of the directors of the Board of Management can be dismissed by the government or another institution and their tenure lasts until retirement at age seventy. In the end, the juridical position of the Danish Central Bank is autonomous. Parliamentary control is weak (Uusitalo 1984).

What limited the authority and activities of the Danish Nationalbank was the unfavorable position of the Danish economy in the international system. Whenever the Danish central bank lowered the discount rate to boost, for example, housing construction, the economy quickly registered sizable current account deficits. Increased consumption led to increased demand for imported goods. The monetary policies of the central bank were therefore frequently determined by the need to defend the country's international reserves. Social Democrat–led cabinets were also defeated by the vulnerable position of the Danish economy as an expansionary fiscal program threatened to widen current account deficits beyond sustainable levels. The Nationalbank therefore possessed the institutional autonomy to set monetary policy separate from government. But its independence was largely nominal since the structural weakness of the economy did not leave many options open (Pekkarinen 1989).

The Netherlands, too, has a relatively small industrial sector and exports chiefly agricultural commodities and food products. However, it generated substantial surpluses through its specialization in shipping, insurance, and financial services, and later the export of natural gas. The surplus on the invisible trade balance is sufficient to cover the deficits in manufactured trade. Dutch Parliament and government also exercise relatively modest influence on the money and credit policies of the Netherlands Bank. According to the Dutch Banking Act of 1948, the Ministry of Finance reserves the right to give instructions to the central bank. This provision has never been invoked. The Treasury is allowed to take up a low ceiling of interest-free advances. However, these advances may be used only to cover temporary requirements. The Bank, in turn, is not obliged to provide funds to the government. In general, the minister of finance and the central bank governor collaborate amicably (Kurzer 1988).

For the Netherlands Bank, the management of the country's exchange rate and money liquidity is eased by a comfortable surplus on current transactions (usually around 1 percent of GDP). By comparison, the Danish Nationalbank saw the external deficit grow from an annual average of 2.1 percent between 1968 and 1974 to 3.5 percent between 1974 and 1979. It is no surprise that the Netherlands Bank has consistently pursued the twin goals of low inflation and a balance of payments equilibrium with considerable success until the turmoil of the mid-1970s and that it actively promoted the guilder as an international reserve currency and a substitute for the German mark (Schotsman 1987). It also follows that the healthy external position of the Netherlands adds to the political weight and visibility of the central bank. With a great variety of instruments at its disposal, the Netherlands Bank is an influential voice in policy making (Fase 1985).

The ability of the Belgian National Bank to go against the desires of the government is limited by its awkward institutional status. Its responsibilities are distributed among different agencies and its governing board is filled with appointments from government and established interest groups. The greatest institutional impediment for the National Bank was that the Banking Commission, a separate agency, supervised financial institutions and set credit restrictions/quotas while the Bank formulated monetary decisions (Kurzer 1988; Mastropasqua 1978). The incomplete powers of the National Bank tempted both politicians and business to abuse the gaps in regulation by avoiding accountability for irresponsible financial behavior. The cartel parties—Socialist, Liberal, and Christian Democratic—appointed their own loyalists to the Bank and the financial groups tended to underreport their financial activities.

Denmark: Economic Recession and Slow Revival

The economic recession hit Denmark harder than most other countries. Unemployment rose in one decade by a factor of eleven from 1 percent in 1973 to 11 percent in 1983. Deficits on the balance of payments increased fivefold (in current terms) between 1975 and 1980. Public-sector debt skyrocketed. To reduce the number of unemployed, government agencies increased their share in the total labor force to 31 percent in 1982 from 10 percent in 1960 (OECD 1988,

37). More public-sector employment and greater social expenditures produced a gross debt of 74 percent of GDP in 1984. Interest rate payments accounted for 2 percent of public expenditures in 1973 and rose to 13 percent in 1983. Net interest payments increased from zero to 5 percent of GDP from 1970 to 1985 (OECD 1988, 40).

As in other European countries, the political elite in Denmark was sharply divided about the meaning of the crisis and the sort of solution needed to pull the country out of a deep recession. Social Democrats and their allies saw the cumulation of negative trends as a sign of the collapse of capitalist production and as an opportunity for thorough economic restructuring. Conservative and Liberal parties blamed the growth of public sector for cost–push inflation and suggested a reorganization of the welfare state and budget cutting. Voters were equally divided and elected unstable coalitions whose support in Parliament was fragile and inhibited the adoption of forceful or painful measures. Crisis management was virtually nonexistent. Denmark had seven elections between 1973 and 1987. Insofar as governments took the initiative they usually led to mandatory wage accords as happened in 1975, 1977, 1979, and 1985. (Einhorn and Logue 1989, 246; Damgaard 1989).

Left-wing governments were committed to budget cutting and stabilization of the public sector but they wanted to act through the consent and cooperation of trade unions. Socialists passed major proposals on incomes policies, tax increases, and devaluations, and cut back some welfare programs to combat inflation and the burden of the foreign debt. In the 1970s, contrary to the trends in other countries, the Social Democratic governments tightened banking regulations and controls over external capital flows in an unsuccessful effort to keep domestic interest rates below those of its major trading partners. This was part of a "sheltering" strategy aimed at expanding the public sector to absorb the unemployed and at avoiding a depletion of foreign exchange reserves. The Nationalbank and professional economists in the major research institutes suggested an entirely different approach that consisted of financial liberalization and deregulation.

The president of the Nationalbank repeatedly pointed out that capital controls were ineffective. However, in the absence of a credible commitment to a fixed exchange rate, the Nationalbank retained the various controls with the purpose of divorcing domestic from international interest rate fluctuations. The removal of exchange and capital controls, therefore, could be administered only after the government had broken with its traditional dependence on small devaluations (Thygesen 1984, 59–65).

In the summer of 1982, the crisis package of the Socialists failed to win parliamentary approval and they resigned. A Liberal–Conservative coalition replaced them and presented its own budget that fall. The thrust of the new government program was to promote competitiveness of private business through a reduction in interest rates, inflation, and wage scales. It froze wages for five months, suspended the wage indexation for two years, increased taxes, and raised employee contribution to education and social security (ETLA et al. 1987, 67).

The Danes themselves noted the inherent danger of liberalizing the financial system and removing capital controls. The Nationalbank, though it had never been very successful, would now have zero prospects of regulating the supply and price of credit (ETLA et al. 1987, 68). However, the price appeared minor. Net central government debt amounted to 40 percent of GDP in 1983 and its consolidation started right after the installment of the new cabinet. Membership in the EMS has helped to arrest public-sector growth as the liberalization of capital movements influenced interest rates and brought them in line with the international level. By adhering to a fixed exchange rate policy the authorities sent a clear signal that were willing to use instruments other than devaluation to restore the economic balance. This, in turn, allowed for lower interest rates as confidence in the Danish crown stabilized (OECD 1988, 57–58).

Danish authorities, for a while at least, thought that they could get away from the rules of collective exchange rate management. In 1979, when the Socialist-led coalition was still struggling to design a crisis package, the Danish crown was devalued by 5 percent to improve competitiveness. It was part of a package that also included permanent modification of indexation mechanisms. Danish officials proceeded very informally and called the Council of Ministers to report their decision and acted unilaterally. In February 1982, the Socialist-led cabinet wanted to devalue again to improve competitiveness and approached the members of the Monetary Committee with the request for a 7 percent devaluation. The Council of Ministers and central bank officials rejected the request but approved a smaller realignment of 3 percent. A few months later, the Socialist cabinet had resigned. Membership in the EMS has eliminated the option of competitive (though small) devaluations and has increased the economic exposure of Denmark. Since international (European) trends had a distinctive deflationary and restrictive bias, the Danes had no choice and soon followed. In the meantime, the Nationalbank has been able to accomplish what it had tried to achieve in the past decade: a stable exchange rate combined with relatively low interest rates. However, this has been at the expense of goals associated with social democracy such as universalistic social entitlement rights and income redistribution.

The Netherlands: Return to Monetary Restrictiveness

The healthy financial position of the economy heightened the reputation of the Netherlands Bank. In the 1970s, the Bank suddenly faced two ominous developments that were more or less beyond its control. Wage negotiations in the Netherlands were based on consensual and centralized negotiations in bilateral or tripartite committees. One of the important preconditions for the smooth implementation of annual wage agreements was the authority of the top leadership to enforce the stipulations of the central accords. By 1970, however, wildcat strikes of unorganized workers or militant unions in the Socialist trade union federation interrupted the cozy arrangements of peak-level negotiations. In the 1970s, industrial militancy and the disappearance of cultural/religious animosity led to a transfer of power from the confederation to the constituent unions and the system of postwar wage restraints gave way to a more fluid and combative era of unenforceable central agreements and large wage drift. The Socialist cabinet intervened after 1974 with mandatory wage agreements but coercive incomes policies were usually aimed at narrowing wage differentials of different groups and it continued to protect the value of real incomes of workers (Braun 1987; Wolinetz 1989). In short, wage and pay ceilings were set to guarantee the purchasing power of wage-earners and salaried employees and did not arrest the growing danger of cost–price inflation.

The second development that interfered with the operations of the Bank was the unanticipated effect of natural gas wealth on the domestic economy. Since the price of natural gas is linked to the spot price of crude oil, government revenues received an enormous windfall after 1974. Natural gas receipts of the central government tripled from 1979 to 1982 and accounted for 7.2 percent of total government revenues in 1982 (OECD 1984b, 35). With these royalties, the government could finance or maintain the social expenditures and transfer payments despite an economic turndown. Generally, public-debt interest payments were not large by international standards, but the rapid growth in public outlays and the sudden collapse of energy prices after 1982 led to a rapid increase in public indebtedness to 55 percent of GDP in 1985.

In addition, royalties from natural gas and the external surplus increased liquidity growth against which the Netherlands Bank fought by trying to keep interest rates as low as possible. Since low interest rates stimulated private and public borrowing, the overall effect was mixed. Hence, interest rate policy and quantitative restrictions on bank lending had to be supplemented by a revival of the earlier centralized corporatist arrangements. For a long time, the Bank really believed that centralized wage negotiations could cope with the twin burdens of rising public expenditures and economic stagnation. However, divisions within the trade union federations and competition between public-sector workers and blue-collar workers made a return to an era of wage restraints and labor unity impossible.

Subsequently, the Netherlands Bank asked for extensive deindexation of wages and salaries, and the removal of a coupling mechanism that tied public-sector salaries and social benefits to private-sector wages. So long as the Social Democrats were in power, the likelihood of a direct attack on the welfare state was small. In 1977, after winning the national elections, the Social Democratic party searched desperately for coalition allies among the Christian Democratic bloc. Disagreements inside the Christian Democratic party ruled out a continuation of a center–left coalition government. Instead, the Christian Democrats formed a coalition with the Liberal party but they refused to deviate from the postwar pattern of union consultation and social spending.

Proponents of market-led recovery and small government received an important endorsement for their own approach from the new winds blowing through the EMS area after 1982. When a second center–right cabinet was elected to office, it resolutely went for budget deficit reduction, austerity, and mass unemployment. Since 1982, the neoliberal cabinet has made enormous strides in reducing the budget deficit and eliminating so-called market rigidities. In rapid succession, it suspended the automatic indexation of public-sector wages and social benefits and secured a wage freeze. Public-sector salaries were reduced by 3.5 percent, welfare payments were reduced, and eligibility criteria tightened. Sickness benefits dropped from 80 percent of previous wage to 70 percent in 1986. Disability payments were scaled down to 70 percent of minimum wage. As in Denmark, unions were not consulted and the program was implemented without their full consent (Fobben 1989).

The achievements of the center–right cabinet also had political ramifications. In the 1970s, Dutch labor had taken advantage of the procedures of collective tripartite bargaining to push for solidarity between private- and public-sector workers and between employed and unemployed. The cabinet, however, proceeded to delink private-sector wages from social benefit payments and public-sector salaries. Among all these changes, one feature has remained unaltered, namely the basic orientation of monetary policy. The Netherlands Bank is convinced that the stability of the guilder–DM exchange rate sends an important message to investors and leads to lower real interest rates, which the Bank claims benefits manufacturing and employment. As before, the Bank defines the broad boundaries of economic policy making, though this time it is by pointing to its obligations to the EMS and absolving itself from any responsibility, claiming that its hands are tied. Economic growth has picked up in the last two years but this is only after a prolonged recession of several years. In addition, the economic upturn is not shared by all citizens and has divided the population into opposing groups with access to widely divergent resources.

Belgium: Debt Crisis and Devaluation

Throughout the 1970s, the worsening economic climate and the uneven developments in the different parts of the country fueled a resurgence of communal clashes and polarized Belgian politics. The split in the party system into hostile francophone and Flemish blocs also affected government stability. Coalition formations, which had always suffered from a lack of consensus, became now even more fragile. Weak governments produced haphazard and contradictory policy measures that were often aimed at appeasing both linguistic groups and resulted in a remarkable growth in public expenditures. Quite obviously, local authorities and central government could not finance the increased expenditures during an economic recession when tax revenues had begun to fall as well. Borrowing was the best alternative and the gross public debt reached first 90 percent of GDP in 1982 and then an astonishing 120 percent in 1988. Interest payments on public debt were 6.6 percent of central government expenditures in 1983. Foreign-denominated debt rose from 22 percent in 1979 to 63 percent in 1984 (OECD 1988, 54). The chaotic public finances and the chronic trade deficit eroded the confidence in the Belgian franc. From 1979 until 1982, the Belgian National Bank made desperate attempts to defend the franc in the foreign exchange markets and spent in the process 430 billion francs (10 billion 1982 dollars) of its reserves (Dancet 1988; Pijnenburg 1989; Smits 1983).

While governments with weak mandates struggled to save basic industries through massive subsidization, the industrial relations system broke down due to the economic strain. Centralized wage formation was never was widely accepted as in the Netherlands. Yet, for brief periods, consensual negotiations between the peak leadership of labor and business managed to link productivity gains to pay compensation increases. After the first oil price crisis in 1974, growing unemployment and declining profit margins in many domestic manufacturing firms brought out escalating labor–management antagonism. Central negotiations gave way to company-level deliberations in which union delegates and management fought hard for their class interests. Fragile coalitions, communal unrest, and a deadlock in the industrial marketplace interfered with the formulation of positive restructuring programs to rescue ailing industries and move the economy into the direction of more specialized high-technology production. In the absence of a shift to more competitive export composition, the external balance could not recover and worsened in the early eighties

The National Bank agreed that the only realistic solution was a steep devaluation. But as in Denmark, it refused to consider a devaluation until certain features of the postwar settlement had been dismantled. To help unstable governments with the formulation of a crisis package, the National Bank presented an elaborate economic plan in 1981 whose major theme was the abolishment of the indexation clause and widespread pay freezes (Craeybeckx and Witte 1983, 444–47; de Ridder 1986, 45–73; McClam and Andersen 1985, 253). As in Denmark, an exchange rate adjustment had to be accompanied by a phasing out of centralized voluntary wage negotiations and a reduction in social transfer payments to be obtained by tightening of eligibility criteria and lower payments.

A year later, the National Bank scored a minor victory and approached the Monetary Committee of the EMS to announce that Belgium was ready to accept a devaluation of 12 percent. The German reaction was to reject the request as excessive and to suggest instead a 8.5 percent devaluation. It approved a realignment after the Belgian government had outlined how it intended to safeguard the advantages of a cheaper currency by removing the comprehensive indexation system. Since 1982, the National Bank has tried to stimulate private savings and a stable exchange rate in the hope that this will result in lower interest rates.

Interest payments in the combined public sector are still around 11 percent of GDP. The Bank has not been able to lower the debt/GDP ratio. With the fixed exchange rate, interest rates are determined by international factors and reflect movements of the BF in the exchange rate grid of the EMS. Because the devaluation was not sufficient to give Belgian producers a real competitive price advantage, aside from drastic changes in the political economy, recurrent central bank intervention was required as the Belgian franc frequently sank to the bottom of the exchange rate band (Giavazzi and Giovannini 1989, 66). Real interest rates were also relatively high. Social security contributions and taxation rates have been lowered but the debt servicing requirements of the government present a genuine barrier to further reductions in tax revenues. In other words, membership in the EMS blocked a more radical exchange rate adjustment but it also aggravated speculative pressures.

Interestingly, the Bank now has greater authority than before to control credit institutions. Since late 1988, it is allowed to impose required reserves for financial intermediaries and its relationships to government and the private sector are more straightforward. It is also finally authorized to sell its gold assets and can count the proceeds of the sale toward its reserves. Though the state receives the net annual interest income of the sold gold stock, the National Bank retains control over the new reserves (OECD 1989, 74–78).

Monetary Unification and the European Central Bank

What can we learn from this comparatively successful endeavor to secure a zone of monetary stability in the Community? The least arresting conclusion is that monetary integration means a real loss of national sovereignty. The objections against a transfer of sovereignty were muted only because domestic interest groups and a powerful section of the state bureaucracy encouraged this sort of external straitjacket to get rid of remnants of the postwar settlements. We should not jump to the conclusion that similar kind of antiwelfare state coalitions will rise in other countries or will coalesce around the central bank, which in turn will legitimate the costs of monetary restrictiveness (Lindberg, chapter 6 in this volume). In some countries, central bankers who are the main cheerleaders of the EMS possess less administrative independence and are not likely to become a vocal point for organizing a new business offensive. In addition, these three countries are special in that they comprehend the narrow limits of national policy autonomy in an interdependent free market economy.

The second conclusion is that harmonization, thus far, has meant convergences with the German model. Recent events suggest that this is becoming a larger problem. The Mediterranean democracies would have to go to considerable lengths to bring their inflation rates down to the German level at a period when inflation is rising and when they are supposed to give up capital controls. Instead, a new proposal by Britain, backed by Spain and several other Community members, involves the creation of a fully convertible hard common currency. This would be managed by a European Monetary Fund to coexist alongside national central banks and currencies.

Britain's hostility to phase three of the EMU is not shared by Denmark, Belgium, and the Netherlands. Insofar as there are differences, the Dutch stick very closely to the German position and argue that the new central bank should not be set up until the end of phase two when everyone is ready for a single currency. The German and Dutch also support financial penalties against countries that refuse to cut their budget deficits. But they all are in agreement on the basic shape of phase three and on the need to fight inflation first and then support EC economic policy. This suggests that the parameters of economic policy making have undergone the greatest shift in Denmark, where financial regulation and credit restrictions were an outright part of budget and incomes policy decisions. It also suggests that social democracy and the postwar settlement, as we know it, have quietly passed away.

Notes

1. All member-states participate in the EMS but not all have joined the Exchange Rate Mechanism. The ERM is the agreement through which the exchange rates are fixed bilaterally. Rates may not vary more than +/–2.25 percent. When the national currency slides down and is close to the bottom limit, the central bank must intervene by selling the currency that is appreciating relative to its own while the central bank of the stronger currency buys the depreciating currency.

2. Belgium administered a dual exchange rate system that operated like capital controls but was less effective.

References

Artis, M. J., and M. P. Taylor. 1988. "Exchange Rates, Interest Rates, Capital Controls and the EMS: Assessing the Track Record." In F. Giavazzi, S. Micossi, and M. Miller, eds., *The European Monetary System*. New York: Cambridge University.

Braun, D. 1987. "Political Immobilism and Labour Market Performance: The Dutch Road to Mass Unemployment." *Journal of Public Policy*, 7:310–29.

Burdekin, R. C. K., and L. O. Laney. 1988. "Fiscal Policymaking and the Central Bank Institutional Constraint." *Kyklos*, 41:647–62.

Cameron, D. R. 1984. "The Politics of Business Cycles." In T. Ferguson and J. Rogers, eds., *The Political Economy: Readings in the Politics and Economics of American Public Policy*. Armonk, NY: M. E. Sharpe.

Craeybeckx, J., and E. Witte. 1983. *De Politieke Geschiedenis van Belgie*. Antwerpen: Standaard Uitgeverij.

Damgaard, E. 1989. "Crisis Politics in Denmark 1974–1987." In E. Damgaard, P. Gerlich, and J. J. Richardson, eds., *The Politics of Economic Crisis*. Aldershot: Avebury.

Damgaard, E., P. Gerlich, and J. J. Richardson, eds. 1989. *The Politics of Economic Crisis*. Aldershot: Avebury.

Dancet, G. 1988. "From a Workeable Social Compromise to Conflict: The Case of Belgium." In R. Boyer, ed., *The Search for Labor Market Flexibility: The European Economy in Transition*. Oxford: Clarendon Press.

de Grauwe, P. 1987. "International Trade and Economic Growth in the EMS." *European Economic Review*, 31:388–98.

de Ridder, H. 1986. *Geen Winnaars in de Wetstraat*. Leuven: Davidsfonds.

Einhorn, E. S., and J. Logue. 1989. *Modern Welfare States: Politics and Policies in Social Democratic Scandinavia*. New York: Praeger.

Esping-Andersen, G. 1990. *The Three Worlds of Welfare Capitalism*. Princeton, NJ: Princeton University Press.

ETLA, IFF, IUI, and IOI. 1987. *Growth Policies in Nordic Perspective*. Helsinki, Copenhagen, Stockholm, and Oslo: ETLA, IFF, IUI, IOI.

Fase, M. M. G. 1985. "Monetary Control: The Dutch Experience." In C. van Ewijk and J. J. Klant, eds., *Monetary Conditions for Economic Recovery*. Boston: M. Nijhoff.

Fobben, J. W. 1989. "The Netherlands and the Crisis as a Policy Challenge: Integration or Ideological Maneoeuvres?" In E. Damgaard, P. Gerlich, and J. J. Richardson, eds., *The Politics of Economic Crisis*. Aldershot: Avebury.

Giavazzi, F., and A. Giovannini. 1989. *Limiting Exchange Rate Flexibility: The European Monetary System*. Cambridge, MA: MIT Press.

Grahl, J., and P. Teague. 1989. "The Cost of Neo-liberal Europe." *New Left Review*, 174:33–50.

Grilli, V. 1989. "Seigniorage in Europe." In M. de Cecco and A. Giovannini, eds., *A European Central Bank? Perspectives on Monetary Unification after Ten Years of the EMS*. New York: Cambridge University Press.

Kurzer, P. 1988. "The Politics of Central Bank: Austerity and Unemployment in Europe." *Journal of Public Policy*, 8:21–48.

Kurzer, P., and C. S. Allen. 1992. "United Europe and Social Democracy: The EC, West Germany, and Its Three Small Neighbors." In C. Lankowski, ed., *Germany and the European Community after the Cold War: Hegemony and Containment*. New York: St. Martin's Press.

Mastropasqua, C., S. Micossi, and R. Rinaldi. 1988. "Interventions, Sterilization and Monetary Policy in European Monetary System Countries, 1979–87." In F. Giavazzi, S. Micossi, and M. Miller, eds., *The European Monetary System*. New York: Cambridge University Press.

Mastropasqua, S. 1978. *The Banking Systems in the Countries of the EEC*. Alphen a/d Rijn: Sijthoff & Noordhoff Publishers.

McClam, W. D., and P. S. Anderson. 1985. "Adjustment Performance of Small, Open Economies." In V. E. Argy and J. W. Neville, eds., *Inflation and Unemployment: Theory, Experience, and Policy Making*. Boston: Allen & Unwin.

McDonald, R., and G. Zis. 1989. "The European Monetary System: Towards 1991 and Beyond." *Journal of Common Market Studies*, 27:183–202.

Mommen, A. 1987. *Een Tunnel zonder Einde*. Amsterdam: Kluwer.

OECD. 1983. *Economic Survey of the Netherlands, 1982/83*. Paris: OECD.

OECD. 1984a. *Economic Survey of Denmark 1984*. Paris: OECD.

OECD. 1984b. *Economic Survey of the Netherlands, 1983/84*. Paris: OECD.

OECD. 1988. *Economic Survey of Denmark., 1987/88*. Paris: OECD.

OECD. 1989. *Economic Survey of Belgium,. 1988/89*. Paris: OECD.

Padoa-Schioppa, T. 1984. *Money, Economic Policy, and Europe*. Brussels: Commission of European Communities.

Pekkarinen, J. 1989. "Keynesianism and the Scandinavian Models of Economic Policy." In P. Hall, ed., *The Political Power of Economic Ideas*. Princeton, NJ: Princeton University Press.

Pijnenburg, B. 1989. "Belgium in Crisis: Political and Policy Response 1981–1985." In E. Damgaard, P. Gerlich, and J. J. Richardson, eds., *The Politics of Economic Crisis*. Aldershot: Avebury.

Putnam, R. 1988. "Diplomacy and Domestic Politics." *International Organization*, 42:427–60.

Rey, J.-J. 1988. "Discussion." In F. Giavazzi, S. Micossi, and M. Miller, eds., *The European Monetary System*. New York: Cambridge University Press.

Sandholtz, W., and J. Zysman. 1989. "1992: Recasting the European Bargain." *World Politics*, 42:95–128.

Schor, J. B. 1985. "Wage Flexibility, Social Welfare Expenditures, and Monetary Restrictiveness." In M. Jarsulic, ed., *Money and Macropolicy*. Boston: Kluwer-Nijhoff.

Schotsman. 1987. *De Parlementaire Behandeling van het Monetaire Beleid in Nederland sinds 1863*. The Hague: Staatsuitgeverij.

Smits, J. 1983. "Less Democracy for a Better Economy." *Res Publica*, 25:130–51.

Thygesen, N. 1984. "Exchange Rate Policy and Monetary Targets in the EMS." In R. S. Masera and R. Triffin, eds., *Europe's Money: Problems of European Monetary Coordination and Integration*. New York: Oxford University Press.

Ungerer, H., O. Evans, T. Mayer, and Ph. Young. 1986. *The EMS: Recent Developments*. Washington, DC: IMF.

Uusitalo, P. 1984. "Monetarism, Keynesianism and the Insitutional Status of Central Banks." *Acta Sociologica*, 27:31–50.

Willett, T. D., and K. Banaian. 1988. "Explaining the Great Stagflation: Toward a Political Economy Framework." In T. D. Willett, ed., *Political Business Cycles: The Political Economy of Money, Inflation, and Unemployment*. Durham, NC: Duke University Press.

Wolinetz, S. B. 1989. "Socio-Economic Bargaining in the Netherlands: Redefining the Postwar Policy Coalition." *West European Politics*, 12:79–99.

Wood, G. 1988. "European Monetary Arrangements: Their Functioning and Future." In D. E. Fair and C. de Boissieu, eds., *The European Dimension: International Monetary and Financial Integration*. Boston: Kluwer.

Woolley, J. T. 1985. "Central Banks and Inflation." In Leon N. Lindberg and Charles S. Maier, eds., *The Politics of Inflation and Economic Stagnation*. Washington, DC: Brookings Institution.

Woolley, J. T. Forthcoming. "1992, Capital, and the EMS: Policy Credibility and Political Institutions."

Woyke, W. 1985. *Erfold durch Integration: Die Europapolitik der Benelux-Staaten von 1947 bis 1969*. Bochum: Studienverlag Dr. N. Brockmeyer.

8

1992, The Community, and the World
Free Trade or Fortress Europe?

John A. C. Conybeare

In theory, the 1992 Project calls for the removal of all internal barriers to trade, labor, and capital movements and the harmonization of all external barriers. The rest of the world is reacting with some ambivalence. Will this be a further opportunity for foreigners to penetrate a market as large as that of the United States, or will it be the beginning of Fortress Europe? The purpose of this essay is to suggest that there are both theoretical and historical reasons to believe that the latter is a possible outcome. These reasons are discussed below in terms of different categories of effects (e.g., EC trade policy, industrial market structures). These effects may also be conceptualized according to the level at which the bargaining process takes place, and in the course of the essay I place them in the context of a three-level game between the EC member nations and the rest of the world, among the EC nations, and among groups within each country. These games are both constant sum (i.e., redistributive) and variable sum (i.e., offering joint gains or losses from cooperation or conflict).

External Effects: The European View

The 1985 White Paper prepared for the European Commission prescribed the removal of the major remaining forms of physical, technical, and fiscal barriers within the EC. Eliminating border controls and harmonizing standards of goods are its most important economic components. The Single European Act, in force since 1987, will assist implementation of the required legislation by mandating qualified majority rule in the Council of Ministers. Proponents of integration believe there is little doubt that 1992 will benefit the EC member-states, at least in the aggregate (e.g., Emerson 1988). The Cecchini report (1988) estimated an increase in output of 2.5 percent to 6.5 percent, producing a onetime increase in GDP of the same magnitude, mostly by way of economies of scale and increased competition. Further effects on savings, investment, and growth in the capital stock could increase the *rate* of growth, producing longer-term increases of up to 35 percent in GDP (*Economist*, 11–18–89, 77). Critics have suggested that the benefits of 1992 have been vastly exaggerated in the quest for political support, a point that will be taken up below, since disappointing results may well have an effect on the EC's external policies that will be to the detriment of the rest of the world.

Negotiations on the major issues have been relatively productive. Borders will be open to all EC banks. The EC Commission will have expanded veto powers over mergers. Major parts of the telecommunications and the life insurance industry will be deregulated. More competitive rules on air transport have been agreed upon, and talks on monetary union are at least still proceeding, despite British resistance.[1] Difficulties still persist in areas such as automobiles (primarily the continuation of import quotas on Japanese vehicles), public procurement ("buy local" still prevails, even with respect to other EC countries), taxes (talks on harmonization of VAT rates have broken down), and workers' rights (Britain is resisting European-style codetermination rules).

What will be the effects of 1992 on countries outside the EC? Formally, the EC does not have an *external* 1992 policy. The White Paper did not discuss post-1992 levels of protection against non-EC goods, services, or capital movements. The official EC position is that fears of Fortress Europe are nothing more than silly paranoia on the part of foreigners (mainly Americans!) who do not understand how the EC works.[2] The EC, Community officials believe, will become a global hegemonic leader, guiding the world toward freer trade.

More specifically, they make two arguments. The main one is that the world should accept (presumably as a leap of faith, and in contrast to the past policies of the EC) that "the Community must adopt a liberal, open approach in order to enhance its own, as well as worldwide, socioeconomic equilibrium" (EC 1989b, 2). The implication is that we should expect that the harmonization of external trade barriers will be in a downward rather than an upward direction. Their secondary argument is that, irrespective of post-1992 external EC trade barriers, countries outside the organization will receive huge benefits. These gains will derive both from the removal of barriers to internal trade in the Community and from the income elasticity effects on world trade of the 1992-induced increase in the EC's GDP. Pelkmans (1989) states this argument most eloquently. Putting it more colloquially, the line is "Don't worry, we won't become more protectionist; and even if we do, you will still gain!" This issue is especially important for the

United States, since 24 percent of U.S. exports (in 1988) went to the EC. Almost half of these exports are high-technology goods, a commodity group that may be particularly vulnerable to further EC protection as "strategic" industries.

There are at least five reasons to believe that the results of 1992 may not be so benign for the world. First, a large economic power is more likely to adopt predatory international economic policies, since it is likely to find itself in a variable-sum game of trade restrictions in which it may benefit from unilateral restrictions, possibly even in the face of foreign retaliation. Second, the division of the world into three large trading blocs may exacerbate conflict in distributive (constant-sum) games, and have adverse distributional implications for the amorphous group of countries left out of the blocs. Third, 1992 will promote oligopolistic conflict and cooperation in world markets, producing patterns of international industrial organization that will hurt consumers globally. Fourth, a powerful, unified EC will create conflicts in other areas because of the temptation to link its economic power to noneconomic issues. Finally, 1992 will add another layer of government, and so European policy making will become increasingly difficult for foreigners to understand and influence.

Leadership

The EC will certainly be in a position to exercise global economic leadership, or at least triopolistic hegemony. In 1987 the EC accounted for 17.7 percent of world exports and 16.6 percent of world imports, averaging slightly more than the United States (10.6 percent and 17.5 percent, respectively), and considerably more than Japan (9.8 percent and 6.2 percent). One must question the assumption that global leadership by the EC will necessarily be benign—for two reasons, one relating to the bargaining games within the EC (distributional issues that are solved by shifting the costs onto foreigners) and one general factor that has always encouraged large economic powers to choose uncooperative tactics in variable-sum trade restriction games with smaller trade partners.

Harmonization—In Which Direction?

Any customs union will create some welfare-reducing trade diversion, as consumers substitute from lower cost world suppliers to higher cost suppliers within the community. The more important question is how trade barriers will be made uniform across the member-states after 1992. It is unclear why harmonization implies (as the promoters of 1992 contend) a downward movement of external trade barriers, especially in areas outside the purview of the General Agreement on Trade and Tariffs (GATT), such as quotas and dumping rules. Most tariffs are "bound" under GATT rules, cannot be raised without offering compensation, and are now relatively unimportant. Average levels of tariffs in 1988 were 7.8 percent in the EC, 6.2 percent in the United States, and 8.0 percent in Japan.

Contemporary protectionism is practiced by way of nontariff barriers.

The EC seems to have little difficulty in justifying such protectionism. The Cambridge School in Britain emphasizes the need to protect European manufacturing industries in the pursuit of full employment, and French arguments focus on the need for "autonomy" in an interdependent world, advocating "managed trade," reduced dependence on world markets and macrolevel planning (Kahler 1985). In practice, all of these measures would produce protectionist, market-sharing policies. Increased competition in EC markets after 1992 may enhance the appeal of such arguments. There appears to be strong sentiment in the EC that the benefits of 1992 should be reserved for EC firms. Calingaert (1988, 93) noted two main EC justifications for post-1992 protectionism: that EC firms will need "temporary" protection from increased levels of competition after 1992, and that foreign countries should not get a "free ride" into EC markets. The last proposition implies that non-EC countries will be threatened with greater EC protection in the absence of concessions on their part, promoting the bilateralization of the world economy, discussed below.

The EC has a plentiful arsenal of weapons with which to implement such a policy. Article 115 of the Treaty of Rome provides the classic "escape clause" mechanism, whenever an EC industry is being "disrupted" by imports. In 1987 alone, 157 applications for escape clause protection were granted, mostly to firms in France (EC 1989a, 16). Since 1980 the EC has also made extensive use of antidumping rules. Between 1981 and 1987, 530 antidumping cases were initiated, and (as of mid-1989) 63 resulted in punitive duties and 113 required price increases on the part of the foreign supplier (EC 1989a, 20). These administrative measures at the Community level will be increasingly attractive as national quotas are phased out.

There will also be the problem of formal and informal quotas. Existing national quotas will have to be abolished, since (given the projected absence of internal trade barriers after 1992) they will become unenforceable. The effects may, however, be easy to maintain or enhance. Quotas on Japanese cars, for example, currently differ widely across the Community, France and Italy being the most restrictive (under 3 percent of the market), Germany and Denmark being the most liberal, with no restrictions. If limits on Japanese cars are to be harmonized, why should we expect them to go down to the German level rather than up to the Italian level? Countries whose domestic producers will lose market shares are far more likely to block agreement than are countries whose producers have already lost markets. More trade restriction will simply be politically easier than less restriction, as has been exemplified in the EC Commission's recent decision to ask the Japanese car manufacturers to observe voluntary quotas to the EC until the late 1990s, quotas that will apply not only to imports but also to cars produced in the EC.[3]

Other areas of quota activity—notably with respect to textiles and electronics—are likely to receive similar treatment: national quotas will simply be replaced by equally or even more restrictive EC-wide Voluntary Export Restraints (VERs). The national telecommunications bureaucracies will insist on similar types of quota-induced market sharing rather than abandon national monopolies. The president of the Commission (Delors) has proposed formal EC quotas for U.S. television programs (*New York Times*, 2–23–90, C1), and the EC recently forced Japanese computer chip manufacturers to set minimum prices.

Public procurement is another major source of protection, particularly since the EC state procurement market is 15 percent of GDP. Public procurement is generally closed to foreign firms. The Commission has itself proposed for 1992 a 50 percent local content rule and a 3 percent "Buy European" preference margin (Hufbauer 1990, 41–43). Other areas of governmental rule-making may be increasingly manipulated for protectionist purposes, even as direct trade barriers appear to decline. Health regulations have been frequently used by the EC for this purpose, the most recent example being measures against U.S. hormone-treated beef exports in 1989. Rules of origin reinforce quotas, making them even more restrictive. In 1989 the EC adopted new rules of origin for semiconductor chips, requiring more local content for electronic components to be regarded as European made, inflicting major costs on U.S. and Japanese chip producers (Flamm 1990, 270–73). France declared (also in 1989) that Japanese Nissan cars produced in Britain would be regarded as part of the (very small) Japanese quota for the French market, unless more than 80 percent of the vehicles' content were sourced in the EC. This will become an increasingly difficult trade issue between the United States and the EC, since Japanese automobile exports to the EC will be produced by their U.S. subsidiaries. Stringent quotas on Japanese cars will result in trade confrontations directly with the United States.

Finally, one should note that 1992 will have little effect on the Common Agricultural Policy (CAP). The cost of CAP is about 50 percent of the value of agricultural output in the EC (Blandford 1989), and there is no indication that 1992 will combat the vested interests behind the policy. On the contrary, the abolition of the border adjustments now necessary to make the CAP work, will make the policy less cumbersome to administer and therefore more durable. In December 1990, the EC chose to allow GATT negotiations to collapse rather than make concessions on agriculture; by the middle of 1992 GATT negotiators were still stymied by the same issue.

Post-1992 protectionism will not affect all foreign firms equally. Those which are already supplying the EC from direct investments in member countries may well benefit even more than indigenous European firms, because foreign subsidiaries have been more inclined to treat Europe as a single market.[4] Half of all U.S. foreign direct investment is in Europe, and in 1988 sales from U.S. affiliates in Europe were $260 billion, which may be compared with the $75 billion of U.S. exports to the EC (Hufbauer 1990, xix). Hufbauer is surely correct in suggesting that "whatever EC–1992 may hold for U.S. exports, it basically holds great promise for General Motors, International Business Machines, Merck, American

Telephone and Telegraph, and a long list of other U.S. firms with a strong presence in Europe" (1990, 25). This list of U.S. firms with direct investments in the EC is constantly expanding. In 1989 U.S. firms were involved in 182 mergers in the EC, with a total value of $15.2 billion (*New York Times*, 7–5–90, C1).

1992, Regional Inequalities, and Recession

One of the classic negative effects of customs unions is that they may exacerbate regional inequalities within the union, primarily by way of factor agglomeration (i.e., labor and capital move to the more developed areas to take advantage of the larger markets, social overhead capital, and external economies). Radical critics of 1992, such as Cutler et al. (1989), argue that German economic dominance (especially through its chronic balance-of-payments surplus), combined with the upsurge in mergers and direct foreign investment, will deprive the poorer members, regions, and sectors of the EC of the benefits of 1992. The benefits, they contend, will be confined to northwestern Europe. Their argument appears to be entirely speculative. Empirical studies show little agreement on where the benefits of 1992 will be concentrated. One study, sponsored by INSEAD, suggested that opportunities for economies of scale and further intra-EC specialization may skew the benefits toward the poorer members in southern Europe (*Economist*, 4–21–90, 75). Others have speculated that benefits will be concentrated on Germany, Austria, Switzerland, and the Netherlands—countries that are well placed to take advantage of expanded market opportunities (*Economist*, 6–2–90, 71–72).

Regardless of where the benefits of 1992 are distributed, there remains the question of how an asymmetric distribution might affect the EC's policy toward the rest of the world. If, as Cutler et al. (1989) believe, the losers will be the labor-abundant agricultural areas of southern Europe, we may expect 1992 to bring added pressure for agricultural protection. If the losers are the older industrial areas of northern Europe (as argued by the INSEAD report), the result would be demands for protection of both these declining industries and for protection of the newer high-technology industries in which these countries are attempting to develop a comparative advantage. Whichever sectors or countries suffer relative or absolute losses as a result of 1992, they should be expected to seek recompense at the expense of the rest of the world, with "beggar-thy-(non-EC) neighbor" policies.

The protectionist effects of regional or sectoral losses resulting from 1992 will also be manifested if recessions in countries such as the United States and Great Britain, plus the current stock market crash in Japan, should foster a global recession. If 1992 arrives during a period of global recession, there will be even more reason to doubt that we would see downward rather than upward harmonization of external trade barriers. If countries have declining marginal utility for income, international redistributions via protection will be even more attractive during a recession. Import competing interest groups will also be more highly motivated to demand protection. The tendency for trade barriers to rise during recessions (as during the 1930s and the 1970s) is well documented (McKeown 1984), as is the incidence of trade wars beginning during such periods (Conybeare 1987).

A recession might not even be necessary to induce this effect. The beneficial results of 1992 have been exaggerated (see Cutler 1989; Holmes 1989; Grilli 1989; Hufbauer 1990, 8). Disappointed expectations may have the same effect on protectionist sentiments as a genuine recession, as producers lobby to achieve these anticipated gains by other means.

The transition to 1992 will, in short, generate intra-EC constant-sum games over market shares and shares of the EC total product. EC producers will encourage cooperative solutions that will shift the distributive costs of 1992 onto foreigners, resulting in a variable-sum game in which the rest of the world (and EC consumers) suffer losses in excess of the aggregate gains to intra-EC producers. Community-wide barriers will replace the previous mix of national barriers, and desire for agreement will cause the new restrictions to cluster around the most restrictive common denominator. Relatively free trading countries (such as Germany) will accept, for example, EC quotas on Japanese cars in order to please the French.

Hegemonic Predation

A more general issue is that the pure theory of trade suggests that large economic powers will maximize their economic gain by taxing trade more heavily (Conybeare 1987). This optimal tariff argument generates two basic types of variable-sum games: a Prisoners' Dilemma between large economic powers and asymmetrical games between a large and a small state. The temptation for the EC to seek gains from other large powers by way of trade restriction may be reduced by the threat of debilitating retaliation (the Prisoners' Dilemma scenario); but apart from Japan and the United States, one would expect a Community intent on maximizing economic gain to prey upon smaller countries rather than engaging in benevolent trade creation. The game thus produced has a variable-sum, within which the EC may gain by preying on smaller countries even in the face of retaliation. This is to assume, of course, that there are no political goals more important than economic gain, and that smaller countries could not coordinate retaliation against the EC.

Historically, large countries have raised trade barriers. When Athens controlled the eastern Mediterranean, it imposed high taxes on third-party trade, as did the Romans in taxing trade that crossed the boundaries of the empire. England steadily raised trade barriers during its long rise to commercial hegemony from the fourteenth to the eighteenth century. Its brief adherence to free trade from the 1840s to World War I was due less to a national interest in free trade than to the power of the cotton textile producers, who were both importers of raw materials and produced over half the value of British exports. They believed that free trade in Britain would encourage reciprocity on the part of other countries. However, it has been calculated that free trade actually cost Britain 4 percent of its national income (McCloskey 1980).

The United States has been, for most of its commercial existence, a country with high trade barriers. The period from 1945 through the 1960s may be an exception, but even then the United States negotiated on a strict "principal supplier" basis (i.e., it would only lower barriers on goods for which one or a few other countries were the principal U.S. source, on the condition that these countries lowered barriers on goods for which the United States was their principal source). This technique precluded free benefits to countries not granting concessions, with the result that even during the Kennedy Round, 80 percent of U.S. concessions went to only ten countries (Finger 1979). Furthermore, much of the tariff protection lost during the twenty years after the war was regained through nontariff barriers during the 1970s.

In brief, if 1992 results in a powerful Community that promotes global free trade, it will be a historical and a theoretical anomaly. Apart from the United States, which would clearly retaliate at some cost to the EC, the Community may be unable to resist the temptation to exploit the asymmetries in its post-1992 trade relationships with smaller countries.

Economic Blocs and Bilateralism

The second issue is the effect of 1992 in promoting a bilateral, rather than multilateral, pattern of global bargaining in which most of the negotiations will be conducted between the EC, North America, and Japan. The United States and the EC alone produce more than half the world's income, and each is the other's largest trading partner. Bilateral bloc negotiations are particularly likely as GATT moves into areas where agreement can be reached only among subsets of GATT (e.g., reciprocity in the treatment of trade in services). Will this be good or bad for the world?

Blocs, Trade Diversion, and the Terms of Trade

The consolidation of the world economy into trading blocs may enhance the incentives to increase trade barriers for the purpose of manipulating terms of trade. Larger trading units are better able to influence their terms of trade, and the resulting competition in predatory transfers is likely to reduce world welfare compared to what it would have been in the absence of blocs (Krugman 1989). However, such losses may might not be large. General equilibrium models of the world economy suggest that if the three blocs (and the rest of the world acting in unison) raised tariff rates to 175 percent, global income losses would be about 4 percent—a not insignificant, but hardly catastrophic, cost (Whalley 1985, 248).

Despite the rhetoric one hears about protectionism leading to global recession, simulation exercises confirm that the effects of trade policy on the economies of *large* powers are minor compared with other types of economic policy, such as monetary and fiscal measures.

Transaction Costs, Public Goods, and Free Riding

Furthermore, bilateralism may be preferable to multilateralism, because the latter creates two problems. One is transaction costs: multilateralism complicates the negotiations when a large number of bargainers has to be satisfied and each can veto the outcome. The other is that multilateralism in the presence of Most Favored Nation (MFN) rules creates "public good" problems that discourage cooperative behavior because predation cannot be directly punished (i.e., the public good cannot be withheld from those who do not contribute to its provision). The MFN rule on which GATT is based provides that bilateral trade concessions must be extended to all members of GATT. The result is that all countries may agree that high tariffs are bad for the world as a whole, but each chooses not to negotiate, knowing that it will get the benefit of everyone else's trade concessions via the MFN rule.

Prior to World War I, this problem was solved by having the MFN rule subsumed by a two-tier tariff structure that was used to punish free riders. The United States still has a two-tier tariff; any country not a member of GATT pays the Smoot–Hawley rates of 1930. It was multilateralism that caused the system to break down in the 1920s, as countries attempted to free ride on the MFN system. The United States was a major offender in this regard: the Fordney–McCumber tariff of 1922 proclaimed that the United States would not negotiate any of its tariffs, demanded MFN benefits from all other countries, and would retaliate if not granted such privileges. This is exactly what one would expect from a country that emerged from the war as the largest world trading power (perhaps another cautionary note for 1992).

In any case, it was the return to principles of bilateralism in the 1930s, through quotas, exchange controls, regional blocs, and principal supplier negotiations, that began again to open up the world trading system. Even the GATT system, which is often seen as a triumph for the principles of multilateralism, has been successful more because it has been based primarily on bilateral principal supplier negotiating techniques.

Redistributive Consequences

If 1992 promotes bilateralism, it may also have at least two redistributive consequences. The first is in the domestic politics of protection. Bilateralism, with its emphasis on reciprocity and the unilateral determination of retaliation, may create more conflict since there are domestic interests for whom retaliation generates no costs. During the late middle ages commercial disputes would often escalate because the perpetrators of predatory actions could not be directly punished. English pirates would seize ships of the Hanseatic League, which, since it could not punish the pirates, would issue letters of marque entitling Hanse merchants to seize the goods of English merchants, who would in turn obtain letters of marque from English authorities, and so on, with the result that any single commercial dispute could rapidly escalate. During the 1980s, U.S. steel producers were unrestrained in their lobbying for protection because they knew the EC could only retaliate against *other* U.S. industries exporting to Europe. Multilateralism, based more on the extension of concessions to all parties through MFN principles and the international determination of retaliation, is less likely to generate such patterns of lobbying.

The protection-promoting effects of bilateral reciprocity may be seen in both the EC and the United States. The U.S. Omnibus Trade Act of 1988 directly promotes bilateralism and invites sectoral rent-seeking with its "super 301" provision. This part of the Act not only makes retaliation against "unfair" foreign trade practices mandatory, but invites the STR to self-initiate 301 cases against countries with "priority" unfair trade practices (Wright 1989). The EC has made it clear, in *official* statements, that where international obligations do not constrain it, access to post-1992 EC markets will be based on reciprocity;[5] and it may even delay completion of the Uruguay Round of GATT negotiations if the outcome threatens to limit its desire to reach reciprocity agreements with its major trade partners (Calingaert 1988, 87, 120, 124). Strict reciprocity ("comparable market access" in Brussels terminology) appears especially likely in the financial services area (Pelkmans 1989, 14), though the United States has apparently been assured that this is a weapon aimed primarily at Japan (Cooper 1989, 333). European car manufacturers have been lobbying Brussels to link Japanese car imports to European exports of vehicles to Japan (Smith and Venables 1990, 138).

The second negative redistributive effect of bilateralism is on small and developing countries. Most concessions in GATT are exchanged between a few countries on a principal supplier basis, and small countries get left out. This has been a constant complaint from the United Nations Conference on Trade and Development (UNCTAD), a body established in an attempt to counteract the lack of developing-country bargaining power in GATT. The problem also occurs in market-sharing arrangements concluded outside of GATT. In 1984, for example, the United States decided to reduce steel imports from 27 percent to 18 percent of the U.S. market. In order to avoid further conflict with Europe and Japan, this reduction was achieved almost entirely by reducing the quotas (by 50 percent in many cases) of small- and developing-country steel exports. Bilateralism produces an asymmetric distribution of the gains from trade negotiations, usually as a result of "minimum winning coalitions" imposing solutions on constant-sum market-sharing games. In the context of 1992, the most likely coalition is Europe and the United States against Japan. Most of the measures taken by the

EC to constrain import shares of the EC market are crafted so as to impose most of the burden on Japan and to avoid angering the United States, notably in the electronics and motor vehicle markets (Flamm 1990; Smith and Venables 1990). Although the European Court of Justice has declared GATT law legally binding in the EC, it has never attempted to stop the EC from violating GATT rules in this manner (Petersmann 1986, 40–45).

Thus, insofar as 1992 helps consolidate the trend toward bilateral bloc negotiations in trade, the effect on the United States and Japan may be minor (negotiations will just get tougher, in both the constant-sum market-sharing games and the trade-taxing Prisoners' Dilemmas), but countries that are small or less developed will undoubtedly be the losers, unless they are ex-colonies with special access arrangements.

EFTA and Eastern Europe

The one exception to this tendency to produce negative effects on outside countries may be with regard to EFTA (European Free Trade Area) and eastern Europe. As the EC struggles to absorb the former East Germany, and subsequently perhaps other former eastern European countries, an increasing amount of the EC's aid (including quasi aid, such as trade preferences) is likely to be diverted away from non-European destinations, both toward eastern Europe and to the poorer members of the EC who currently fear that rebuilding eastern Europe will be at their expense. Even prior to the political changes in eastern Europe, the EC had planned to increase its efforts to redistribute wealth toward the poor areas of the EC, presumably to the detriment of external aid. The coming of the 1992 Project will force the EC to focus on eastern Europe more than might otherwise have been the case, because the abolition of intra-EC economic barriers will magnify the potentially disruptive effects of imports of labor and subsidized goods from the east. Eastern European exports may well fill quotas currently supplied by non-European sources.

There may also be a reciprocal effect. Events in eastern Europe may help or hinder progress toward 1992. Delors, president of the Commission, hopes to accelerate the pace of agreements on unity, cementing the ties of the current twelve members prior to dealing with the east (*Economist*, 2–24–90, 45). Germany may, however, delay 1992 if the absorption of the former East Germany becomes problematic.[6] The situation will be further complicated by the proposed agreements with EFTA for free trade in goods, services, capital, and labor (the so-called European Economic Space), but without requiring EFTA to adopt the CAP, EC external trade policy, or to remove frontier controls.

The expansion of the EC may make protectionism an even more tempting solution to adjustment problems. A larger range of commodity production encompassed by the EC will both reduce the trade diversion costs to EC consumers of protection and increase the range of industries that may demand protection.

Hufbauer, who generally takes a benign view of 1992, makes the following prediction with respect to the EC's policies toward eastern Europe:

> Greater competition for intra-European aid resources, together with increased imports from the East, will inevitably put pressure on the Commission to find new means of addressing economic dislocation. The Commission could respond with a more leisurely pace of EC trade liberalization relative to the outside world, especially in agriculture and low technology products such as textiles and apparel, footwear and consumer durables. (Hufbauer 1990, 19)

Bilateralism and Military Externalities

The combination of 1992 and the democratization of eastern Europe may weaken European security ties to the United States, and promote multipolarity in international security affairs. The unification of Germany, and the consequent diminution of the already waning power of France and Britain, and the economic crisis in the Soviet succession states will reinforce this trend. The effect might be to reduce the perceived need for cooperation in trade relations. Post-1992 Europe appears likely to develop its own forms of security organization. Opinion polls report that 85 percent of Germans favor the removal of nuclear weapons, and the NATO Nuclear Planning Group is expected to endorse the withdrawal of some U.S. tactical nuclear weapons in Germany (*Economist*, 6–30–90, 45; 4–28–90, 52).

Gowa (1989) argues that bipolarity may enhance the incentives for free trade within military blocs because the welfare-increasing effects of trade creation will indirectly promote military capacity. Insofar as 1992 accelerates the decline of military bipolarity it may, conversely, reduce the incentives to adhere to free trade principles within the former anti-Communist alliance system, further reinforcing the conflict inducing effects of bilateralism in trade negotiations.

Industrial Organization

1992 will promote market concentration in the EC, through mergers, joint ventures and bankruptcies. The trend has already started (Rosenthal 1990). In 1989, $55 billion of cross-border mergers alone were effected (*Economist*, 10–28–89, 17). The efforts of the EC Commission to prevent state aid that inhibits intra-EC competition (by, for example, taking France to court in order to force it to cut subsidies to Renault) will accelerate this process. Within the EC this may have detrimental effects on small businesses and labor unions. In industries that are already oligopolistic, we will see further concentration. It seems unlikely that post-1992 Europe will be able to support six car manufacturers when the United States and Japan have only three each. The same may be true for the twelve European airlines, the eleven producers of telephone exchanges (there are four in the United States), and many other industries. Mergers and cooperative arrangements are already occurring in banking, insurance, airlines, and the car industry. Externally, market concentration may present new opportunities for both conflict and cooperation. Such opportunities may be exhibited by way of oligopolistic collusion and strategic industry policies on the part of governments. The fact that a substantial part of European industry is state owned (about one-third of French and Italian GNP is produced by state enterprises), will make anticompetitive policies even more tempting after 1992.

Private and State-Induced Collusion

Collusion may be promoted from within the industry or by the EC itself. There is a problem of prediction here. Oligopolists may try to put each other out of business, with a little help from their home governments. But they may also collude, as Freddy Laker discovered when he tried to compete with British Airways and Pan American on the North Atlantic air routes. The most likely scenario is that European oligopolists will seek globally collusive arrangements, with the costs falling on consumers and countries outside of Europe. If collusion results in formal mergers between United States, EC, and Japanese oligopolies, there will arise equally conflictual questions of taxation and national control.

The airline and automobile industries provide examples of oligopolistic cooperation transcending even the large confines of the EC, and which may well reduce any competition-enhancing effects of 1992. Although the EC transport ministers have agreed that from January 1993, existing capacity-sharing and price-fixing agreements between European airlines will be prohibited, the decline in competition through partial mergers may nullify the effects of competition. Though U.S. carriers are considerably more efficient than their European counterparts,[7] corporate cooperation both within Europe (e.g., Air France plus Lufthansa, Swissair plus Scandinavian, KLM plus British Airways plus Sabena) and between European and U.S. carriers (e.g., KLM plus Northwest, Swissair plus Delta, and British Airways plus United, the last-mentioned subsequently abandoned) may prevent the air-traveling public from seeing the benefits of added competition. Competition within EC national markets is disappearing even more rapidly with a number of intra- and inter-state mergers and acquisitions.

We are likely to observe a similar outcome in the motor vehicle industry, as 1992 encourages mergers and joint ventures both as a means of dealing with a more competitive environment and as a way of making it less competitive. The recent joint venture announced between Mitsubishi and Daimler-Benz is only the latest in a long stream of such arrangements: Ford with Volkswagen, Nissan, Fiat, and Mazda; GM with Toyota and Saab; Peugeot with Fiat; Rover with Honda; Mitsubishi with Chrysler and Hyundai; Renault with Peugeot and Chrysler; Toyota with Volkswagen—to name but a few! (*Economist*, 2–24–90, 74). Some of these will have ramifications far beyond the car industry, resulting in large conglomerates spanning vast areas of high-technology industry. The

Daimler-Benz arrangements with Mitsubishi, for example, will encompass not only motor vehicles, but the aerospace and defense industry, complementing proposed links with British Aerospace and Matra.

However, multinational conglomerates in the automobile and other sectors may, in the longer term, make protection more problematic for the EC, even if only because it will be difficult to determine what is a "European" firm. Smith and Venables (1990, 153) note that in the 1990s a large proportion of the British automobile output will be from Japanese-owned plants. It will be difficult for the Europeans to treat British Hondas differently from U.S.-built Hondas without causing a major trade dispute. Mergers and joint ventures will make the car companies themselves increasingly averse to protectionist measures, as they attempt to obtain components from the plants (inside or outside the EC) with lower costs.

Collusion may also be promoted by governments. The governments of Italy, France, and Germany are resisting total liberalization of the post-1992 telecommunications equipment market, hoping to retain some sort of cartelistic arrangement to preserve a large market share for their current national monopolists. In the semiconductor industry, the EC recently concluded a price-fixing agreement with Japan (*Economist*, 1–13–90, 19), in order to keep prices high enough to protect less efficient EC chipmakers, despite having protested vigorously about a similar deal between Japan and the United States, which the EC feared would divert Japanese chip exports to the EC. There is here an ideal situation for intergovernmental collusion between the EC and the United States, concocting a market-sharing arrangement to protect their indigenous chip producers from Japanese competition.

Porter (1990) argues that collusive arrangements between firms (whether formal mergers or not) may be the biggest danger of Fortress Europe in the longer term. Interfirm cooperation, he believes, stifles competition, produces lower productivity and a general loss of competitive advantage. Mistakenly believing that Japanese success was based on cartelization and collaboration, "Europe has rushed to embrace cooperation between competitors, . . . misunderstanding and misapplying the Japanese model." Internationally successful Japanese firms, he argues, have been those which, despite being in industries with few producers, are highly competitive with each other. The long-term result of fostering collusion, he predicts, is that European firms will be less able to compete in world markets and will fall back on demands for "transitional" (i.e., permanent) protection from non-EC firms. Unfortunately, 1992 is helping to promote European industrial concentration, in the belief that it will enhance the competitive advantage of European firms.

Given the hectic pace of such cross-national corporate cooperation, one may be skeptical of the claims that 1992 will herald a new era of welfare-enhancing competition in global, or even EC, markets. The major incentive for the EC to encourage collusion is to prevent non-EC firms from benefiting from the enlarged market. Hence we might also register some doubt as to whether the rest of the world will, as EC spokespersons claim, derive great benefit from the larger internal market—unless these beneficiaries have collusive arrangements with EC firms.

Strategic Industry Policy

There is a new branch of trade theory known as "strategic" trade theory (Krugman 1987). In globally oligopolistic industries possessing increasing returns to scale, there will exist pools of supercompetitive, or monopolistic, profits that may be acquired by any firm that can credibly threaten to underprice its competitors and drive them from the market. Internationally, governments become important players in such games because they have the capacity to subsidize their own oligopolists so that they can make such credible threats. Recent empirical work suggests that although internal economies of scale are insignificant (given the large size of existing national markets), there may be substantial external economies of scale[8] within the EC (especially France), benefits that might be enhanced by strategic industry policies (Caballero and Lyons 1989).

This is the kind of conflict we have seen with the Boeing-Airbus situation; Airbus has been subsidized quite directly and Boeing indirectly through its defense contracts (Dixit and Kyle 1985). The U.S. Department of Commerce charges that Airbus has received $16 billion in subsidies from the United Kingdom, France, Germany, and Spain. Insofar as 1992 will help generate large EC firms operating in globally oligopolistic markets that are subject to increasing returns, we should expect to see fewer of the traditional chicken, steel, and pasta wars, and more conflicts based on the global distribution of oligopoly profits in areas such as aircraft, telecommunications, semiconductors, financial services, and pharmaceuticals.

The EC already devotes a considerable amount of resources to industrial subsidies—8.6 percent of output, as compared with less than 3 percent in the United States and Japan (*Economist*, 2–24–90, 71). Though the EC is committed to abolishing subsidies that inhibit intra-EC competition between indigenous firms, it is by no means clear that subsidization will be abandoned with respect to foreign competition.

The potential for destructive competition and the generation of social losses is great, particularly since the firms benefiting from strategic industry policies are most likely to be those with political influence, rather than those actually operating with increasing returns in oligopolistic industries. In a more optimistic vein, it should be noted that strategic industry policies may become increasingly hard to implement. As international capital markets become more integrated, and cross-national mergers and joint ventures become more common, it will become difficult to distinguish between "their" oligopolists and "our" oligopolists. Increasing Japanese direct investment in the EC through joint ventures will make it harder for the EC to implement discriminatory treatment of goods and services produced by Japanese corporations.

In general, then, 1992 will promote market concentration in the EC and this will generate both situations of strategic industry conflict with the United States and Japan, and raise issues of global collusion. These games are mostly in the nature of Prisoners' Dilemmas, since they present the prospect of joint gains and losses.

Issue Linkage

It is likely that the enhanced economic power of the EC will encourage it to link its economic strength to other issues. Linkage of unrelated issues is usually used as a way of trying to increase the costs to the other side of not cooperating. During the Chicken War of the 1960s (when the United States and the EC got into a trade war over the Community's increased tariffs on frozen U.S. chickens), the United States hinted at a link between U.S. troop levels in Europe and the chicken tariff. In the 1880s, France attempted to use its superior power in a punishing trade war with Italy as a means to force Italy to withdraw from the Triple Alliance with Germany and Austria-Hungary. In the early 1980s, Brazil threatened to default on its debt to U.S. banks if shut out of the U.S. steel market.

Such linkages are rarely successful. The tactic creates confusion and forces policy makers to think about trade-offs they are unprepared to make. Linkage may create such large risks that it is either not taken seriously (such as the U.S. linking of chickens and NATO) or would have major consequences if it were taken seriously (e.g., had Italy allowed itself to be forced out of the Triple Alliance by French tariff policy).

However, linkage can constitute an effective threat when it creates very large, asymmetric, and credible costs. In 1893, Germany moved quickly to end a tariff war with Russia when the latter entered a military alliance with France. Economically dominant powers are obviously most likely to be able to make such links. As the EC gains in economic power, there is no reason to assume that it will not make linkages to other issue areas, as all great economic powers have done in the past. One example is when France used the weapon of access to EC markets to force New Zealand to release the French secret service agents who had bombed and sunk the Greenpeace ship "Rainbow Warrior" in Auckland harbor. Such links will create confusion, conflict, and potentially resentment on the part of the smaller powers that are their most frequent object.

Information and Institutional Structure

Finally, the agglomeration of rule-making power at the Community level may contribute to the increasing mystification of the EC decision-making process to outsiders seeking to understand and cope with multiple overlapping institutions. Americans have to understand not just the individual countries but the Community level and how the two levels interact. It has been reported that U.S. businesspeople view 1992 with some trepidation, even if only because they will be unable to "monitor the shifting winds inside the labyrinthine EC bureaucracy" (*Business Week*, 12–12–88, 55). At the Commission level alone, foreigners must deal with twenty-two Directorates, some of which are working at cross-purposes. Greenwald (1990, 346) notes that although the External Relations Directorate (DG–1) is working for a successful completion of the Uruguay Round, and is concerned to prevent the evolution of a Fortress Europe, the Internal Market Directorate (DG–3) is equally busy fostering cartelistic arrangements and "temporary" protection for European producers.

The introduction of majority voting in the Council may make protectionist measures easier to implement, since free trading countries like Germany will no longer be able to veto anticompetitive measures. The increasing role of the European Parliament in decision making is also likely to skew policy decisions against freer trade, in the same way that the more active role of the U.S. Congress in trade policy since the late 1970s has clearly moved trade policy in a more restrictive direction. Representatives respond to the concentrated interests of industries in their districts that demand protection. The European Parliament is unlikely to behave differently as its power over European trade policy expands.

What happens when one side does not understand policy making on the other side? One of the most common misperceptions in international politics is the tendency to perceive the other side as more unified and potentially more malevolent than it really is, and this misperception is powerfully fueled by lack of information (Jervis 1976). As Richard Neustadt (1970) has documented, lack of information, leading to misperceptions about the policy-making process, caused major problems in Anglo-U.S. relations after World War II, notably the Suez and Skybolt crises.

Americans have less difficulty seeing Europe as a single entity than do many Europeans, but in this instance such a perception may be unhelpful because it leaves Americans (especially those exporting to the EC) unable to understand and influence the real policy-making process and prone to assuming that the EC is a unitary actor with unfriendly designs. During the Chicken War neither party fully understood the domestic politics of the other side, and in particular, that domestic politics prevented compromises that appeared reasonable to the other side.

Lack of information is a major reason for the American ambivalence about 1992, and the fears of a Fortress Europe. When we do not understand something we use what the Pentagon cheerfully calls "the worst-case scenario." The same sorts of misperceptions of U.S. policy making may exist on the European side, though one may suspect that the Europeans understand the U.S. policy-making process somewhat better, since it is based on the institutionalization of the venal but honest system of porkbarrel and logrolling.

The problems here go beyond mere perception. The multiplicity of organizations is a fertile breeding ground for protection. Referring to the telecommunications market, Cowhey suggests that "EC rules will leave national leaders with some latitude for hidden but curtailed protectionism. This blend of credit taking, blame avoidance and hidden protection provides an ideal backdrop for a political process that relies on building of a consensus over time" (1990, 196). American observers complain that one consequence of the multiplicity of institutions in Brussels being very different and less transparent than their counterparts in the United States is that the EC fails to inform interested foreign parties about issues under consideration until decisions have already been made (Calingaert 1988, 100, 125, 126). U.S. firms are routinely excluded from European standard-setting bodies, effectively producing a nontariff barrier. Ford and GM are excluded from the Committee of Common Market Car Manufacturers, though they may be consulted individually by regulators (Smith and Venables 1990, 146). U.S. firms are likely to be excluded from European high-technology research consortia, such as RACE and Esprit (Hufbauer 1990, 36).[9] Since a large part of the static gains from 1992 are alleged to derive from the elimination of national differences in product standards (Cooper 1989, 327), the exclusion of non-EC countries from standard setting will diminish these gains to both the EC and especially to foreign countries exporting to the EC. It should be reiterated here that the EC argues that foreigners will benefit from 1992 even if trade barriers rise, because of the larger market; but exclusion from standard setting will partially nullify these gains.

Conclusion

It is not impossible that 1992 will produce a powerful advocate for global liberalization. The United States has apparently been reassured by the EC that this will be the case, and President Bush has pronounced that "the U.S. welcomes the emergence of Europe as a partner in world leadership," administration officials believing that 1992 might make the EC less "insular" and "more aware of its external responsibilities" (*Economist*, Supplement, 7–7–90, 6). In November 1990 the United States and the EC agreed to hold biannual talks. Perhaps the EC will behave in a manner that is historically unprecedented for economically hegemonic powers. Unfortunately, history and social science theory would suggest that the EC might become an economic predator, bargaining bilaterally with other predators, promoting oligopolistic restraints on world markets, linking its economic power to noneconomic issues, and baffling outsiders as to how it makes decisions. U.S. trade policy is moving in the same direction, with the passage of the 1988 trade bill endorsing aggressive reciprocity as its basic principle (Wright 1989). Assertive trade actions between large powers are likely to reinforce the incentives for such policies on both sides.

These effects may easily be conceptualized as bargaining games played out at three levels: within the EC member countries, among EC members, and between the EC and the rest of the world. There are three basic variations of games, which are linked and blend together. First, there are distributional (i.e., market-share) issues within the EC, between firms, and between countries. They usually begin as simple constant-sum market-share games, when domestic interests lobby for protection, as may well occur with the increased levels of post-1992 competition. They are resolved by turning them into variable-sum games, restricting competition within the EC by cartelistic market-sharing arrangements and blocking imports with nontariff barriers and strategic industry polices, effectively shifting the costs onto foreigners. The outcome is likely to be a variable-sum game (in this case, negative-sum), since the costs to the foreigners and EC consumers are likely to be greater than the gains to the EC producers. Second, there are purely international variable-sum games, created because of the gains that the EC may derive from using its size to impose optimal trade taxes on smaller trade partners—this is the classic optimal tariff argument familiar to economists. Again, the outcome is negative-sum for the world as a whole, but the EC may gain despite foreign retaliation. Third, there are international "minimum winning coalition" games, largely between the EC, the United States, and Japan. Such coalitions have been common in the international steel trade in the 1970s and 1980s (e.g., U.S. steel quotas that gave the EC favored treatment at the expense of Japan), and as the collective power of the EC grows, such behavior should become more common. Semiconductors and automobiles are likely candidates.

Notes

1. Statutes are being prepared for the creation of a common currency, a European central bank, and the necessary institutions for the coordination of macroeconomic policies (*Economist*, Supplement, 1990, 20–26).

2. The author heard remarks to this effect from Mr. Henning Christopherson, Vice President of the EC Commission, during his keynote address to a colloquium on 1992, sponsored by the European Institute of Public Administration in Maastricht, the Netherlands, October 27, 1989.

3. As the *Economist* (12–16–89, 15) wryly noted, quotas applied to internal EC production defeat the competition-promoting objectives of 1992.

4. Foreign subsidiaries may, however, still be excluded from some of the benefits of 1992; for example, by exclusion from the setting of product standards, allegedly one of the major benefits of 1992 (Cooper 1989, 327).

5. The Commissioner for External Relations stated in 1988 that "where international obligations do not exist, we see no reason why the benefits of our internal liberalization should be extended unilaterally to third countries" (quoted in Hufbauer 1990, 20, note 41).

6. Friction has been reported between France and Germany, as the latter has been induced to slow down the pace of monetary union, in consideration of the costs of reunification.

7. Revenues per passenger kilometer (in $U.S.) were (in 1989) 1.6 for the eight major U.S. carriers, 1.1 for British Airways, 0.8 for Lufthansa, 0.8 for UTA, and 0.7 for Alitalia (*Economist*, 12–9–89, 71).

8. Internal economies of scale occur when a firm's cost of production declines with

volume, for reasons relating to the technology of production (e.g., it is cheaper, per unit, to produce ten cars than one car). External economies of scale occur when industry expansion generates cost reductions benefiting all firms in the industry (e.g., an expansion in the computer industry will cause the educational system to expand the supply of computer programmers and lower their cost to the industry).

9. RACE is a $1.5 billion program for the development of high-speed data telecommunications. Esprit is a microelectronics program, half funded by the EC budget.

References

Blandford, David. 1989. "Bringing Agriculture into the GATT." *Canadian Journal of Agricultural Economics*, 37:813–23.

Business Week. Various issues.

Caballero, Ricardo, and Richard Lyons. 1989. "Internal versus External Economies in European Industry." Discussion Paper Series No. 427. Department of Economics. Columbia University.

Calingaert, Michael. 1988. *The 1992 Challenge from Europe*. Washington, DC: National Planning Association.

Cecchini, Paolo. 1988. *The European Challenge: 1992*. Aldershot: Gower.

Conybeare, John. 1987. *Trade Wars*. New York: Columbia University Press.

Cooper, Richard N. 1989. "Europe Without Borders." *Brookings Papers on Economic Activity*, 2:325–40.

Cowhey, Peter. 1990. "Telecommunications." In Gary Hufbauer, ed., *Europe 1992*, pp. 159–224. Washington, DC: Brookings Institution.

Cutler, Tony, Colin Haslam, John Williams, and Karel Williams. 1989. *1992—The Struggle for Europe*. New York: Berg.

Dixit, Avinash, and Albert Kyle. 1985. "The Use of Protection and Subsidies for Entry Promotion and Deterrence." *American Economic Review*, 75 (March): 139–52.

Economist. Various issues.

Economist (Supplement). 1990. *An Expanding Universe: A Survey of the European Community*. 7 July.

Emerson, Michael. 1988. *The Economics of 1992*. New York: Oxford University Press.

European Community. 1989a. Section of External Relations, "1992 and the Community's External Trade," EXT 68, Brussels, 27 June.

European Community. 1989b. Economic and Social Committee, "1992 and the Community's External Trade," EXT 68, Brussels, 12 July.

Finger, J. M. 1979. "Trade Liberalization." In R. Amacher, G. Haberler, and T. Willett, eds., *Challenges to a Liberal International Economic Order*. Washington, DC: American Enterprise Institute.

Flamm, Kenneth. 1990. "Semiconductors." In Gary Hufbauer, ed., *Europe 1992*, pp. 225–93. Washington, DC: Brookings Institution.

Gowa, Joanne. 1989. "Bipolarity, Multipolarity and Free Trade." *American Political Science Review*, 83 (December): 1245–56.

Greenwald, Joseph. 1990. "Negotiating Strategy." In Gary Hufbauer, ed., *Europe 1992*, pp. 345–92. Washington, DC: Brookings Institution.

Grilli, Vittorio. 1989. "Financial Markets and 1992." *Brookings Papers on Economic Activity*, 2:301–24.

Holmes, Peter. 1989. "Economies of Scale, Expectations and Europe 1992." *The World Economy*, 12 (December): 525–38.

Hufbauer, Gary. 1990. "An Overview." In Gary Hufbauer, ed., *Europe 1992*, pp. 1–65. Washington, DC: Brookings Institution.

Jervis, Robert. 1976. *Perception and Misperception in International Politics*. Princeton, NJ: Princeton University Press.

Kahler, Miles. 1985. "European Protectionism in Theory and in Practice." *World Politics*, 37 (July): 475–502.

Krugman, Paul. 1989. "Is Bilateralism Bad?" Paper prepared for a conference on international trade, Tel Aviv, 21–22 May.

Krugman, Paul. 1987. "Is Free Trade Passe?" *Economic Perspectives*, 1 (Fall): 131–44.

McCloskey, Donald. 1980. "Magnanimous Albion: Free Trade and British National Income." *Explorations in Economic History*, 17 (July): 303–20.

McKeown, Timothy. 1984. "Firms and Regime Change: Explaining the Demand for Protection." *World Politics*, 36 (January): 215–33.

Neustadt, Richard. 1970. *Alliance Politics*. New York: Columbia University Press.

New York Times. Various issues.

Pelkmans, Jacques. 1989. "Europe—1992: A Handmaiden to GATT." Paper presented to the eighth Erenstein Colloquium, organized by the European Institute for Public Administration, Kerkrade, Netherlands. 27–28 October.

Petersmann, Ernst-Ulrich. 1986. "The EEC as a GATT Member." In Meinhard Hilf, ed., *The European Community and the GATT*, pp. 23–72. Deventer: Kluwer.

Porter, Michael. 1990. "Europe's Companies after 1992." *Economist*, 9 (June): 17–20.

Rosenthal, Douglas. 1990. "Competition Policy." In Gary Hufbauer, ed., *Europe 1992*, pp. 293–344. Washington, DC: Brookings Institution.

Smith, Alasdair, and Anthony Venables. 1990. "Automobiles." In Gary Hufbauer, ed., *Europe 1992*, pp. 119–58. Washington, DC: Brookings Institution.

Whalley, John. 1985. *Trade Liberalization among Major World Trading Areas*. Cambridge, MA: MIT Press.

Wright, Richard. 1989. "The 1988 Trade Act—Refinement or Major Change to U.S. Trade Laws?" *Brigham Young University Law Review*, 2:533–48.

9

U.S. State Government Responses to EC–1992

A Survey of State Development Agencies

Frances H. Oneal

The European Community's completion of the single internal market by the end of 1992 (EC–1992) is officially welcomed in the United States for the "free flow of capital, goods, products, services, and people" it will bring. Secretary of Commerce Mosbacher has stated that EC–1992 is in the United States' best interests, both commercially and strategically, and that the United States stands to gain from this market integration (Mosbacher 1990). While U.S. policy statements emphasize the opportunities that will follow from EC–1992, an undertone of caution is present. Calls for close monitoring of specific sectors, warnings against protectionism, and above all, concern that non-EC producers and service providers may be unequally or unfavorably treated under the new EC legislation are evident in Commerce Department statements.

Governmental concern about the economic consequences of EC–1992 for the United States is also felt among the states. This chapter examines the effect that EC–1992 has already had on state governments, and considers the implications of the states' reactions to date for EC–state relations after 1992. Focusing on the states' views of EC–1992 emphasizes that complex governance, a term Hughes (chapter 3, this volume) employs to describe the development of multilevel governing arrangements in Europe, applies equally to the evolving intergovernmental relations between the U.S. states and the EC.

State Governments and the International Economy

The growth of state governments' role in international economics is part of a larger trend, that is, the emergence of subnational actors as significant players in the international arena.[1] In the United States, this development has been fostered by governmental decentralization. Devolution of the federal government's responsibilities in the 1980s placed greater emphasis on state and local governments' role in promoting economic stability and growth.[2] This role has been especially pronounced in the area of export promotion and investment seeking by state development agencies (SDAs). The National Association of State Development Agencies (NASDA) reports that the budgets of state development agencies doubled every two years in the early 1980s. The average SDA budget reached $20 million per year in 1988. An average of $1 million per year was spent on export promotion, and $3 million in seeking foreign investment (NASDA 1989a).

Additionally, many states maintain overseas liaison offices to foster good communication and better relations with their major trading partners, particularly in Europe and Japan. This high level of formalized activity suggests that an important new intergovernmental relationship will develop as a result of EC–1992: EC (supranational) to U.S. state (subnational) relations. To preview the nature of this relationship, a survey was sent to the fifty SDAs in late 1989. The questionnaire had three main areas of concern: the SDAs' views of the likelihood and importance of possible economic results of EC–1992; the SDAs' perceptions of the attitude of various economic sectors in their states toward EC–1992; and the SDAs' programmatic responses to the coming common market.

SDAs in twenty-two states participated in the survey (see Table 9.1). These states comprise 46 percent of the U.S. population and 59 percent of its Gross Domestic Product. Examination of the data reveals that the sample is a very closely representative cross-section of all fifty states. They fully represent the geographic range of the United States. There is no significant difference between the average state population size in the sample and the average state population in the United States; and no significant difference between the sample's average income per capita and that of the entire United States. Finally, the states surveyed vary widely in terms of (1) their economic involvement with the EC, and (2) their level of programmatic response to EC–1992.

State Development Agencies

State government activity in the area of international economic promotion is a relatively new phenomenon. Only fifteen states had such agencies in the early 1970s, but all states had established at least one by the early 1980s (Neuse 1982, 57). State development agencies dealing with international matters are variously organized in the state governments. The most common arrangement is a division of international affairs within an economic development agency, most often within the state's Department of Commerce. Some economic development offices rank at the departmental level themselves, while others are constituted as special commissions or boards. All such agencies, whether departments, divisions, or commissions, are referred to here as SDAs.[3]

Table 9.1

Region, Income, and Population of States Surveyed (1986)

State	Region	Income Per Capita	Population
1. Alabama	Southeast	$13,472	4,083,000
2. California	Pacific	$19,297	27,663,000
3. Delaware	Northeast	$18,177	644,000
4. Florida	Southeast	$14,782	12,023,000
5. Hawaii	Pacific	$17,839	1,083,000
6. Idaho	West	$13,196	998,000
7. Illinois	Midwest	$18,103	11,582,000
8. Montana	West	$15,035	809,000
9. New Hampshire	Northeast	$17,519	1,057,000
10. New Jersey	Northeast	$20,173	7,672,000
11. New Mexico	West	$15,735	1,500,000
12. New York	Northeast	$20,350	17,825,000
13. Ohio	Midwest	$16,358	10,800,000
14. Pennsylvania	Midwest	$15,379	11,900,000
15. South Carolina	Southeast	$13,059	3,425,000
16. South Dakota	West	$13,825	709,000
17. Tennessee	Southeast	$14,898	4,855,000
18. Texas	Midwest	$18,078	16,800,000
19. Utah	West	$14,290	1,680,000
20. Virginia	Southeast	$17,641	5,904,000
21. Washington	Pacific	$17,130	4,535,000
22. Wisconsin	Midwest	$16,002	4,807,000
Average income per capita, States above		$16,379	
Average income per capita, Total U.S.		$16,808	
Total U.S. Population			243,400,000
% of U.S. Total Population, States above			62.6%

Source: U.S. Department of Commerce, Bureau of the Census. 1989. *Statistical Abstract of the U.S.*

As early as 1976, the overseas activities of SDAs attracted the attention of political economists, who were interested in studying the SDAs' techniques, the problems they encountered, and their successful strategies. A Commerce Department–sponsored study of six SDAs concluded that their internationally oriented programs were "a prime economic development factor in the growth and expansion of state and regional economies." (U.S. Department of Commerce 1977, 15).

Analyzing the Survey of SDAs

This survey's focus is state government activity with regard to one particular international development: EC-1992. Some SDAs (notably California and Virginia) stressed that while the SDA was the locus of the state's response, other departments were also involved. The states' Departments of Agriculture, for example, are developing new policies and programs because of EC-1992, and these activities are separate from the SDAs'. While the SDAs' responses to EC-1992 do not represent the entire reaction by state governments, they can be taken to be the most significant part, and as representative of the states' outlooks on the single internal market. In the following sections, the SDAs' general attitudes and separate assessments of the likelihood and importance of outcomes of EC-1992 are discussed.

General Attitudes toward EC-1992

The SDAs were asked to indicate their general attitude toward EC-1992, using a scale of one (Strongly agree) to five (Strongly disagree).[4] While on average the states agreed that EC-1992 will be economically beneficial to EC member countries (1.5), they did not feel that European unification would benefit only Europe (3.9). They felt that EC-1992 will in the long run benefit the global marketplace (1.9), the United States (2.2), and their state in particular (2.1). The SDAs judged that EC-1992 may be more beneficial for eastern Europe than for the United States, but they did not think that it will be more beneficial for Japan and the Soviet Union than for the United States. Asked if EC-1992's effect on them will be significant, most states agreed, but allowed that it might be beneficial only for certain sectors of their economy.

The SDAs were also asked to speculate on the prospects for the creation of a single European currency and a unified European government. A single currency was seen as a likely long-term outcome of EC-1992, beneficial for the global marketplace and for the United States. The SDAs did not feel that a unified European government was a likely long-term outcome of EC-1992, although such an outcome would be generally beneficial for the United States.

Finally, the SDAs were asked for their views of the U.S.-Canada Free Trade Agreement (FTA). There was strong agreement that the FTA is generally beneficial to the United States (1.9) and to the individual states (1.8). When asked if the state's economy has been or will be more affected by the FTA than by EC-1992, the SDAs gave mixed responses, but the average response of 2.0 shows that this is the belief of most states. This is significant, given that only four of the twenty-two states border Canada. A state's view of the advantageousness of the FTA correlates positively with its view of EC-1992's benefits for the state ($r = .27^*$, $n = 19$), as does a state's view of the benefit of the FTA and EC-1992 for the United States ($r = .45^{**}$, $n = 19$).[5]

Private-Sector Views of EC–1992

The SDAs were asked to share their perceptions of others' attitudes toward EC–1992. From a list of eleven economic sectors, the state legislature, and the governor's office, the SDAs perceive little variation in attitudes.[6] On a scale of one (Very favorable) to five (Very unfavorable), attitudes in all sectors were on average favorable (3). The most favorable attitudes were perceived from the governor's office, the state legislature, business leaders, manufacturers, and the energy producing sector. Less favorable attitudes were perceived among agricultural interests and cultural industries (those representing printed media, television and cable firms, film, radio, and recorded music).

The SDAs were then asked which of these sectors had expressed the greatest interest in EC–1992. On a scale of one (High interest) to five (No interest), all sectors on average showed more than a moderate (3) level of interest. Exporting firms, the governor's office, manufacturers, business leaders, agricultural interests, and banks and financial concerns were reported to have a very high level of interest in EC–1992. Tourism-related firms, the energy sector, and cultural industries were reported to have less interest in EC–1992. No state reported low interest (3) among exporters.

Possible Outcomes of EC–1992

The SDAs were asked to assess the likelihood of many possible outcomes of EC–1992, both for the United States and their own state. Using a scale of one (Not a likely change) to five (A very likely change), the SDAs indicated on average that they foresee positive outcomes as more likely than negative outcomes. For instance, increased EC foreign direct investment (FDI) is seen as more likely than decreased; increased tourism as more likely than decreased; increased employment in export-related industries rather than decreased. Asked about possible disruption in the economic relationship between the United States and the EC, and between the state and the EC, short-term disruption is seen as unlikely (2.2 for the U.S.–EC relationship, 1.9 for the state–EC relationship). Medium-term and long-term disruption are discounted even more so.

The Significance of Possible Outcomes of EC–1992

The SDAs were then asked to assess the importance of some possible outcomes of EC–1992 for the United States and their state. On a scale of one (Not important) to five (Very important), the possibility of reduced employment in export-related industries (4.3) and in industries representing FDI from the EC (4.1) were seen as clearly important outcomes. Greater difficulty exporting to the EC (4.3) and more restricted access to the EC marketplace (4.1) were also seen as significant. Of less importance were greater difficulty importing from the EC (2.0) and

Table 9.2

States' Level of Concern* Over EC–1992:
Rank Order, Least to Most Concerned

1.	Illinois	1.40	12. Montana	3.20
2.	New York	1.50	13. New Hampshire	3.20
3.	Ohio	2.30	14. Utah	3.20
4.	Idaho	2.60	15. New Jersey	3.20
5.	Delaware	2.67	16. Pennsylvania	3.29
6.	South Dakota	2.80	17. Texas	3.38
7.	New Mexico	2.86	18. Virginia	3.44
8.	Wisconsin	3.00	19. Florida	3.50
9.	California	3.00	20. South Carolina	3.90
10.	Hawaii	3.00	21. Tennessee	3.90
11.	Washington	3.00	22. Alabama	4.29

*Concern is the state's view of the likelihood and importance of five possible outcomes of EC–1992. An average of one would indicate that all outcomes are considered unlikely and not important; and average of five would indicate that all are considered very likely and very important.

short-run economic disruption of the economic relationship between the state and the EC (3.4).

An index of concern over possible outcomes of EC–1992 can be derived by combining the two previous sections of the survey. The average of the responses to questions regarding the importance and the likelihood of the possible outcomes is an indicator of the states' concern for each outcome. On a scale of one (Not likely and Not important) to five (Very likely and Very important), five important areas of concern were identified: restricted access to the EC marketplace (3.3), greater difficulty exporting to the EC (3.3), reduced EC FDI (3), reduced employment in export-related industries (2.9) and in industries representing FDI (2.9). If the states are ranked according to the average score on these five issues, Illinois ranks lowest, while Alabama leads the list. It is notable that the five southeastern states score highest in concern. The rankings are shown in Table 9.2.

SDAs' Responses to EC–1992

"State entrepreneurship" (Eisinger 1988) refers to innovative strategies of intervention, guidance, and initiative in developing state and local economies, in contrast to traditional macroeconomic strategy conducted at the federal level. One of the survey's principal aims was to discern the varieties of state entrepreneurship in this policy area. The SDAs were asked to describe their programmatic responses to EC–1992, given the interests and concerns of various economic sectors in each state. Of the twenty-two states, all but three of them

(86 percent) report having created programs or begun initiatives specifically in response to EC–1992. Seven have created a new informational service; seven have initiated a new research effort; eleven have held a special conference; one has created a new division within the department; twenty-one other special types of efforts have been inaugurated. These include a metric conversion program, developing a new state promotional brochure, holding seminars, establishing a program to identify European trade shows of interest, creating an EC–1992 guidebook for businesses, and opening additional offices overseas.

Half the states (including two of the states that did not initiate any new programs) have modified existing programs in response to EC–1992. New facets have been added to existing informational services, trade show participation has been expanded, and research efforts have been modified to include a focus on EC–1992. Eighty percent of the states have used at least one source of assistance provided by the federal government, most often from the Department of Commerce and the U.S. Trade Representative.

Apparently there has been very little interstate cooperation regarding EC–1992. The only exception is among the western states, where the Western Governors' Association has dealt with EC–1992 concerns. Further coordination is being considered. Only three states have conducted a study of the potential impact of EC–1992 on their state's economy; these studies examined the impact on exports, tourism, imports, and employment. Five states estimated their departmental expenditure directly related to EC–1992. An average of $107,000 was the outlay for 1990 among these five departments. Given the close correlation ($r = .99^{**}$, $n = 5$) of estimated expenditure and Gross State Product (GSP), costs related to EC–1992 can be estimated for the other states. An average of $491,000 would have been spent by the SDAs in 1990 if the same relationship of expenditure to GSP held for all fifty states.

Seminars and dissemination of information are the most common contribution of the SDAs to aid companies in adjusting to EC–1992.[7] Many of the SDAs have focused on small and medium-sized firms, especially manufacturers, who can benefit most from the department's assistance. A major mission of SDAs in the 1980s was assisting firms in establishing export relations, and promoting the most competitive of the state's firms in the world market. That expertise is now being utilized to encourage more companies to make overtures in Europe before 1992.

A simple index of an SDA's level of activity related to EC–1992 was created based on each state's programmatic responses. The index adds the number of positive responses to questions concerning programs created or modified, efforts coordinated with other states, federal assistance sought, and impact studies conducted. Six states have a score of only one or two on the activity index; highest were Texas and California, who scored nine and twelve, respectively (see Table 9.3). In the following sections, this index is related to the level of economic ties to the EC and to state wealth.

Table 9.3

Index of SDA Activity Related to EC–1992: Rank Order, Least to Most Active

New Hampshire	1
Illinois, Ohio, Pennsylvania, Washington, and Wisconsin	2
Hawaii, New Mexico, and Tennessee	3
Delaware, Florida, South Dakota, and Virginia	4
South Carolina and Alabama	5
Montana, New Jersey, New York, and Utah	6
Idaho	7
Texas	9
California	12

Economic Sensitivity and Views of EC–1992

It is reasonable to assume that the greater the state's economic links to the EC, the more attentive that state would be to EC–1992. As in the literature on interdependence (e.g., Keohane and Nye 1977), the measure of economic ties will be referred to as the sensitivity of a state to EC–1992. One index of sensitivity to EC–1992 is derived by averaging (1) the employment due to EC FDI as a percent of a state's total employment, and (2) the value of EC FDI as a percent of Gross State Product (GSP). Table 9.4 lists the FDI sensitivity index by state, from the least sensitive (Hawaii) to most (South Carolina).

Another sensitivity index is based on the value of exports from a state to the EC as a percentage of GSP. However, only fourteen states were able to estimate the percentage of their total exports that are destined for the EC. Unfortunately, the U.S. Department of Commerce does not collect data on the destination of exports by state of origin.[8] For the fourteen states for which data are available, a second sensitivity index, EC Exports/GSP, can be derived. The index of export sensitivity is also shown in Table 9.4, from least sensitive (Washington) to most sensitive (Virginia).

The two sensitivity indexes are not closely correlated ($r = .17$, $n = 14$), indicating that, at least for fourteen states, EC investment and investment-related employment are not a good predictor of export involvement with the EC. While export sensitivity is most widely used to measure interdependence between countries (Cameron 1978; Tetreault 1980), the FDI sensitivity index is also useful since data are available for all states. The following two sections separately discuss the relationship of FDI sensitivity and export sensitivity to the other variables of interest.

FDI sensitivity is positively correlated with SDA activity ($r = .33^*$, $n = 22$), indicating that the states with the most EC investment have responded more vigorously to EC–1992. FDI sensitivity is also positively associated with the index of concern ($r = .32^*$, $n = 22$). Therefore, close investment ties to the EC raise the SDA's concern over the effects of EC–1992 upon the state. For instance,

Table 9.4

Sensitivity to EC–1992: Rank Order, Least to Most Sensitive

State	FDI Sensitivity	State	Export Sensitivity
1. Hawaii	.62	1. Washington	.004
2. Idaho	.79	2. Hawaii	.028
3. Washington	.94	3. New Mexico	.182
4. New York	.97	4. Florida	.559
5. South Dakota	1.01	5. Tennessee	.756
6. New Hampshire	1.43	6. Utah	.808
7. Florida	1.75	7. Montana	.959
8. Wisconsin	1.90	8. Wisconsin	1.173
9. Delaware	2.03	9. New Jersey	1.260
10. Virginia	2.04	10. California	1.316
11. New Mexico	2.09	11. Texas	1.411
12. Illinois	2.18	12. Idaho	1.574
13. Montana	2.22	13. New Hampshire	1.773
14. Alabama	2.31	14. Virginia	2.864
15. California	2.37	15. Alabama	n.a.
16. Pennsylvania	2.44	16. Delaware	n.a.
17. Tennessee	2.44	17. Illinois	n.a.
18. Ohio	2.56	18. New York	n.a.
19. New Jersey	2.76	19. Ohio	n.a.
20. Texas	4.47	20. Pennsylvania	n.a.
21. Utah	4.56	21. South Carolina	n.a.
22. South Carolina	5.37	22. South Dakota	n.a.

Source: U.S. Department of Commerce, *Foreign Direct Investment in the U.S.*, Table D–14, "Gross Value of Property, Plant and Equipment of Affiliates," and Table F–8, "Employment of Affiliates"; *Statistical Abstract of the U.S.*, 1989; and state surveys.

FDI Sensitivity = (EC FDI/GSP) + (EC FDI Emp./Tot. Emp.) / 2
Export Sensitivity = (EC Exports)/GSP
n.a. = not available
Year is 1989 or most recent year available.

the more sensitive states feel more strongly that restricted access to the EC marketplace and greater difficulty exporting to the EC are likely outcomes. The more sensitive states also see a greater likelihood of reduced employment in industries representing EC FDI. They also attach greater importance to the possibility of reduced EC FDI and FDI-related employment in their state than do the others. This is as would be expected, given an index based on EC FDI and FDI employment. The states with smaller investment links to the EC have a more sanguine outlook. In general, greater FDI sensitivity is associated with a more pessimistic outlook on the results of EC–1992 for the state.

Export sensitivity is also positively correlated with SDA activity ($r = .24$, $n = 14$), indicating that, to a degree, the states exporting most to the EC have responded more vigorously to EC–1992. Furthermore, export sensitivity is positively associated with the index of concern ($r = .15, n = 14$). SDAs in states exporting more to the EC are more concerned over the effects of EC–1992 on the state.

In particular, the more export-sensitive states feel more strongly that greater difficulty exporting to the EC is a likely outcome. They also attach greater importance to this outcome, and to reduced employment in exporting than do the less export-sensitive states. This is as would be expected, given an index based on exports as a percentage of GSP. Overall, greater export sensitivity is also associated with a more pessimistic outlook on the results of EC–1992 for the state.

State Wealth and Views of EC–1992

Another assumption to be tested is that the wealthier states will be more responsive to EC–1992 than the poorer states, due to a greater availability of resources. A state's wealth is measured by its Gross State Product per capita. The average income among these states is $16,379, ranging from South Carolina's $13,059 to New York's $20,350. The wealthier states have been more attractive to EC investment than the poorer states; but as a percentage of state income, EC FDI is more important in the poorer states. Therefore, a state's wealth is inversely related to its FDI sensitivity ($r = -.14, n = 22$). At the same time, state wealth is positively related to SDA activity. Thus, the poorer states responded less actively to EC–1992, despite their greater FDI sensitivity to the European economy and concern over EC–1992.

In terms of export sensitivity, the wealthier states export more to the EC, both in absolute terms and as a percentage of their GSP. A state's wealth is therefore positively correlated to export sensitivity ($r = .19, n = 14$). The positive relationship of state wealth to SDA activity is also more easily understood in this case: the more sensitive (and wealthier) states have more actively responded to EC–1992.

Further, the wealthier states are more likely to believe that EC–1992 will be beneficial to the EC, to the United States, and to the state. The poorer states are more likely to agree that EC–1992 will benefit other states more than itself. Business leaders in wealthier states are reported to hold more favorable views of EC–1992; the same is true (but less strongly so) for agricultural interests and manufacturers in wealthier states.

Regarding the outcomes of EC–1992, the poorer states responded that more restricted access to the EC marketplace, greater difficulty exporting to the EC, and reduced employment in export- and FDI-related industries are more likely than did the wealthier states. The wealthier states felt that increased FDI in their state was more likely than did poorer states. In general, the poorer states are more pessimistic in outlook, while the wealthier states are more positive.

At the same time, the wealthier states attach greater importance to possible outcomes of EC–1992 for their state than do the poorer states. The wealth of a state is positively related to the level of importance attached to more restricted EC access, greater difficulty exporting, reduced EC FDI, and reduced export- and FDI-related employment. Thus, while the poorer states are more pessimistic in outlook, they attach less importance to the negative outcomes they foresee. This, in addition to having fewer resources, may explain why the poorer but more investment-sensitive states have had less SDA activity related to EC–1992.

Geographic Region and Views on EC–1992

In analyzing the surveys by geographic region, one might reasonably expect decreasing sensitivity and therefore lower SDA responsiveness looking from east to west. As expected, FDI and export sensitivity are inversely related to region ($r = -.20, n = 22; r = -.51^{**}, n = 14$, respectively). The western states are less closely tied to the EC economy in terms of investment and exports. Both sensitivity indexes are on average greatest in the Southeast and least in the Pacific region.

Some interesting differences in attitudes and outlooks on EC–1992 are found when the data are analyzed by region. Confidence in EC–1992's widespread benefits is strongest in the Midwest, whereas the Southeast is more doubtful of EC–1992's benefits outside the EC. SDAs in midwestern states most emphatically disagree that EC–1992 will have a negligible impact upon them, while the northeastern states feel most strongly that they will be more affected by the Canadian FTA than by EC–1992.

Explaining Levels of Concern and SDA Activity

Regression analysis of ten independent variables[9] reveals that per capita income is the single best predictor of a state's level of concern over EC–1992, while a state's total wealth (GSP) is the best predictor of the level of SDA activity related to EC–1992. In regression equations explaining the level of SDA concern and activity, FDI sensitivity has a positive coefficient as expected, but it is not statistically significant, as shown in equations 1 and 2.[10] Export sensitivity was even less significant as an explanatory variable for SDA concern and activity, using the fourteen-state subset for which data were available.

$$\text{SDA Concern} = 4.9 - .44 \text{ (GSP/cap)} + .15 \text{ (Sensitivity)} \qquad (1)$$
$$(.000) (.035) \qquad (.195)$$
$$R^2 = .22 \ F = .0356 \ N = 22$$

$$\text{SDA Activity} = 1.98 + .53 \text{ (GSP)} + .55 \text{ (Sensitivity)} \qquad (2)$$
$$(.074) (.010) \qquad (.189)$$
$$R^2 = .32 \ F = .0106 \ N = 22$$

Therefore, in looking at the twenty-eight states that did not participate in the survey, greater concern can be expected from those states with lower per capita income, while a greater degree of SDA activity can be expected from those states with the larger economies. If the parameters in equations 1 and 2 are applied to data from all fifty states, an average level of SDA activity of 4.15 and an average level of concern of 2.97 are produced. This suggests a variety of SDA responses in each state, prompted by only a moderate level of concern.

Conclusions and Implications for the Future

While predictions regarding the number of SDA activities do not suggest what type of programs will be developed, informational services, conferences, and seminars are the most likely. Export promotion, which has outpaced investment-seeking programs in recent years (Eisinger 1988, 294) is also likely to be the major emphasis. The survey responses, commentary on the surveys, and SDA publications received all indicate that most states perceive EC–1992 as an opportunity, not a threat. A more competitive international environment was often mentioned as a positive challenge arising from Europe's market unification.[11] While a measure of caution exists for certain sectors, the SDAs' predominant reactions toward these fears was to monitor EC policy, to encourage firms to position themselves strategically in advance of 1992, but otherwise to "wait and see." The SDAs were attempting to prepare their states for 1992, but refrained from further action until actual consequences are felt.

However, the survey reveals a notable lack of economic impact studies. Without a statistical examination of potential areas of impact, the SDAs' optimistic views of EC–1992's effect on the states' economies may be misplaced. The surveys also show that regional coordination and consultation is lacking, illustrative of the competitive approach of many states in the area of economic development (Grady 1987). Interstate cooperation, especially among neighboring states with limited international staffs, seems a cost-effective approach in responding to EC–1992. Just as the supranational EC structure may be only one step in the evolution of a more complex, multilayered governance structure to provide a variety of public goods (Hughes, chapter 3 in this volume), so may be the development of a regional SDA orientation for more rational provision of economic development.

Finally, states do not maintain data on importing firms, whose interests are not considered as a group by the SDAs as are exporting firms' interests. As a result, the concerns of importers and the possible ramifications of EC–1992 for them have not been considered by the SDAs. As noted at the outset, the past decade has seen a devolution of economic responsibility to the state governments. This means that the trade balance and economic interdependence may increasingly become a matter of concern for each state, not just for the United States as a whole. Collecting data on imports and defining the interests and influence of state importers will be an important task for SDAs in the future.

From the EC's point of view, a refined understanding of and closer communications with state governments is advisable for two reasons. First, the states now exert more influence on U.S. foreign economic policy than ever before (Kline 1983), further complicating the bargaining games at the level of U.S.–EC interaction. Second, the states' economic policy variations shape the United States' domestic economic landscape. Internal trade barriers, as defined by the EC, are designed by state governments, and come in the form of: sales, excise, income, and corporate tax policies; government procurement regulations; financial services regulation; technical barriers; and certain transportation laws (Pelkmans 1988, 65). The EC, now in the process of eliminating these types of trade barriers, must continue to deal with internal variations within the U.S. market for the foreseeable future.

For the next two years, trade with Europe will receive considerable attention. Yet, the U.S.–Canada FTA is only now coming into full effect, and Canada will remain the United States' single largest national trading partner. Asia remains of great economic importance to many states: NASDA lists as many SDA overseas offices in Japan, Korea, Taiwan, and Hong Kong as in all European countries (NASDA 1988, appendix A). Further, the United States' merchandise trade balance with Europe is more favorable for the United States than is the trade balance with Japan and other Asian partners. Therefore, state relations and trade policy with Canada, Japan, and the Pacific Rim will vie with the EC for the SDAs' attention in the current climate of growth in international trade.

In sum, the states are on balance very favorably disposed toward expanding economic relations with Europe in the wake of EC–1992. However, many SDAs lag in preparing themselves for the heightened level of activity that will be necessary for dealing with the unified EC. The role of SDAs in guiding the states in the international economy must evolve in the 1990s from what it has been in the 1970s and 1980s. The heightened level of state activism in economic development which began during this period is likely to endure, "because many contemporary economic challenges are more amenable to public action at the regional and local level, and because for the moment, the federal government has willingly relinquished its leadership role in domestic policy" (Fosler 1988, 311). But the SDAs must go beyond the entrepreneurial development of programs and trade promotion strategies. The SDAs are well positioned to become "miniembassies," acting as official liaisons, troubleshooting, arbitrating, and otherwise representing the subnational economies in this country to the supranational economy of Europe. In accepting the challenge to fulfill this greater role, the SDAs may ultimately play the leading role in U.S.-European economic problem solving and policy making.

Notes

1. Rosenau (1990, 9, 133) argues that the present dominance of subnational governments, subgroups, and transnational organizations on the world stage constitutes an era of "postinternational politics."

2. The trend toward greater state and local government economic responsibility in Europe is described in Page and Goldsmith (1987).

3. The list of participating state agencies is available from the author.

4. All continua were on a five-point scale, with a zero option for "Unable to say." Zeros were treated as missing values. Averages for all states with nonzero responses are reported in parentheses.

5. Significance of correlation coefficients is designated by: ** = significant at the .05 level; * = significant at the .10 level; no symbol = not significant at the .10 level.

6. SDAs in eleven states reported that they were "Unable to say" regarding importers, in fifteen states with regard to the energy producing sector, in ten states with regard to cultural industries, and in nine states with regard to agriculture.

7. Several SDAs also mentioned private-sector programs sponsored by universities, chambers of commerce, and private research and development centers. The SDAs are augmenting their own efforts by referring companies to these programs. In the same spirit, one state's major response to EC–1992 has been the creation of a public–private partnership program for export promotion to the European market.

8. The Commerce Department has stated that "currently there exists a paucity of accurate and reliable empirical commodity flow data about merchandise shipments by state. . . . The one time cost of a survey that would produce reliable data at the state level for domestic and international shipments is almost equal to the current annual budget for all foreign trade statistics" (Farrell and Radspieler, n.d., 6–7).

9. FDI sensitivity, export sensitivity, concern, the value of EC FDI, numbers employed by EC FDI, exports to the EC, region, population, total state government expenditure, state wealth, and income per capita were tested.

10. Beta coefficients, t-statistics, and adjusted R^2s are reported in each equation.

11. See, for example, *Europe 1992: Implications for California Businesses*, 1989, pp. 5–15.

References

California State World Trade Commission. 1989. *Europe 1992: Implications for California Businesses*. Sacramento: California State World Trade Commission.

Cameron, David R. 1978. "The Expansion of the Public Economy." *American Political Science Review*, 72, 4 (December): 1243–61.

Eisinger, Peter K. 1988. *The Rise of the Entrepreneurial State*. Madison: University of Wisconsin Press.

Farrell, Michael G., and Anthony Radspieler. No date. "Origin of Merchandise Exports Data." U.S. Deparment of Commerce, Bureau of the Census, Foreign Trade Division.

Fosler, R. Scott, ed. 1988. *The New Economic Role of American States*. New York: Oxford University Press.

Grady, Dennis O. 1987. "State Economic Development Incentives: Why Do the States Compete?" *State and Local Government Review*, 19, 3:86–94.

Keohane, Robert O., and Joseph S. Nye. 1977. *Power and Interdependence*. Boston: Little Brown.

Kline, John M. 1983. *State Government Influence in U.S. International Economic Policy*. Lexington, MA: Lexington Books.

Mosbacher, Robert A. 1990. "U.S.–E.C. Cooperation Increases as the Single Market Takes Shape." *Business America*, 15 January 1990, pp. 2–3.

National Association of State Development Agencies. 1988. *NASDA State Export Program Database*. Washington, DC: NASDA.

National Association of State Development Agencies. 1989a. "Survey Shows States Shifting Focus to In-Place and Homegrown Industry." Press Release, 20 June 1989.

National Association of State Development Agencies. 1989b. "Survey of States on FDI

Efforts." *The NASDA Letter*, October 13, 1989, pp. 1–4.

Neuse, Steven M. 1982. "State Activities in International Trade." *State Government*, 55, 2:57–65.

Page, Edward C., and Michael J. Goldsmith. 1987. *Central and Local Government Relations: A Comparative Analysis of West European Unitary States*. Beverly Hills, CA: Sage.

Pelkmans, Jacques. 1988. "The Internal Markets of North America." *Research on 'The Cost of Non-Europe.'* Brussels: Commision of the European Communities, vol. 16.

Rosenau, James N. 1990. *Turbulence in World Politics*. Princeton, NJ: Princeton University Press.

Tetreault, Mary Ann. 1980. "Measuring Interdependence." *International Organization*, 34, 3 (Summer 1980): 429–35.

U.S. Department of Commerce, Bureau of the Census. 1987. *Foreign Direct Investment in the U.S.*

U.S. Department of Commerce, Bureau of the Census. 1989. *Statisical Abstract of the U.S.*

U.S. Department of Commerce, Domestic and International Business Administration. 1977. *State Government Conducted International Trade and Business Development Programs.*

10

European Security Policy and the Single European Act

Frederic S. Pearson

European unity will remain incomplete without any consideration for the security policy dimension [loud applause]. The formulation of a common European security policy is one of the priority tasks in the immediate future.

—Helmut Kohl,
Speech to the European Parliament,
Strasbourg, March 9, 1988

Introduction

It is difficult to say whether the momentous debates heard since 1984 in the European Community (EC) concerning renewed integration eventually will achieve either full economic or political union among the member-states. The resulting agreements so far fall short of European unification, or even full confederation on the pre-1787 American model. While Europe is on course at least for a common internal market by 1992, some of the most difficult issues even for that limited agreement remain to be resolved, issues including tax harmonization, monetary cooperation, and welfare policy. In addition, rapidly changing East and central European events add to the financial and political pressures on a twelve-nation West European economic community.

While visions of a unified economic market predominate, external security policy also is drawn into the debate because of the close association these days between such policy and technological innovation, and because of the pace of changing political relations in Europe. The uncertain future of NATO and the demise of the Warsaw Treaty Organization mean that both larger and smaller European states will be struggling to define and assure their security as well as their welfare requirements as the century draws to a close (Kolodziej 1987; Kolodziej and Pearson 1989). Europe's assertive role both in offering diplomatic alternatives and dispatching various military forces during the Iraq–Kuwait crisis of 1990–91 also indicates a potentially growing EC weight in extra-European regional settlements.

The unemployment shocks of the 1980s, following as they did the oil and inflation shocks of the 1970s, at first led to greater European economic nationalism, to the expulsion of guest workers, and reversion to deflationary policies. Yet additional factors seemed to spark a subsequent realization that there was, in many respects, greater safety in numbers than in autarchy. Perhaps it was the growing belief that old manufacturing industries had to give way to new service and high-technology industries, and that these in turn required vastly enlarged markets to take advantage of economies of scale and to recoup research and development costs (Moravcsik 1990). Perhaps it was revival of the traditional European penchant for large conglomerated corporate structures. Perhaps it was Japan's unmistakable success in penetrating trade markets, and along with the United States, in controlling important communication and electronics technologies that alarmed Europeans about the viability of their own economies. It was time to reconsider the basic europolitical/economic structure, and to pay more than lip service to a combined population and market size greater than that of either the United States or the former USSR.

This study is designed to focus on a different but related set of factors, that is, the possibility of the integration process itself stimulating the development of an EC security policy at a time when the venue for a new eurosecurity system is being debated (among the candidates: revised NATO; the Conference on Security and Cooperation in Europe [CSCE]; the Western European Union [WEU]; and bilateral arrangements). Most initial accounts of the Single European Act (SEA) of 1985, the "enabling legislation" for a reinvigorated European Community, and particularly those in North America, attributed it to concern about: the tangle of separate rules, regulations, and impediments holding Europe back from exploiting the potential of its market size, and from competing effectively with other western economic powers; and the crisis of unprecedented postwar unemployment levels. (See, for example, Greenhouse 1988; Yemma 1988a; U.S. Department of State 1988.) Indeed the agencies and organizations that promoted renewed integration, that is, the Commission, the European Parliament (EP— popularly elected after 1979), and the European Council, largely were concerned with promotion of economic development as opposed to matters of security policy. The Treaty of Rome itself (Article 223) exempted armament production and trade from necessary EC jurisdiction. Security policy resided with separate national governments, with broader Atlantic institutions (NATO), and with the WEU, containing, in contrast to the EC, only NATO-aligned states (and excluding NATO mavericks Denmark and Greece).

And yet, security policy concerns cannot be separated entirely from economic development, because of the pivotal importance of high technology for both issues, because of European trade interests in arms, and because the EC also has developed competence to consider foreign policy matters. Indeed, provisions of SEA relating to European Political Cooperation (EPC), the coordination of foreign policy, for the first time give the EC the legal (ratified treaty) and political sanctions to proceed into the security realm (the Solemn Declaration at the Stuttgart Summit of 1983 mentioned economic aspects of security in a political context; see Kirchner 1989, 2–3). This extended mandate is confined so far only to political and economic rather than explicitly military aspects of security (see Garnham, this volume, chapter 11), but as we review past discussions on these matters it is apparent that such lines of distinction are extremely difficult to maintain.

It may be coincidental, or it may be fundamentally important, that the renewed integration impetus corresponded to increased European skepticism about the direction of western security policy in the first Reagan administration. To many West Europeans, American policy seemed dangerously aggressive in military and specifically nuclear strategy toward the USSR. While Americans were responding to a basically European request for nuclear weapons to offset growing intermediate-range Soviet capabilities, the size and destabilizing potential of the U.S. response, and talk in Washington about the possibility of fighting and winning a "limited" nuclear war in Europe, alarmed Europeans of all political persuasions. Both continued doubt about the reliability of American security commitments, and a tremendous upsurge in "peace movements" resulted. At the same time, Washington's tendencies not to consult allies regarding security policy commitments in the Third World, sometimes involving forces stationed in Europe, fostered concern that reliance on American leadership could lead European states into unpopular and dangerous entanglements.

With the Reagan–Gorbachev rapprochement, and with Mr. Gorbachev's subsequent efforts to reduce East–West tensions while encouraging reform movements in eastern Europe and the USSR, a western European consensus developed that military threats from the East were negligible. However, subsequent U.S.–Soviet plans for conventional force reductions, and the unexpectedly serious prospect of German reunification also fostered a dilemma about the extent, timing, and institutional locus of greater euro-self-reliance in defense. In the words of one EC Commission official, such changes foster "a rivalry in the division of labor between the changing North Atlantic Treaty Organization and the European Community." The EC "may interfere on security questions, and no doubt it will infringe on political questions. . . . The EC is the only stable institutional setting on the continent." (Quoted anonymously in Kaslow 1990.)

The basic question for discussion, then, is whether the formation of a coherent western European entity in the early 1990s offers policy incentives or imperatives for further EC security coordination, and whether the EC is likely to be a major actor in a redefined eurosecurity system. Furthermore, how will the EC deal with the Soviet-successor states in the Commonwealth of Independent States, and the former Soviet allies in eastern Europe? Do uncertainties about the future of NATO, French or British strategy, Middle East peace and petroleum supplies, or ethnic nationalism and economic crises in the East increase or diminish prospects for a coordinated West European security policy either inside or outside the Community? In the process of answering these questions, it will become apparent that the interest groups and coalitions pushing toward and away from such coordination are subnational, national, and transnational. Certain of the initiatives, especially those in the European Parliament, also involve euro-institution-building *per se*, while others relate to Europe's continued technological viability as well as its foreign policy coherence.

Background Developments

The main initiatives for greater West European integration came both from the European Commission and Parliament, but included certain intergovernmental proposals as well. Increased pressures for European union generally coincided with the direct EP election of 1979; but renewed stirrings of interest in joint security policies and weapon procurement can be traced to 1978 with a WEU study claiming that the West European NATO arms market could be economical even without arms exports to the Third World. Such joint security approaches, largely based on economic, budgetary, and euro-institutional incentives, would prove politically difficult, however, because only four states produced most of Europe's weapons, because national governments varied in force preferences, and because the Rome Treaty, in addition to restricting security concerns, allowed states to protect their security information and their domestic arms industries (Pearson 1988).

In the early 1980s, EC commissioners, conscious of the growing importance of high technology, of a mounting economic recession, and of the American and Japanese "challenges," advocated greater technological collaboration within the Community. Armaments manufacture, as a reflection of high technology and as a leading export sector, was included in such proposed collaborative endeavors. Impending enlargement of the Community also made institutional reform more timely.

Meanwhile, the West German and Italian governments collaborated on a draft treaty, the Genscher–Colombo initiative of 1981, aimed at strengthening EPC, the foreign policy arm of the Community, along with legal and cultural coordination. A secretariat was included, existing procedures of foreign policy formation codified, and limited majority voting introduced (a veto could still be implemented in writing). Indeed, this initiative related to earlier French Gaullist suggestions regarding "Europe of the Fatherlands," in which Paris would have played a prominent leadership role in a coordinated and assertive foreign policy (Haywood 1989, 124).

In this draft EPC treaty, two controversial provisions were added on security, and were to find their way as well into later EC reform proposals and the SEA:

(1) recognition of the benefits of closer cooperation on European security to strengthen a European identity, and readiness to coordinate more closely on economic and political aspects of security; and (2) determination to maintain "technological and industrial conditions" necessary for security. The former appears to represent concerns about American leadership, the same concerns expressed in the subsequent 1984 revival of WEU machinery. The latter provision was seen by critics as sanctioning common European arms production and security standards. Even these provisions, however, did not go beyond prevailing practice or levels of commitment in prior agreements. Nothing here would mandate a common Community security policy even in the economic and political, let alone the military, spheres. However, common arms procurement and R&D in space and defense sectors theoretically could emerge if envisioned common industrial policies were to materialize (*Bulletin of the European Community* 1985, 16; European Community, *Official Journal*, December 11, 1985, pp. 112 and 176; McSweeney 1988).

Members of the European Parliament also sought a greater *raison d'être* in enhanced legislative powers (Lodge 1986; 1985, 204–207; Scharpf 1985; Verminck 1985; Hrbek and Laufer 1986; Chaban-Delmas 1985; Albertini 1985; Chiti-Batelli 1986). While such powers would not have been much bolstered by the Genscher–Colombo proposal, the Parliament responded in 1984 with its own draft treaty on European Union (EUT), derived through extensive committee consultation with interest groups and scholars, which was submitted to the member-states. The EUT entailed a federalized western European government, centered on a bicameral (EP and Council) legislative and budgetary authority, and on the Commission as a powerful driving force for that legislation. Confederal aspects were retained in the area of foreign policy cooperation, and separate states were to retain authority in matters more efficiently handled at the national level. The Commission followed in 1985 with a White Paper on the technical implementation of an enlarged euromarket, identifying 300 needed directives (Ferri 1984; Wille 1985).

In response to this bold initiative for European union, and in part to preempt or control that impetus, the European Council, representing the member governments, substituted the Single European Act in December of 1985 (signed in January 1986). Based loosely on the Council's Dooge Committee Report (1985) on institutional structure, which itself contained features of both the Genscher–Colombo and EUT approaches, SEA had some features in common with EUT, such as enhanced EP budgetary authority and qualified majority voting on many issues in the Council. However, in retaining unanimity principles on important policy matters and in denying Parliament full legislative (initiative and amending) authority, SEA fell well short of union. Indeed, the Danish prime minister at the time expressed satisfaction with SEA since it did not involve *any* erosion of sovereignty (*Bulletin of the European Community* 1985, 18).

SEA appeared aimed mainly at facilitating industrial, commercial, technological and trade development through the free movement of capital and products, and secondarily, persons, that is, the completion of the Rome Treaty (although there would be no legal sanctions for not meeting the new 1992 deadline). Heads of state rejected Commission and EP proposals for greater monetary coordination, and provided for only unanimous voting on most matters of fiscal (monetary and tax) policy, free movement of persons, or rights and interests of labor. Only taxes needed to bring about the internal market would be harmonized (i.e., turnover, excise, and other indirect taxes), and foreign policy coordination remained voluntary. Thus, the Council seized upon the programmatic approach of the 1976 Tindemans Report to the EP, which stressed loose Community cooperation in foreign, security, and monetary policy, rather than the more revolutionary constitutional approach of the EUT, as enunciated by the Spinelli Report to EP from its Committee on Institutional Affairs in 1983 (Schoutheete 1986; Lodge 1985, 1986).

Key reservations about European unification were voiced by Britain, Denmark, Greece, and Ireland, and these views still complicate the evolution toward a eurosecurity policy. The British government reluctantly accepted SEA as a commercial venture and in part for EPC, but impeded moves toward supranational decision making and monetary union (Aeppel 1988; Baum 1988; Yemma 1988b; "Euro Summit," *German Tribune* 1988). Although tentatively supporting SEA, Danish political leaders were concerned about being caught up in the foreign policy initiatives and, particularly in the security policy area, in the military-industrial complex of the dominant European powers, France, Germany, and Britain. SEA provisions about relations with states outside the Community in part were inserted to satisfy interests, such as Denmark's, in continued ties to European Free Trade Association (EFTA). The Greek government and political parties voiced similar concerns about large state dominance, extra-EC ties, and uneven development policies. The Greek Left was especially dubious of increased NATO militarization and defense collaboration. Ireland found difficulties for its neutrality and inter-Irish policies in close coordination with NATO members, and particularly with the UK.

Thus, to preserve consensus within the Council, states more supportive of EUT, such as Italy and BENELUX, and those at least lukewarm, France (worried about EPC) and Germany (concerned about agricultural subsidies and monetary restrictions), settled on the far less ambitious SEA.[1] Continuation of the "Luxembourg Compromise," that is, veto power in the Council for states with overriding national interests at stake, was a necessary concession to states such as Denmark and Britain, although other EC members, including France, were increasingly willing to override vetoes (namely Britain's) on matters considered tangential to issues under general agreement (Haywood 1989, 127–29).

In reaching this accord to complete the internal EC market by 1992, the Council also endorsed Commission proposals on technical cooperation, or as some termed it, a "Technological Community." This was understood to include support for the French EUREKA civil high-technology project, although no specific project references or funding commitments were made in SEA, and although EUREKA remained open to states outside the Community. A parallel military technology project subsequently was launched outside the EC, known as the European Research and Technology Program (EUCLID) under the NATO-related Independent European Programme Group in 1990 (see Garnham, chapter 11 in this volume).

The Security Policy Debate

Aspects of security policy coordination were slipped into the various reports underlying SEA, and into the final act itself. In fact, Britain seemed more interested in defense policy coordination than other aspects of EPC, while German, Dutch, and Italian officials wanted joint foreign policy actions, and political/economic more than security coordination. The French were somewhat skeptical of Community efforts to define common security policy, although Paris and Bonn already had established a permanent consultative committee (1982) to begin bilateral security policy coordination (Feld 1989, 152–54). Under SEA, common positions arising from EPC consultations would be communicated to security institutions such as NATO and WEU. Thus, closer security cooperation would be feasible, and nothing in SEA was meant to impede membership in these other security organizations.

While the topic remained controversial, a number of EP committee reports in the past decade have advocated greater security policy coordination, and in December 1989 the Parliament affirmed its support for "parallel development of common foreign and security policies" under EPC by a vote of 275–33 (eight abstentions; see European Parliament, *EP News* 1989). Some of the earlier committee reports also had been influential, though not decisive, in the debate over EUT. As a result of doubts about U.S. strategic and euromissile policy, the EP Political Affairs Committee, in its second "Klepsch Report" (April 1984), recommended a common EC stance on security policy *vis-à-vis* Washington. Irish, Danish, Greek, and other MEPs (members of European Parliament) expressed strong reservations, and these committee recommendations were not explicitly included in the draft EUT, adopted in February 1984. Instead, economic and political aspects of security, all the EC at that time felt comfortable treating, were lumped into the sphere of political cooperation in foreign policy. But under EUT, the European Council would have been authorized to extend this sphere to cover other aspects of security policy, namely arms procurement and sales, as well as defense and disarmament (European Community, *Debates* 1–313, 1984b, 108–109; European Parliament, *Working Documents*, January 1984).

In light of the recently changed European political map, one wonders whether the aborted EUT impetus toward an EC military security role will be renewed, and whether the suspicions of states such as Britain, Denmark, Greece, and

Ireland have been reduced or reinforced by a reunified Germany and reduced super-power presence. Incentives could develop for an integrated EC voice on arms control and territorial issues, particularly as a subgroup of CSCE. Prospective EC membership for Austria and other neutral states could complicate such incentives, although with a changed or reduced NATO mandate, some of the EC disharmony on security approaches and reticence to deal with the topic could erode.

There is already long precedent for such security harmonization and consultation even under the restricted provisions of EPC; in 1983 the EC foreign ministers discussed the INF talks in Geneva and the stationing of Pershing and cruise missiles under NATO. Similarly, common EC positions have been attempted regarding UN disarmament negotiations and in prior meetings of CSCE (Kirchner 1989, 3–4). The changing incentives for smaller or more suspicious EC members also are reflected in Greece's reduced opposition to security coordination upon assuming the Council Presidency in 1988. As Western Europe has emerged from the U.S. security blanket, Greece has gained interest in steering both European and American policy in desired directions vis-à-vis Turkey. Therefore, matters of lingering national interest interact with European regional concerns potentially to increase the tendency to use EPC as a security vehicle. This is reinforced for states such as Britain and Denmark, traditionally worried, albeit in different ways, about patterns of dominance and dependence and Germany's role in the Community.

If we want to understand the likely position of EC governments as the security debate unfolds, we must appreciate the diversity of actors and their positions even in the evolution of SEA. For example, in the early stages, the importance of EUT for security was interpreted differently by various national and transnational political factions. In the words of one German Christian Democrat in the European Parliament, EUT contained only "a nod in the direction of security policy." However, the wording was permissive enough to allow a Conservative to observe that the Council could extend the role of the Union beyond merely political/economic aspects of security "to the very teeth of defense itself" if it should wish. A Socialist saw the draft treaty as giving Europe a common direction, and moving it toward equal partner status in the North Atlantic Community at a time of U.S.-European strain. This would be crucial in allowing Europe's future security to be determined in Europe. A French Liberal envisioned a future president of a United States of Europe moving decisively, on the basis of a unified European nuclear strike force, to end arms races and boost solidarity with the Third World: "As high technology in industry conditions economic and social well-being, so high technology in armaments conditions diplomatic influence" (European Community, *Debates* 1–313, 1984b, 31–33, 80–81).

While U.S.-European strategic strains formed a backdrop for EUT, more immediate economic (especially unemployment) and political concerns, including EC budgetary and programmatic stalemate at the Athens Council summit, were the driving forces. Scientific and technological advancement were seen as the keys for European resurgence, world power, and by implication, security:

> The level of power and degree of independence of each State today in international affairs is commensurate with the level of scientific and technological development of that State. If we succeed in being competitive in the new key sectors we shall be treated with dignity, and as equals. (Statement by Zecchino, European Community, *Debates* 1–309 1984, 35)

With the substitution of SEA for EUT in 1985, the Council made additional somewhat vague references to necessary eurosecurity preparations under political cooperation (noted above). In parliamentary debates concerning SEA, the technological rationale for security policy again was emphasized, along with new European assertiveness. Although certain states and political parties expressed misgivings about the wisdom of SEA (and particularly the diminished EP role in comparison to EUT) and/or of greater integration, the fundamental political consensus to support the agreement was based largely on two perspectives. Parties on the Right, that is, Conservatives, Christian Democrats, and nationalists, pointed to the technological-commercial-security benefits, and to defense of European civilization with a strong separate voice in NATO. SEA supporters on the Left tended to stress economic and employment benefits, and to voice suspicions both of militarized technology and American security leadership.

Various EC governments and political parties have continued forming new perspectives on security, in these days of the dissolved Soviet threat and diminished American leadership, as well as uncertainties about the fate of political and economic reforms in Eastern Europe, and events in nearby regions such as the Middle East. Most European governments, with the traditional exception of France, long have avoided or opposed increased defense budgets. Indeed many have come to see the U.S.-Japanese technological/trade threat as Europe's primary security concern. Even French analysts speculate that post–cold war European security concerns will subordinate defense *per se* to broader political and technological questions. At least prior to the Iraqi crisis, French officials had begun to grapple with appropriate force reductions, especially in light of conventional arms talks. However, spokesmen such as Defense Minister Chevenement still assert a global French role and commensurate force requirements, including a fully independent French strategic capability and the nonnegotiability of the *force de frappe* as long as the superpowers do not reduce their own strategic forces to levels comparable to France (LaFranchi 1990, 4).

Although the mission of the joint French–German military brigade (composed mainly of second line troops because of Germany's NATO ties) remained rather murky as it was inaugurated in 1988, the symbolic precedent was striking, particularly in its status outside the NATO joint command. The accompanying Franco-German Defense and Security Council, with secretariat in Paris, was established to coordinate defense and disarmament policy and further promote joint weapons production. Indeed it would appear that the Mitterrand government is extremely committed to Franco-German economic partnership, and concomitantly to strategic partnership as a foundation of the new European Community (Feld 1989, 155–56).

However, the future of joint Franco-German security institutions, and the ultimate Franco-German willingness to extend *force de frappe* doctrines to a unified Germany remain clouded by French policy traditions, by German anti-nuclear sentiments, NATO attachments, and financial commitments, by Central European uncertainties, and by a presumably declining Soviet nuclear threat. The Federal Republic traditionally has been reluctant to link its defense exclusively to one or two countries, and has sought wider partnerships. France has been reluctant to commit forces to anything other than territorial French defense (Garn-ham 1988, ch. 3). Britain, as both a nuclear and continental power, clearly has interests in such future partnerships as well, as do Italy and the smaller NATO states. Therefore, while complications remain, institutions such as those embodied in the Defense and Security Council or EPC could afford politically useful strategic alternatives for Germany in linkage to western Europe *versus* North America.

Any moves toward wider EC security policy will depend in large part on how assertive the "new Germany" can be, and on a tenuous balance among political forces in various member-states. Among these forces are those taking pro-technology and those taking environmental and antidefense stances. On the extreme Right, euro-nationalists and reactionaries call for increased European military power and security collaboration. They speak of a crisis for European civilization that requires separate states to coalesce, defend themselves technologically from American and Japanese penetration, and form a European pillar within NATO at least as strong as the U.S. MEP Le Pen of France, for example, has lamented the lack of external border defenses as internal European frontiers are dismantled: "Europe must be a power in the world . . . there can be no power without common defense . . . a nuclear umbrella should be erected over the territory of the E.C." by the two European nuclear powers. He further has advocated "proposals for an armaments production plan and a common space weapons plan" (European Community, *Debates* 2–346, 1986, 56–57). Presumably such zest for major defense initiatives is not widely shared in the "post–cold war" Europe.

The center-right parties, and especially the Christian Democrats, have seen SEA less as a defense vehicle than as a way out of perceived economic stagnation and technological vulnerability, which they also interpret as security problems. They tend to stress the free movement of capital, inflation control, progress toward monetary union, the internal market, and advanced technological projects, which will both strengthen Europe internationally and ultimately provide jobs. As one Dutch Christian Democrat put it, with a large enough market in which to sell its high-technology products, Europe would be able to keep up with the U.S. and Japan "the European way . . . the social way," with proper levels of social welfare benefits, increased employment, redistribution of work and reduction of hours (European Community, *Debates* 2–363, 1988, 208). A German colleague also noted that,

> The new world structure—Japan has 160m. inhabitants—needs a new kind of assertion for us Europeans. In the long term even Denmark can guarantee its individuality, its originality, only through a united Europe. (European Community, *Debates* 2–333, 1985a, 177)

While many on the left agree with the need for a strong European voice in (or out of) NATO, and for technological advances, they have stressed, even more than Christian Democrats, economic and social concerns as opposed to military projects and power. They have been suspicious and critical of American strategic policy, and have tended to opt for a separate, some even say neutral European voice, conceivably with minimal or passive rather than extensive European defense preparations. Socialists (not necessarily including the French) tend to be suspicious of military production and corporate conglomerates *per se*, but look to multinational European enterprises to provide employment in the "post-industrial" and "postmilitary" era. Some fear that "Technological Community" projects, outside direct EC control and with a bureaucracy all their own, would benefit mainly large firms with no necessary commitment to European labor and with projects spilling over into the military sphere (European Community, *Debates* 2–333, 1985a, 167–68).

The traditional extreme Left, the Communists, at least in Italy and France, have wavered between suspicion of and in some cases near enthusiasm for West European unity. Some even criticized SEA for not going far enough. Those Communists who support defense preparations generally have advocated European solutions in the weapons economy, whereby the interests of national defense firms, such as Westlands Helicopter in the UK, would take second place to Europe's joint needs to compete worldwide and to the interests of workers. Hence, euroweapons consortia could be developed, under governmental auspices and EC supervision, to keep production facilities from withering or falling into the hands of the Americans or exploitative national firms. Italian Communists also have advocated positive responses to East European and Chinese commercial and technological offers, which is in line with their traditional support for technology as a potential benefit to society. Some French Communists have worried, however, that SEA provisions do not clearly address unemployment, industrial and social policy, regional policy, and peace/disarmament. At the same time, troublesome potential benefits for multinational corporations and U.S. defense contractors, both in the unified European market and in EPC treaty provisions for coordination and preparedness regarding political/economic aspects of security, have been noted (European Community, *Debates* 2–333, 1985a, 151).

In general, leftist supporters of EUREKA and a Technological Community have tended to see these as nonmilitary alternatives to the American SDI programs, while rightist supporters have tended to see them as SDI competitors. Though SDI's momentum has slowed, there is no significant disillusionment about R&D for high technology. The question of where weapons technology fits in the midst of declining worldwide markets has not yet been worked out. Leftist critics of EUREKA have seen the project as inextricably linked to a highly militarized French technology program. Rightist critics saw it as inadequate to the task of making Europe the third superpower (European Community, *Debates* 2–333, 1985a, 144–61). Nevertheless, the EC has been ready to proceed with such projects for lack of ready alternatives and at least to mount some major technological initiatives.

Moderate parties of both the Left and Right, as well as European bureaucrats also have voiced both hopes for and doubts about the adequacy of SEA in bringing about the technological advances considered essential for Europe's future. Commissioners have lamented the lack of majority voting provisions for funding and contracting within the proposed EC Technological Community. They argue that this will impede necessary joint ventures (European Community, *Debates* 2–330, 1985b, 47–49). Some Conservatives and Socialists have doubted that EUREKA has the funding and focus necessary to compete with the United States and Japan. While companies may be able to carry off coordinated development and marketing of specific "high-tech" products, there is little coordination of "upstream" primary research, focused on funding the "best," most up-to-date projects *vis-à-vis* Japan and the United States.

Although proponents, especially those in the EC Commission, of a joint approach to arms production and weapons procurement have stressed the mandate afforded by SEA, their legal grounds remain controversial and weak. SEA wording was a compromise set at the minimal common denominator, which provided for British and French reservations about an EC Commission role in structuring arms production and procurement, together with Irish, Danish, and Dutch concerns about being swamped by large arms producing states. However, again changing political and economic incentives and pressures impinge upon legal considerations; the fact is that most European arms producers and ministries are responding to declining defense markets by promoting massive "restructuring," which involves corporate mergers and acquisitions both within and across national lines and rationalization of production overcapacities. Inevitably this involves arms production in the overall single European market (Brzoska 1990; Pearson 1990).

Europeans sometimes cite their own relatively successful positions in space, telecommunications, and nuclear technology, but tend to see themselves as falling dangerously behind the United States and/or Japan in biotechnology, data processing, and other crucial fields. Increasing technological dependence on the United States and Japan in such areas could, it is feared, make Europe a technopolitical colony. The lack of a unified market, along with disparate rules, standards, research, and contracting, and failure to generate American-style giant "high-tech" firms (IBM, AT&T), to nurture innovative small firms, and to develop university-corporate partnerships all were identified as basic reasons for these disadvantages. In this, the Parliament's Committee on Energy, Research, and Technology joined the Commission in arguing that while "we have heard talk . . . of military technology and civilian technology . . . [t]here is no difference." Large-scale multinational projects are thought to be needed—if not EUREKA, then something else, especially concentrating in biotech, space (presumably including lasers and optics), and electronics. (See Poniatowski, European Community, *Debates* 2–333, 1985a, 18, 30–36.)

The debate on both the ethics and feasibility of military *versus* civilian technology in the "new Europe" has become quite pointed. Socialists and some Communists have argued that science, which struggled for years to free itself from the Church and from despots, should not now be thrown to the military. Some Danish and Dutch parties further maintain that high technology itself is a false and dehumanizing god, and have joined Greek Communists in arguing for "appropriate technologies" and the prerogatives of small states and enterprises (European Community, *Debates* 2–333, 1985a, 24–25, 37–41).

But these views and cautions appeared to remain slightly in the minority, at least prior to the momentous 1989–90 eastern European developments. Christian Democrats tried to portray technology, in providing goods and services, as the basis for humanity, rather than as dehumanizing, and maintained that religion-based European culture depended on being able to reply to SS–20s with more than bows and arrows.[2] Such views now seem more difficult to maintain when the SS–20s themselves no longer dot the horizon.

The confusion about whether Europe can proceed with the development of essentially nonmilitary high technology has been reflected in the committees reporting to Parliament, as they patched together wording to satisfy all major parties. Thus, for example, in the draft resolution from the Committee on Energy, Research, and Technology in 1985, controversial paragraphs called for focus on nonmilitary aims and rejection of SDI research, as well as partnerships with countries (unlike the United States at that time) not restricting technology transfers in joint ventures. Yet, immediately following were paragraphs calling for European coordination with the United States and Japan in research going beyond fusion and space, both of which clearly have military implications. Ultimately, the EP struck the anti-SDI paragraph from the resolution by a vote of 156 to 153, and yet failed to insert a pro-SDI paragraph in its place (European Parliament, *Working Documents* 1985; European Community, *Debates*, 2–330, 1985b, 78ff). Again, reduced European tensions might ease such ambiguity slightly, since Washington presumably will apply fewer pressures to restrict technological transfers on security grounds.

Thus, European leaders want to distinguish themselves from what are seen as the pitfalls of heavy U.S. reliance on military R&D, and yet must grapple with the size of U.S. R&D expenditures and corporate entities. They would prefer to put a "humane face" on high technology, but also realize the close connection between civilian and military applications and the difficulties of racing against countries (United States and Japan) with a head start (Narjes, European Community, *Debates* 2–330, 1985b). They want to include states outside the EC in joint ventures, as with EFTA or eastern bloc states, and Lome Convention or other LDC participants, as well with the United States and other OECD partners. Additionally, they see less threat warranting, and fewer resources available for military R&D.

EC policy statements have continued to stress civilian technology projects, in order to avoid controversies within the Community. Yet, given past production, or overproduction trends, existing or planned multinational partnerships, the need for economies of scale, and declining East–West security restrictions, there remains temptation to subsidize military technology and to become involved in military production and sales projects outside the EC. Prior to the East European thaw, the eurogroup within NATO had agreed that in view of common security interests, the United States must be assured special access to the EC internal market ("Spending," *German Tribune* 1988). This rationale now has lost relevance, but if the deeper motivation was to gain joint technological advantages, then there will still be room for U.S. investment and further EC openings to neutral and East European states, as well as to Japan and the Third World.[3]

Especially in the realm of joint high-technology weapon production, given huge R&D investment requirements, pressure will build to expand the security sphere of SEA, as envisioned in EPC and by various EP committees. Since both West and East Europe as well as the CIS share technological disadvantages *vis-à-vis* the United States and Japan, the logic would entail even joint defense product ventures with the East, although technical and financial disparities act as roadblocks. The reality of Soviet MiGs landing for the first time in Britain for promotion at air shows and of French cosmonauts joining their Soviet counterparts in joint space explorations seem but a hint of things to come, especially since all these developments occurred before the Berlin Wall was breached (Hettne 1988).

U.S. corporations also are being forced by receding defense budgets to shift strategy, either toward more civil and less military production, or toward increased international joint ventures. On the one hand, the cold war thaw lessens the attractiveness of military production investments, but on the other hand it erodes some of the barriers to broad international sharing of military technology. This is reinforced by the reality of continued regional conflicts, as in the Persian Gulf. Joint ventures between North American, West, Central, East and South European firms may offer particular advantages in penetrating markets, particularly in certain parts of the developing world. Japanese links to European defense firms also will make it increasingly difficult for Washington to dictate the terms of joint U.S.-Japanese weapons projects (as in recent debates about a Japanese fighter plane). Hence, through leaner but more transnational defense production, as well as through debates about the strategic future of Germany, NATO, regional security issues, and the Atlantic–Pacific partnership, the EC would appear to be driven inexorably toward a more assertive security policy role. Much depends, however, on whether the overall difficulties in SEA implementation can be surmounted.

Conclusions

Security policy has entered the planning for the Single European Act mainly through a rather unbridled multiparty (of course with notable exceptions and growing environmental concerns) enthusiasm for the saving graces of technology in Europe's future. In response to perceived EC policy stagnation, eroding competitiveness, and persistent unemployment levels, technology was seized upon as something of a cure-all. With structural reforms to clear the way for, and increased investment in high-technology partnerships, Europe was expected to regain world stature and influence, repel foreign penetration and domination, and employ the multitudes. Along with disappearance of the Soviet threat, rejuvenation of the Western European Union, and growing French–German strategic consultation, trust grew that Europe might be freed from the vagaries of U.S. strategic leadership as well. Finally, Europe's redrawn political map and Middle East policy concerns bring a new set of incentives about coordinating security policy through EPC.

However, apart from the uncertainties of overreliance on technology *per se* (e.g., possible future energy and environmental crises), certain structural contradictions still impede the fulfillment of these hopes and dreams. Since parties have agreed on SEA and the importance of technology for different reasons, developments could prompt disillusionment. If technological projects and enlarged markets include major military applications, or fail to stimulate employment of European workers, leftist parties and smaller states might withdraw their support. If, on the other hand, decisions for technological funding are delayed, if a "dirigist" EC approach to Technological Community regulations is adopted, or if projects do not produce breakthroughs enhancing Europe's competitiveness, parties on the Right and conservative governments could lose faith. If the benefits of technology and new joint ventures are derived mainly by large British, French, or German firms, other member-states could cry "foul." And finally, if Germany's EC attachments are threatened, or if Germany becomes too dominant, a number of neighboring states would be alarmed about the viability of SEA.

Community decision-making authority in SEA remains weak; the coalition supporting the plan is subject to fragmentation; opinions on the wisdom of military projects in SEA are nearly evenly divided; and pressures to enlarge the Community cause uncertainties. In particular, as it is not clear that military and civilian technology can be separated fully, it is also not clear that European Community technology and/or security can be separated effectively from the rest of western and eastern Europe, and the Western Hemisphere or the Orient. If the U.S. and Japanese challenges are seen to persist or increase, if Washington becomes increasingly preoccupied with the Pacific or increasingly at odds with Europe over agricultural or military policy, or if NATO falls apart, new thinking about European security could take on continentwide dimensions, conceivably leaving an EC role as only a subregional caucus. On the other hand, with each new member and with successful implementation of SEA, EC prominence as a stable institution is enhanced.

The EC market is indeed large, but also inevitably will absorb products and techniques from other regions. And as a security community, the EC has yet to develop machinery and structures to play a prominent collective defense or eurowide security role. It must formulate Franco-German and British defense coordination and come to terms with prosperous neutrals, EFTA, and poorer states on the periphery. In the momentum toward a larger Community or wider community ties, however, lies the danger of financial, if not security, overcommitment.

SEA has provisions for expansion and outside connections. But key questions remain. Is size and commitment enough to stimulate technological "takeoff" among twelve or more disparate states? How can West Europe emerge as an industrial and political, let alone a military superpower, without a functioning West European government? SEA provisions for small subgroups of states to go ahead with joint technological and security projects if full EC participation proves infeasible reflect prudent planning for uncertain commitments and policy disagreements.

Security policy offers an example of these dilemmas in cases such as the Westlands Helicopter decision, in which a firm's own preferences, and those of its national government, ran counter to the preferences of other states and institutions in the EC. In the end, American penetration of the European defense helicopter market was sustained and enlarged because of the primacy of national decision-making centers and the priorities of those evaluating technological and funding capabilities. These decision-making prerogatives have not fundamentally been diminished under SEA, although lately they have been invoked more by states with weaker European commitments, such as Britain and Denmark, than by the Community at large.

Thus, while many, especially on the Right, had hoped for a West European pillar in NATO equal to the United States, that prospect appears increasingly complicated if not irrelevant, at least until the future of Atlantic cooperation and eurodefense is determined, and something more on the order of EUT is adopted for Community governance. Nevertheless, enthusiasm for increased integration remains high, and the impetus for a West European strategic alternative to NATO, as seen in various EP committee reports, has grown, brewing in conflicts over security policy and SDI implications, U.S. technological dominance (stealth technology is the latest area where sharing appears minimal), the urge throughout NATO for defense budget cuts, arms control initiatives in the post-Soviet era and the need for coordinated responses, developments in eastern Europe, and uncertainties over markets and requirements for conventional weapons.

SEA contains language legitimizing and conceivably expanding collaborative European weapons production and export consortia. However, in the midst of collaboration is continued national armament production (sometimes, as in the case of French aircraft, competing with collaborative projects), persistent, though declining, myths of national arms autarky (seen, for example, in the British decision to produce a new generation of tanks; Baum 1988a), and persistently depressed LDC arms markets outside the Middle East (conceivably the Iraqi crisis and declining superpower competition could restimulate arms purchases in such areas as South and Southeast Asia).

SEA, along with the revival of WEU, may indeed be the first steps toward greater western European strategic self-reliance; uncertainties about Germany could hasten rather than retard integration as France presses to link her neighbor ever more securely to the West. But SEA *per se*, basically a technocommercial venture—even in the security area—seems unlikely, in its present form and in the near term, to spill over into full strategic collaboration or political unity among the EC membership.

Notes

1. Depending upon the issue, under SEA the European Parliament would have a "consultative, collaborative, or joint action" role in relation to the Council. Collaborative legislative powers would allow EP deliberation on Commission proposals before referral to Council; consultation with EP would take place if Council disagreed. However, joint legislative action would allow merely delay of Council action; the EP could only accept or reject initiatives or propose changes, rather than amend legislation. Council could override EP rejection with a unanimous vote. See Lodge 1986, 214–18.

2. Of course, much political opportunism can be reflected in these philosophical positions; for example, the Christian Democratic mayor of Toulouse, a French city increasingly oriented toward high-technology investment, in 1985 called for European manned space shuttles and a coordinated space policy. French Communists, while critical of military applications, managed to approve certain high-technology projects with potential military spinoffs, such as Ariane, Airbus, and Esprit, which also happened to be French initiated (European Community, *Debates* 2–333, 1985a, 36–37).

3. Note reports of an impending aerospace merger between Daimler of Germany and Mitsubishi of Japan. Both parties are seeking ways to offset the gigantic American dominance of this industry, to overcome their own inexperience in production, and to take advantage of market and labor access (National Public Radio report, 7 March 1990).

References

Aeppel, Timothy. 1988. "British Balk at Attempts to Create European Central Bank." *Christian Science Monitor* (June 29).
Albertini, Mario. 1985. "L'Europa sulla soglia dell'unione." *Il Politico*, 50, 4:557–69.

Baum, Julian. 1988a. "Britain Can Make its Own Tanks, Thanks." *Christian Science Monitor* (December 23), p. 11.

Baum, Julian. 1988b. "Thatcher Attack on European Unity: More Bark than Bite?" *Christian Science Monitor* (September 22), p. 9.

Baum, Julian. 1988c. "Thatcher Puts Limits on a United Europe." *Christian Science Monitor* (July 29), pp. 1, 8.

Brzoska, Michael. 1990. "The Structure of Arms Production in Western Europe beyond 1992." Paper presented to the Conference on Restructuring of Arms Industries in Western Europe. Hamburg, Germany (June).

Bulletin of the European Community. 1985. Vol. 18, no. 11.

Chaban-Delmas, Jacques. 1985. "Perspectiven fur die politische Zukunft Europas." *Europa-Archiv.* Vol. 40 (March 10), pp. 121–32.

Chiti-Batelli, Andrea. 1986. "Riflessioni sulle vicende del progetto di Unione Europea." *Affari esteri.* Vol. 69 (January), pp. 60–70.

"Euro Summit Shows Limits to Any Leap Foward." 1988. *German Tribune* (December 11), pp. 1–2.

European Community. 1984a. *Debates.* No. 1–30.

European Community. 1984b. *Debates.* No. 1–313.

European Community. 1985a. *Debates.* No. 2–333.

European Community. 1985b. *Debates.* No. 2–330.

European Community. 1986. *Debates.* No. 2–346.

European Community. 1988. *Debates.* No. 2–363.

European Community. 1985. *Official Journal of the European Communities. Debates of the European Parliament.* No. 2–333 (December 11).

European Parliament. 1984. *Working Documents, 1983–84.* Doc. 1–1200/83/B (January 30).

European Parliament. 1985. *Working Documents, 1985–86.* Doc. A2–109/85/A (September 30).

European Parliament. 1989. *EP News* (December 11–15).

Feld, Werner. 1989. "Franco-German Military Cooperation and European Unification." *Journal of European Integration.* Vol. 12 (Winter/Spring), pp. 152–56.

Ferri, Mauro. 1984. "Le projet de Traite d'Union Europeene." *Annales de Droit de Liege.* Vol. 29, no. 4, pp. 275–91.

Garnham, David. 1988. *The Politics of European Defense Cooperation: Germany, France, Britain, and America.* Cambridge, MA: Ballinger, ch. 3.

German Tribune. 1988. "Spending Dominates Defence Agenda." December 11, p. 2.

Greenhouse, Steven. 1988. "Making Europe a Mighty Market." *New York Times* (May 22), sec. 3.

Haywood, Elizabeth Z. 1989. "The French Socialists and European Institutional Reform." *Journal of European Integration.* Vol. 12 (Winter/Spring), pp. 124–29.

Hettne, Bjorn. 1988. *Europe: Dimensions of Peace.* London: Zed Books and United Nations University.

Hrbek, Rudolf, and Thomas Laufer. 1986. "Die Einheitliche Integrationprozess." *Europa-Archiv.* Vol. 41 (March 25), pp. 173–84.

Kaslow, Amy. 1990. "European Community Sizes Up Its Growing Voice in Geopolitics." *Christian Science Monitor* (March 7), pp. 1–2.

Kirchner, Emil J. 1989. "Has the Single European Act Opened the Door for a European Security Policy?" *Journal of European Integration.* Vol. 13 (Fall), pp. 2–4.

Kolodziej, Edward A. 1987. *Making and Marketing Arms: The French Experience and its Implications for the International System.* Princeton, NJ: Princeton University Press.

Kolodziej, Edward A., and Frederic S. Pearson. 1989. "The Political Economy of Making and Marketing Arms: A Test for the Systemic Imperatives of Order and Welfare."

Occasional Papers, No. 8904. St. Louis: Center for International Studies, University of Missouri-St. Louis.

LaFranchi, Howard. 1990. "France Ponders Military Changes." *Christian Science Monitor* (February 5), p. 4.

Lodge, Juliet. 1985. "European Union: A Qualitative Leap Forward?" *World Today*. Vol. 41 (November), pp. 204–207.

Lodge, Juliet. 1986. "The Single European Act: Towards a New Euro-Dynamism?" *Journal of Common Market Studies*. Vol. 24 (March), pp. 203–23.

McSweeney, Bill. 1988. "The European Neutrals and the European Community." *Journal of Peace Research*. Vol. 25 (September), pp. 205–21.

Moravcsik, Andrew. 1990. "The European Armaments Industry at the Crossroads." *Survival*. Vol. 32 (January/February), pp. 65–85.

National Public Radio Report. March 7, 1990.

Pearson, Frederic S. 1988. "Problems and Prospects of Arms Transfer Limitations among Second-Tier Suppliers: The Cases of France, the United Kingdom and the Federal Republic of Germany." In *Arms Transfer Limitations and Third World Security*, ed. Thomas Ohlson (Oxford: Oxford University Press and SIPRI), pp. 126–56.

Pearson, Frederic S. 1990. "Political Change and World Arms Export Markets: Impacts on the Structures of West European Arms Industries." Paper presented to the Conference on Restructuring of Arms Industries in Western Europe. Hamburg, Germany (June).

Scharpf, Fritz W. 1985. "Die Politikverflechtungs-Falle: Europaische Integration und deutscher Foderalismus im Vergleich." *Politische Vierteljahreschrift*. Vol. 26 (December), pp. 323–56.

Schoutheete, Philippe. 1986. "Le Rapport Tendemans: dix ans après." *Politique Etrangere*. Vol. 51 (Summer), pp. 527–38.

U.S. Department of State. 1988. "The European Community's Program for a Single Market in 1992." *Western Europe: Regional Brief*. (November).

Verminck, Mieke. 1985. "Le Parlement europeen de 1979 a 1984: La perte en potentiel de pouvoir d'une institution faible." *Res Publica*. Vol. 27, no. 2–3, pp. 287–95.

Wille, Emilio. 1985. "Federal and Confederal Aspects of the Draft Treaty Establishing the European Union." *Il Politico*. Vol. 50, no. 3, pp. 481–92.

Yemma, John. 1988a. " 'No Going Back' for EC, Biggest Market in the World." *Christian Science Monitor* (May 27), p. 75.

Yemma, John. 1988b. "Should Britain Throw the Pound into Europe's Monetary Pot?" *Christian Science Monitor* (June 10), p. 13.

11

European Defense Cooperation

The 1990s and Beyond

David Garnham

Recent events have remade the European security landscape. In April 1989, when NATO celebrated its fortieth anniversary, Alliance leaders expected the Atlantic Alliance to soldier on indefinitely as the principal structure for western European defense. By mid-1990, as the Soviet threat evaporated, even former Prime Minister Margaret Thatcher, an ardent hawk, conceded that "the cold war is over." This chapter examines prospects for European defense cooperation as America and Russia disengage from central Europe. The analysis stresses those variables that will shape future events.

The Strategic Environment for Defense Cooperation

The following factors will influence the pace and form of European defense cooperation during the next decade:

1. perceived threat
2. economic and technological competition
3. resource scarcity
4. balancing behavior
5. European union

In terms of the multilevel games metaphor discussed by Dale Smith and James Ray in their introductory chapter, four of these factors (excluding only resource scarcity) are predominately international (Level I). However, several of the other factors are strongly influenced by outputs from Level II games within the EC countries. This is particularly true of threat perceptions, perceptions of North American and Japanese competition, and balancing behavior.

The Threat

The Warsaw Pact is defunct. Troops of the former Soviet Union left Czechoslovakia and Hungary in 1991 and will quit eastern Germany by 1994. This transforms central Europe from a potential staging area for a Russian offensive against western Europe to a buffer zone that insulates NATO–Europe from any eastern threat.

As fear of the Soviet Union diminished throughout Europe and North America, marked differences emerged among the NATO members. As Table 11.1 indicates, the British and French publics were relatively more apprehensive (albeit less so than the Poles), and official thinking in London and Paris reflected this pessimism. Moreover, Level II factors loomed larger in some countries, for example, Britain compared to France, where opinion was more fragmented and partisan differences sharper.

Most NATO countries retain defense establishments whose structures evolved to counter the now defunct Soviet threat. Nonetheless, real defense expenditures by most member-states have ebbed for several years and are now declining more precipitously. The largest reductions are occurring in Germany. Even before unification, several significant cuts were enacted: The West German Bundeswehr contracted by 12 percent. In mid-1990, for the first time in the FRG's history, the defense budget declined (by 8 percent) in current deutschemarks, and despite unification this amount was frozen during 1991. In addition, the government shortened conscription from fifteen months to twelve effective 1 October 1990. Additionally, West Germany's traditionally high rate of conscientious objectors rose even higher, from 8.5 percent of draftees in the 1950s to 12 percent in 1988 (Schulte 1989) and then doubled between 1990 and 1991 (see "Number of Conscientious Objectors," 1992). It is also increasingly less likely that the Anglo-German-Italian-Spanish European Fighter Aircraft (EFA) program will proceed despite billions of dollars of sunk costs. EFA is opposed not only by the opposition Social Democrats but also by the Free Democrats from within the government coalition. In August 1991 Germany withdrew from the project to develop EFA's electronic warfare system. Even more significantly, between 1992 and 1994 the German Bundeswehr will decline from 454,000 to 370,000 men, the level set by Chancellor Kohl and then President Gorbachev in July 1990. Before unification, the combined German armies equaled 667,000.

In Britain, defense expenditures grew by 12 percent in constant pounds between 1980 and 1985, but then declined 6 percent between 1985 and 1989, and total British force levels dipped by 20,000 between 1985 and 1990. As a percentage of GNP, British military spending exceeded 5 percent in 1984–85 but declined below 4 percent during 1990–91. This is the lowest level of defense effort since World War II, but spending will fall 6 percent more in real terms between 1990–91 and 1994–95.

In July 1990, Defense Secretary Tom King announced the results of Options

Table 11.1

Opinion of Changes in Eastern Europe (percentage responding "yes")

Question: Do you think that the changes in Eastern Europe . . .

	Italy	FRG	Spain	Hungary	France	UK	Poland
Will guarantee a lasting peace in Europe?	58	44	42	40	31	30	17
Do not really remove the risks of serious conflict in Europe?	29	31	23	38	50	49	56
Could provoke another world war?	3	6	11	15	13	11	19
No response	10	19	24	7	6	10	8

Source: Isabel Hilton. February 19, 1990. "East Meets West as the Old Order Passes." *Independent,* p. 14. Surveys were conducted between 8 January and 30 January 1990 with national samples ranging from 941 (FRG) to 1,193 (Hungary) among respondents aged eighteen and older. For more details of the surveys, see: Roland Cayrol. 1990. "L'Est pense comme l'Ouest." *Le Journal des Elections,* 11:6–11.

for Change, the first defense review since 1981. Two of the three armored divisions will be withdrawn from Germany, and Royal Air Force (RAF) Germany will decline from 12,000 to 6,000. In October 1991, the House of Commons approved a 25 percent cut in British military forces during five years. Naval cuts include reducing destroyers and frigates from forty-eight to "around forty" and attack submarines from twenty-seven to sixteen. In addition, the MoD (minister of defense) canceled orders for thirty-three Tornado fighters and ordered only 130 Challenger 2 main battle tanks rather than 600 as contemplated earlier. British participation in the multinational EFA program, which would cost the UK approximately $11 billion, is also in doubt. Despite the magnitude of these cuts, Alan Clark (minister for defense procurement) and the Treasury advocated much larger reductions.

The Labour party's position is also important. Party conferences in 1989 and 1990 supported large cuts in military spending (£7 billion in 1990). But party leaders, who vividly recalled how public rejection of Labour's defense policy proposals undermined electoral support in three successive general elections, ignored these votes. Furthermore, Labour's close links to trade unions make it especially sensitive to the unemployment caused by canceled defense contracts. Nonetheless, a Labour government would probably accelerate the decline of British defense spending.

The pattern of America's recent defense spending closely resembles that of Britain. Real defense spending rose sharply during President Reagan's first term but fell steadily after the mid-1980s, and President Bush proposed further annual 2 percent reductions in real spending during each of the next four years. As a percentage of GDP, U.S. military spending has declined from over 6.5 percent to less than 5.5 percent; it will fall to 3.6 percent of GNP in 1996, and perhaps even lower. This is the lowest percentage since 1939, well below the Carter administration level of 5.1 percent of GNP during fiscal 1978 and 1979.

These spending cuts require overall military manpower reductions of nearly 25 percent. The U.S. Army, which has the largest number of European troops, will decline more than 30 percent. Meanwhile, the Defense Department closed or downsized 225 European military installations during 1991. By the end of this decade, not more than 100,000 American troops will remain in Europe, and the likely number is much lower. Even before the Soviet Union imploded, former Defense Secretary James Schlesinger, previously an advocate of large American deployments in Europe, recommended a "residual" force of around 50,000 (Apple 1990). And Senator Sam Nunn, chair of the Armed Services Committee, recommended 75,000 to 100,000.

France's response to the diminished Soviet threat was more cautious. When interviewed on Bastille Day 1990, President Mitterrand (1990) even said that the relevant issue was not reductions but how much to raise military spending to compensate for inflation. Especially among the conservative parties, Iraq's invasion of Kuwait intensified this wariness. Charles Pasqua (RPR) saw "instability" to both the East and the South, and François Fillon (RPR, former National Assembly defense committee chair) argued, "It is out of the question to diminish the defense budget."

Despite this opinion, French forces declined by 12 percent (50,000 men) during the 1980s, and a further reduction of 35,000 is planned over four years. Moreover, the defense burden dropped from 3.85 percent of GDP in 1981 to 3.4 percent of GDP in 1991. President Mitterrand also proposed reducing the period of conscription from twelve months to ten months.

Elsewhere, Belgium announced plans in December 1990 to reduce its forces in Germany to 3,500 (from 22,000) by the end of 1995 while downsizing Belgian armed forces from 82,000 to 66,000. Earlier, the Netherlands announced that 750 (of 5,500) Dutch troops in Germany would be withdrawn while reducing military spending by more than one billion dollars. Italy's defense budget has declined to 1.7 percent of GDP.

As the Soviet threat dissolved, alliance leaders began to defend NATO as necessary protection against "instability." After more than forty years of a fossilized cold war European order, the dizzying pace of change stunned policy makers and analysts. Although governments avoided premature commitments to novel frameworks, the obsession with instability became so distorted that in early 1990 Britain's defense ministry seemed to argue that the end of the cold war actually increased the security threat and justified more defense spending.

The principal sources of domestic and international instability in central and East Europe are unresolved national aspirations and the lack of democratic experience. The dissolution of the Soviet Union and Yugoslavia exemplifies domestic nationalities problems. Latent conflict between Hungary and Rumania illustrates the international dimension. Conflict in Rumania illuminates the difficulty of establishing democratic institutions on an authoritarian base.

It is not clear how NATO can help to manage this situation. Obviously, American troops deployed to defend western Europe against a conventional blitzkrieg and to bolster the nuclear guarantee are poorly qualified to quell the most probable forms of eastern European instability. Nonetheless, European politics will remain volatile, and instability may affect the pace of change. Significant domestic or international violence in eastern Europe could resuscitate the U.S.-dominated postwar security system.

Economic and Technological Competition

As Frederic Pearson noted in chapter 10, the EC has a longstanding concern for the technological implications of defense programs. Moreover, European integration has long been animated by the ambition to compete successfully with North America and Japan. Paul Fabra (1990) recently reminded Europeans that "the single European market of 1992 was conceived as an organic necessity for Europeans threatened in their work and perhaps in their identity by the American superpower and by the Japanese superpower." This also holds for the European Space Agency (ESA), Eureka, and the Independent European Programme Group (IEPG), but the goal is accorded different priority by various European governments. For example, Britain emphasizes the IEPG's role in promoting European competitiveness less than France does. But even Britain shares this concern as revealed by London's preference for mergers that link British military contractors to European partners. According to the *Times*'s defense correspondent (Evans 1990), the MoD sees "Industrial consortia, especially those which have a strong European membership capable of taking on the American giants in the competitive market as the way ahead. . . ." (Also see "Dilemmas in Defence Supply," 1990.)

Resource Scarcity

As military budgets shrink, the absurdity of duplicative weapons systems is increasingly apparent. But NATO members continued plans to build redundant systems including four main battle tanks (M1, Challenger, Leopard 2, and AMX–40) and multiple fighter planes (EFA, Rafale, and various American models). Some analysts think that rising weapons costs and smaller military budgets will increase pressure for "value for money." This implies more open arms competition and greater cooperation among the western allies. While some of the national weapons programs are stalled, including an improved M1 tank in the United States and Leopard 3 in Germany, multinational arms cooperation has yet to bloom.

A second prognosis is less upbeat. Export markets are contracting. The Iraq War may reverse this trend, but arms makers confront smaller markets both at home and abroad. The Stockholm International Peace Research Institute estimated that orders to West European defense industries would decline 30 percent by the mid-1990s. This eventuality stimulated discussion, especially in Germany and within the British Labour party, concerning the "conversion" of defense industries. When combined with a perception of lessened threat, this Level II concern may elevate the priority of national economic effects while deemphasizing security concerns. The likely consequence is greater protection of national defense industries, not progress toward cooperative arms production or a common armaments market (U.S. Department of Defense 1990, 4). This possibility is even more pessimistic than John Conybeare's analysis of protectionism in civilian industries (chapter 8 in this volume), for protection of *national* defense industries may continue even after 1992.

Balancing Behavior

Two balance-of-power considerations arise in contemporary Europe: the traditional security balance and the political-economic equilibrium. The first emphasizes balancing Russia's military potential; the second involves both Germany's weight within Europe and exogenous economic and technological competition from the United States and Japan. This produces three distinct balances: (1) western Europe plus North America are balanced against Russia; (2) the Community is balanced against Japan and the United States; and (3) within the Community France, the UK and others are balanced against Germany.

The Atlantic Alliance has been principally responsible for maintaining the military balance. European leaders still fear a strategic void in central Europe and recall President Mitterrand's warning that "An arms vacuum has always elicited foreign meddling" (quoted in Isnard 1990).

German unification triggered renewed interest in balancing German influence. This concern jeopardized the longstanding Franco-German relationship, which provided the "motor" of European unification during forty years while London displayed what Sir Michael Howard (1990) describes as a traditional "sour mixture of arrogance and timidity towards Europe...."

The Franco-German security partnership has three principal components: deployments of French troops in Germany, the Franco-German Defense and Security Council, and the Franco-German Brigade. The Defense Council first met in April 1989 (Schmidt 1989). By uniting the heads of state and government, the foreign and defense ministers, and the military chiefs of staff, it seeks to harmonize bilateral defense policies. But according to German press reports, at the September 1990 Franco-German summit President Mitterrand and then Defense Minister Chevènement "refused even to discuss a joint strategic concept" (Hort 1990).

The brigade, headquartered in Baden-Württemberg, attained its full strength of 4,200 men in 1990 and became operational in 1991. Although its role remains ambiguous, the brigade's symbolic significance will grow as other French troops withdraw from Germany. France maintained over 50,000 troops at 28 garrisons in southwestern Germany; half of these troops have returned to France, and the others depart in 1994. The multinational brigade will remain and expand to 35,000 and later to 50–80,000 men. It may also widen to include units from other Western European Union (WEU) members.

German reunification awakened substantial interest in Anglo-French cooperation to offset German power. By November 1989, the *Sunday Times* ("The Future for Britain," 1989) was editorializing:

> A new Anglo-French *entente cordiale* has a lot going for it. With a combined might of 115m people it would be potentially more powerful than a united Germany. Both Britain and France are nuclear powers and, as the American nuclear umbrella over Western Europe is folded up in the 1990s, it will make sense for Britain and France to combine their nuclear defences, perhaps even to offer Europe the protection of an Anglo-French nuclear shield. . . . The weight of history militates against such a close alliance. There are plenty of people on both sides of the Channel who could not stomach it, such is the strength of mutual dislikes and historical antipathies. But those who think like that must ponder whether playing a poor second to a Fourth Reich is really a better alternative.

Britain's distrust of German unification was palpable during 1989 and 1990. This smoldering issue exploded during the summer of 1990 in an interview granted the *Spectator* by British Trade and Industry secretary Nicholas Ridley. Ridley called European monetary union, "a German racket designed to take over the whole of Europe." The prospect of British monetary policy being decided by the Bundesbank led to the statement, "being bossed by a German would cause absolute mayhem in this country, and rightly, I think." According to the *Economist* ("Britain, Europe and the Generation Game," 1990, 10) Mr. Ridley expressed "the reflex thoughts of millions of Britons who lived through the second world war and were brought up on an older view of Britain's place in the world." This seemed to include Margaret Thatcher, then the oldest cabinet member. In December 1989 the prime minister told a luncheon gathering that nothing good could ever come from the Germans. When other guests demurred, she responded "I'm beginning to wonder whether any of you are still sound" (Brock 1990).

The French shared British concerns with rising German power, but they were more mindful not to offend Germany. As one of President Mitterrand's advisers reportedly asked, "What could we do with Mrs. Thatcher that was not anti-German?" And a defense ministry official said that the French, "will not do a thing to push Germany away from us militarily." He described their actions as "keeping faith with Germany" while "opening with the U.K." Most French leaders thought it essential to maintain close Franco-German relations. According to Michel Vauzelle (1990), the Socialist chair of the National Assembly's Foreign Affairs Committee, "For France, the only wise response to the current upheavals remains with Germany."

British and French interest in a closer bilateral relationship was illustrated by London's serious consideration of an Anglo-French replacement for 150 WE177A/B gravity bombs. Three air-to-surface alternatives were reviewed for deployment on Tornado aircraft: Boeing's SRAM-T, Martin Marietta's Tactical Air-to-Surface Missile (TASM), and Aérospatiale's ASLP (air-sol à longue portée). ASLP is derived from the shorter-range ASMP and will have a range of at least 1,000 kilometers. London has previously considered nuclear cooperation with Paris, but never so seriously. Both British and French defense ministry officials talked as if it could actually happen, and unlike previously Washington now encouraged this collaboration.

At the end of 1991 Britain and France signed an agreement to jointly develop an antiaircraft frigate. This is Britain's first ever collaborative warship program. There is also planning for the use of French ports by British military forces. Other subjects of possible Franco-British defense cooperation included France's intention to join with Britain and Germany in NATO's Identification System (NIS) and possible cooperation between Rolls-Royce and Snecma on supersonic jet engines.

Confronted by German unification and the prospect of American disengagement, Britain and France hedged their bets. British foreign secretary Douglas Hurd (Dhombres 1990) described British and French interests as "nearly identical." These interests include their desire to contain German influence; their status as Europe's only nuclear powers; their roles as major arms exporters; similar aspirations in European arms control negotiations; and commitment to "serious" military programs.

These shared interests are offset by disagreements regarding European union and centuries of mutual distrust. In 1990, a British international affairs specialist could still refer to Britain's "absolute distrust of the French." Prospects for Anglo-French balancing must be weighed against this obstacle. Moreover, since unification both Britain and France have given renewed attention to bilateral relations with Germany. Prime Minister John Major established a good personal relationship with Chancellor Kohl, unlike the mutual enmity between Kohl and Thatcher, and Paris reignited the Franco-German partnership.

Political Union

Russell Dalton and Richard Eichenberg (chapter 4 in this volume) present data showing that public support for the EC "varies greatly across countries." With the notable exception of Britain, German unification increased European enthusiasm for political union; it was one more reason to move beyond implementation of the Single European Act to Economic and Monetary Union (EMU) and eventual political union. Margaret Thatcher thought events in central Europe demonstrated the errors of European supranationalism and strengthened the case for "widening" rather than "deepening" the Community. Rather than wanting stronger Community institutions to contain a united Germany, she feared "political integration, in which [Britain] should be bossed about by the Germans" (Butt 1990).

The Germans argued differently. President Richard von Weizsacker told *Le Monde* (Rosenzweig 1990) that Germany's "enterprise of unification will not succeed if we simultaneously prevent the European Community from accomplishing the necessary progress. . . . The two objectives are linked." Chancellor Kohl also connected German unification to European unification. He described his goal (quoted in McEwen 1990b) as "the political unification of Europe" and said there was an "unstoppable current" flowing toward full economic and political union. Denmark's foreign minister was fatalistic: "The deepening of the European Community is going to take place whatever, and there is nothing that the U.K. or Denmark could do to stop it" (Usborne 1990).

Although the EC is formally committed to political union, considerable resistance remains, especially in Britain where it is pronounced among the public (see Table 11.2) and within the Conservative party. While still prime minister, Margaret Thatcher even made thinly veiled comparisons between the EC bureaucracy and discredited Marxist regimes of eastern Europe. She urged eventual EC membership for the eastern European states but asserted that if the Community "set down the path of giving more and more powers to highly centralized institutions, which are not democratically accountable, then we should be making it harder for the Eastern Europeans to join. They have not thrown off central command and control in their own countries only to find them reincarnated in the European Community" (Thatcher 1990). Former Conservative party chair Norman Tebbitt is also europhobic. To Tebbitt (1990), "This is not just a row about a common currency or the Social Charter. It is about whether Her Majesty's Government is to be progressively reduced to the level of a provincial administration, the Mother of Parliaments to a regional council enacting bylaws and the United Kingdom to a province of Europe. . . ."

Moreover, John Major was the least pro-European of the three candidates to succeed Margaret Thatcher as Conservative party leader: Michael Heseltine is most pro-European and Douglas Hurd stands between Major and Heseltine on this question. That said, Major's approach to European issues is much more openminded than Mrs. Thatcher's.

Labour party propaganda stresses the party's greater commitment to European union, but Labour is also hesitant compared to continental parties. Labour did urge earlier participation in the European Monetary System (EMS) and supports the Social Charter, but both parties oppose increased power for the European Parliament, a single European currency, and a European central bank free of political control on the Bundesbank model. Thus, the British will remain

Table 11.2

Attitudes toward European Union (percentage)

Question: The member-states of the European Community are planning to complete the single European market by the end of 1992. In general, do you favor or oppose this plan as a means of making progress toward European Union?

	Britain	France	Germany	Spain
Favor	46	66	62	58
Oppose	24	7	11	5
Neither/don't know	30	27	27	37

Source: "Four-country Poll Confirms British Coolness on Europe." November 18, 1989. *Independent*, p. 7. Surveys by Harris Research Centre and associated firms, 2–16 October, 1989. Samples totaled: UK, 1,036; FRG, 1,003; France, 1,074; and Spain, 1,000.

reluctant Europeans even under a Labour government.

In France, more than 60 percent of the public now perceives little difference between Left and Right on the issues of European policy or national defense; only one-quarter perceive large differences (Jeambar 1990). Nonetheless, fissures concerning European policy have opened within both wings of *la classe politique*. Some Socialists (for example, Jean-Pierre Chevènement) and some conservatives (such as former cabinet members Charles Pasqua and Philippe Séguin, both RPR) express nationalistic reservations that mirror British concerns. Nonetheless, France's principal politicians, including François Mitterrand, Valéry Giscard d'Estaing, and Jacques Chirac, still back European goals.

The Forums for Defense Cooperation

Defense cooperation exhibits the pattern of "complex governance" described by Barry Hughes (chapter 3 in this volume). Cooperation occurs bilaterally and also within several multilateral forums characterized by overlapping mandates and memberships, e.g., NATO, EC, WEU, CSCE, and IEPG. This section examines probable developments in these arenas during the coming decade. As the long-time focus of European security, NATO is a logical starting point.

NATO

For more than forty years, American leadership reinforced Europe's defense and moderated intra-European conflicts (Joffe 1984). Now, both objectives are accomplished. The Soviet threat evaporated, and with EMU on the horizon, and subsequent political union a serious possibility, European order no longer requires an American pacifier.

The fundamentally changed European security environment compelled new NATO doctrines. The Alliance modified its longstanding declaratory policy of flexible response to make nuclear arms weapons of "last resort," rather than first-use. At the end of 1991 unilateral steps by presidents Bush and Gorbachev eliminated ground-launched and seabased tactical nuclear weapons.

Meanwhile, the German public's support for foreign troop deployments sagged. A March 1990 survey ("Polls: Most Germans and Americans for German Unity," 1990) found that 56.5 percent of West German respondents would welcome the complete withdrawal of U.S. troops, as compared with 38.6 percent who were opposed. There was also unusual friction between American troops and German civilians during the scaled-down January 1990 Reforger (Return of Forces to Germany) exercise. Some American units were even escorted by German police to prevent civilian harassment (O'Dwyer-Russell 1990).

London and Paris continue to see NATO differently. The British value NATO for its own sake and think it should adapt to new circumstances. It would be desirable, therefore, if France rejoined the integrated military structure. If the Supreme Allied Commander Europe (SACEUR) were a European, it would be difficult for France to remain outside, and a British commander speaking in Bonn endorsed this possibility (Hoagland 1990). There is some French support for reintegration. For example, Giscard ("M. Giscard d'Estaing souhaite," 1990) proposed transforming NATO into "a Euro-Atlantic pact" which France should enter. But in the post–cold war era France considers integrated defense superfluous. With typically Gallic ambiguity, Mitterrand advocated a defense which "while not strictly European (we remain allied to the Americans) should have a specifically European axis. . . . " France continues to rely on NATO while awaiting an evolving EC security role built on the foundation of WEU.

NATO remains the nominal focus of European security, in part because the Bundeswehr is assigned to NATO and no one wants to reorganize German forces on a purely national basis so soon following unification. But the continued deployment of foreign troops in Germany is uncertain. To make the remaining forces more politically acceptable to Germans, and to obscure their role as constraints on German autonomy, non-German divisions will be integrated into multinational corps combining divisions from two or more countries.

European Community

The EC's attention to security issues is erratic. In the early postwar years, European-based security structures seemed an inevitable dimension of integration. This expectation collapsed with the European Defense Community initiative in 1954 and when the EEC failed for decades to become an authentic common market, much less a nascent United States of Europe. The Community's European Political Cooperation (EPC) should have focused on European security (Cahen 1989, 15–16), but the EC was ill-equipped to play this role: Article 223 of the

Treaty of Rome barred security issues, and its membership included neutral Ireland, dovish Denmark, NATO-centric Britain, and nationalistic France. Recently, resurgent interest in possible political union renewed interest in a security role.

Security has returned to the EC agenda. Throughout Europe, there is widespread acceptance of the opinion expressed by a high French Ministry of Defense official (Dominique 1990), that the Community "will not continue for long to speak of a central European bank, a common currency, or regulations covering pollution and free exchange without beginning, one day or another, to address its own defense." Moreover, Table 11.3 shows the substantial public support for an EC approach to defense policy, especially in Germany and France but not in the United Kingdom. A *Eurobarometer* survey conducted in the autumn of 1990 ("Près de sept," 1990) showed that nearly 70 percent of Europeans favored a common European defense. In France, support for an "integrated European army" rose from 50 percent in May 1989 to 61 percent in November 1991 ("La majorité des Français," 1991).

As Frederic Pearson describes in the preceding chapter, the Single European Act (SEA) opened the door to security discussions. Where the Treaty of Rome excluded security issues, the SEA's Article 30, Section 6, explicitly recognized that "closer cooperation on questions of security would contribute in an essential way to the development of a European identity in external policy matters." However, this coordination was limited to "the political and economic aspects of security." When the European Parliament debated security issues in 1989 (*Official Journal* 1989), Irish delegates could not even agree if these were "issues and areas which are outside the scope of European political cooperation and the provisions of the Single European act."

Security issues assumed more prominence as political union took center stage within the Community. At the Maastricht Summit in December 1991, the Community took a major step toward an expanded security role. WEU was designated an "integral part of the development of the European Union" that may "elaborate and implement decisions and actions of the Union which have defense implications." This appeared to ratify Chancellor Kohl and President Mitterrand's wish (Kohl and Mitterrand 1990) to form "a clear organic relationship" between WEU and the Community. Security issues will now be coordinated by the secretariats of WEU and the EC Council of Ministers. The Community may absorb WEU when the Brussels Treaty expires in 1998.

The EC had already begun to address commercial issues raised by military procurement. Typically, the Community's tariff provisions were not applied when defense ministries purchased imports, generally from the United States. This practice was based on Article 223, which suspends the treaty when "vital national security interests are claimed." Now, however, the Commission asserts that the Community's right to set tariffs (Article 28) applies to all defense purchasing except for weapons and other specialized military equipment and material.

Table 11.3

Attitudes toward EC Defense Policy (percentage responding "yes")

Question: Please tell me whether you think that defense policy should be made by the EC as a whole, or whether you think such decisions should be made by each country independently.

	Britain	France	Germany	Spain
EC as a whole	45	63	74	45
Each country independently	40	31	16	29

Source: "Four-country Poll confirms British Coolness on Europe." November 18, 1989. *Independent,* p. 7. Surveys by Harris Research Centre and associated firms, 2–16 October, 1989. Samples totaled: UK, 1,036; FRG, 1,003; France, 1,074; and Spain, 1,000.

This issue is controversial. The Commission sees the U.S. defense industry, which wants a zero tariff on anything European MoDs might import from the United States, pitted against European suppliers (and the Community, which wants the tariff revenues). But Brussels is also at odds with the European MoDs, who oppose higher costs for non-Community purchases. Both British and French defense officials strongly oppose regulations that could regulate their procurement decisions. They accept Brussels' prerogative to set tariffs, so long as the actual tariff is zero.

Western European Union

Seven of the nine WEU members (Belgium, Britain, France, Italy, the Nether-lands, Portugal, and Spain) sent naval forces to the Persian Gulf following Iraq's invasion of Kuwait. Britain, France, and Italy sent combat aircraft while Belgium sent four transport planes, and Britain and France also deployed ground forces. Germany moved eighteen fighter-bombers to Turkey, placed naval forces in the Mediterranean, and agreed to amend its Basic Law to permit future military deployments outside the NATO area. WEU also organized "tight coordination" of these forces including intelligence, logistics, air defense, and possibly rules of engagement. According to Douglas Hurd (McEwen 1990a), this was "an im-pressive display of European solidarity," and it was judged the most important meeting in the WEU's thirty-six year history.

These were significant actions, especially Spain's decision to break a long isolationist tradition. But when Iraq attacked, WEU waited nineteen days before meeting; by then the United States had acted unilaterally and asserted its leader-ship within the United Nations and NATO. Considering European stakes in the Persian Gulf, and WEU's status as the only exclusively European organization with a security mandate, the response was modest.

Protagonists on both sides of the debate concerning European union saw the Iraq conflict as confirming their positions. Proponents thought it underscored the lesson of the nearly disastrous Reagan–Gorbachev summit at Reykjavik in 1986: Europe's vital interests remain vulnerable until European institutions exist to formulate and implement common foreign and defense policies. Opponents of federal institutions, especially the British, said it proved that a deeply divided Europe could not frame a common policy and required American leadership.

For a time in early 1990 EC momentum toward political union appeared likely to doom the WEU to irrelevancy. In the end, however, WEU was the Community's chosen instrument to expand its security role. France visualizes WEU as the EC's defense pole; Britain sees WEU as NATO's European pillar. At NATO's November 1991 summit, the *Rome Declaration on Peace and Cooperation* "welcome[d] the perspective of a reinforcement of the role of the WEU, both as the defense component of the process of European unification and as a means of strengthening the European pillar of the Alliance, bearing in mind the different nature of its relations with the Alliance and with the European Political Union." According to France, NATO had "for the first time recognized that henceforth integrated and multinational European structures could play as important a role in continental defense as NATO's integrated military structure" (Isnard 1991). But Prime Minister John Major (1991) delivered a different message to the House of Commons. He told MPs that NATO had endorsed "the British proposal to use the Western European Union as the means of strengthening the European pillar of the Alliance." Subsequent events at the EC's Maastricht Summit buttressed the French interpretation.

Conference on Security and Cooperation in Europe

The CSCE combines the European states, Canada, and the United States. As the cold war waned, CSCE emerged as a main focus for European security issues, which Italy's foreign minister called "the most important political body for Europe" (Michelis 1990). The Soviet Union and Germany were CSCE's strongest proponents with German foreign minister Hans-Dietrich Genscher (FDP) envisioning the eventual evolution of "an interlocking system of mutual collective security" ("Genscher Proposes East–West," 1990). The Social Democrat's (SPD) platform for the December 1990 all-German elections advocated "a European security system within the framework of the CSCE which would absorb the present military alliances" (Nagelschmitz 1990, 33). The Free Democrats (FDP) described their aim "within the framework of the CSCE . . . to achieve cooperative security through comprehensive disarmament and by using the alliances . . . mainly as political guarantors" (p. 37). And the Greens asserted that "A pan-European order of peace, a system of collective security should replace NATO and the disintegrating Warsaw Pact" (p. 42).

France was less enthusiastic. The French government accorded more prominence to NATO and WEU. Jacques Chirac ("L'appartenance à l'OTAN," 1990) explicitly rejected the concept of "an institutionalized CSCE which would play the role of the European UN." Most leading British politicians also dismissed German hopes for CSCE. Foreign Secretary Hurd (1990) dismissed CSCE's capacity "in the foreseeable future [to] become an organization offering collective military security guarantees of the old traditional kind. So far as members of NATO are concerned, it will not replace NATO."

The Soviet Union's demise undermined CSCE's role as an East–West bridge. The North Atlantic Cooperation Council now provides a forum for discussions between NATO countries and former Warsaw Pact members, and in December 1991 even Russian president Boris Yeltsin expressed Russia's "long-term political aim" of NATO membership. There is, nonetheless, some progress in institutionalizing CSCE, including a small secretariat in Prague, a research office in Warsaw to collect data on elections, a Conflict Prevention Center in Vienna, and annual meetings of the Council of Foreign Ministers.

Like all aspiring collective security systems, the CSCE option assumes that potential aggressors can be deterred if members vow to defend potential victims. Collective security's historical record, for example, the League of Nations and the United Nations, is very poor. The national interests of individual states often diverge from the collective interest, so members are tempted to overlook aggression. Moreover, although Iraq's invasion of Kuwait was especially flagrant, even Iraq convinced some observers that Kuwait's greed and insolence justified its action. In Europe, the principal flaw is that great powers such as Russia are immune from collective security, for collective action against them could unleash global warfare. Timothy Garton Ash (1990) is right: "If I was a German I certainly would not swap an American nuclear umbrella for a Helsinki paper one. I would go further: If I was a Pole or a Czech or a Hungarian, I would like nothing better than to put my fledgling democracy under a West European, or, best of all, an American nuclear umbrella." It is noteworthy that the European Community and the United Nations, rather than CSCE, led efforts to quell warfare in Yugoslavia.

Independent European Programme Group

Current IEPG priorities are EUCLID and the open market initiative. The European Research and Technology Program (EUCLID) is a military R&D program somewhat analogous to the civilian program, Eureka (Brocard 1990). EUCLID builds on the technical strengths of participating states to focus European research and to reduce wasteful duplication. The program concerns intermediate technology rather than basic research or finished products, and companies wishing to join a project must demonstrate relevant past experience. Of the first eleven research foci identified, France and the Netherlands will play a leading role in three each, West Germany and Britain in two each, and Spain, Norway, and Italy in one each. IEPG hopes that the value of EUCLID projects will eventually exceed $100 million. The other priority is an open market initiative. Currently, most European countries have very autarkic military procurement practices. Only 10 percent by value of Britain's equipment purchases are made overseas, and according to the *Economist* ("Open Your Arms," 1989), "France and West Germany buy an even smaller proportion of their defense equipment from abroad than Britain does." In France, 97 percent of MoD expenditures are made domestically, sometimes for collaborative projects. Furthermore, because Europe's national markets are small, research and development costs are high. French R&D costs equal 30 percent of combined spending on R&D and production, and the level is rising by 1 percent annually. To combat this problem, France now requires that 10 percent of new R&D involve collaborative arrangements with foreign partners.

IEPG seeks to address these problems by opening the European military procurement market. The member-states are publicizing their purchasing plans and opening all projects exceeding one million ECUs to competition from the other states. This effort builds on the Anglo-French Reciprocal Purchasing arrangements that began in 1987. During 1989, 244 British firms subscribed to the French contracts bulletin, and 128 French firms received the British bulletin. This initiative has not produced dramatic results, but it has modestly increased cross-buying and is judged a success.

IEPG excludes four categories of purchases from the open market program for political or security reasons: shipbuilding (platforms only, not equipment), nuclear, cryptographic, and CBW. Also, although there is no upper limit on contract size, very large projects like EFA or the Tiger helicopter will be negotiated individually as in the past. Moreover, the program operates on the basis of *juste retour*, so in principle when a country buys abroad it guarantees a reciprocal sale. The smaller states, and those with less developed defense industries, demand *juste retour*. The British, in particular, hope this will be only a transitory stage to a truly open market. The French agree but are less hopeful; Germany, with its large trade surplus but smaller defense industry, is less concerned by this issue. The exclusion of ship platforms, and retention of *juste retour*, means this is only a partial step toward an open military procurement market. But it is a significant advance in a previously neglected field.

In addition to IEPG's efforts, European defense manufacturing is also being transformed by mergers and cooperative agreements among defense firms. A few examples illustrate this trend. First, there is consolidation of defense industries within states, for example Daimler-Benz's takeover of Messerschmitt-Bölkow-Blohm and the expansion through domestic acquisitions of British Aerospace (BAE) and GEC. Secondly, firms are merging across national borders. Recent examples include the creation of the French holding company, Eurocopter. Jointly owned by Aérospatiale (60 percent) and MBB (40 percent), Eurocopter controls the companies' helicopter activities, which equaled $1.8 billion in 1989. Thomson-CSF purchased Philip's defense-electronics business, and Matra plans new relationships with Daimler and GEC. Another ambitious plan, to merge the missile divisions of British Aerospace and Thomson with combined sales of $2.6 billion, collapsed in March 1991. Less formal arrangements include Westland's agreements with *all* the possible suppliers of a new British light helicopter: MBB and Aérospatiale if the Tiger were chosen; McDonnell Douglas if the AH–64 Apache were selected; and a collaborative arrangement with Augusta, CASA, and Fokker to develop a new helicopter derived from the Augusta's Tonal.

Shrinking markets and rising R&D costs stimulate industrial consolidation. Transnational mergers are the obvious way to overcome inefficient national defense markets. These firms also become more competitive with their larger American rivals (all of the ten largest defense firms are American), and they improve their access to procurement decisions in several national markets. Defense industrial consolidation is one facet of a broader European corporate trend spawned by 1992. Until now, governments have animated European defense cooperation; in the future "that task will be done—and done better—by international businessmen" (Fitchett 1990).

Yang and Yin

Yang

There is a multiorganizational smorgasbord of security organizations. During the 1990s, the fortunes of some will rise while others fall. NATO, the reigning champion, will decline as America disengages from Europe. At the opposite extreme, the European Community will gather momentum as the goals of economic and monetary union are reached. Long before Maastricht, Rainer Rupp (1989–90, 22) argued that "whether the European Community governments will make a deliberate decision to bestow on the European Commission security policy responsibilities or not; such responsibilities will accrue to the Commission by the nature of its obligations and day-to-day management of an economically and politically more united Europe." CSCE may also grow in influence, but it will peak at quite a low level of importance.

WEU, and perhaps IEPG, will blossom as NATO fades, but in time the Community is likely to absorb WEU. Bilateral relations will remain significant. The Franco-German relationship will remain crucial unless Britain overcomes its distaste for European institutions. Overall, defense cooperation will be stimulated by the momentum of European union, the competitive threat from North America and Japan, a residual Russian threat and general instability, America's withdrawal and encouragement of cooperation, and efforts to balance a united Germany.

Yin

Alternatively, the diminished threat may permit European states to avoid the price of cooperation despite American withdrawal. Britain may exercise its historic preference and distance itself from continental entanglements while reasserting its maritime vocation. Forgetting recent promises, Germany may become self-absorbed and lose interest in broader European objectives. France may welcome the chance to preserve a semblance of nationalistic autonomy. Existing patterns of Franco-German cooperation could endure, and Anglo-French cooperation might deepen, but without major progress toward strengthening the European pillar.

Pressure for defense cooperation is as likely to be economic and industrial as political. The creation of a pan-European defense industrial base will probably continue even in the absence of political will. The missing ingredient is pressure to integrate military structures and forge a common strategy. Who or what will supply that impulse?

References

Apple, R. W., Jr. 1990. "Bush's Fragile Battalions in Europe." *New York Times*, February 2 , p. 1.

Ash, Timothy Garton. 1990. "The New Continental Drift." *Independent*, March 1, p. 27.

"Britain, Europe and the Generation Game." 1990. *Economist*, July 21, p. 10.

Brocard, Yves. 1990. "Euclid, une structure originale." *Air & Cosmos*, 1271 (February 10): 31–33.

Brock, George. 1990. "Thatcher's Personal Struggle to Accept Reunification." *Times*, July 16, p. 2.

Butt, Ronald. 1990. "Voiceless in the Power Stakes." *Times*, April 11, p. 12.

Cahen, Alfred. 1989. *The Western European Union and NATO: Building a European Defence Identity Within the Context of Atlantic Solidarity*. London: Brassey's.

De Michelis, Gianni. 1990. "Europe: A Golden Opportunity Not to Be Missed." *International Herald Tribune*, March 26, p. 6.

Dhombres, Dominique. 1990. "Un entretien avec le secrétaire au Foreign Office." *Le Monde*, March 30, p. 4.

"Dilemmas in Defence Supply." 1990. *Financial Times*, January 25.

Dominique, Gérard (pseudonym). 1990. "Pour une CEE de la défense." *Le Monde*, April 11, p. 2.

Evans, Michael. 1990. "Defence Implications Need Careful Examination." *Times*, January 9.

Fabra, Paul. 1990. "L'Europe schizophrène." *Le Monde*, January 13, p. 27.

Fitchett, Joseph. 1990. "The Shape of Things to Come: Defense in the 1990s." *The American Enterprise*, 1 (May/June):26–37.

"Genscher Proposes East–West Cooperative Security Structures." 1990. *The Week in Germany*, March 30, p. 1.

Hoagland, Jim. 1990. "Modernizing the American Role in Europe." *International Herald Tribune*, April 12, p. 4.

Hort, Peter. 1990. "Architects of the Draft Plan Want to Hear Bonn's Views." *Frankfurter Allgemeine Zeitung*, October 23. Translated in *The German Tribune*, 4 November 1990.

Howard, Michael. 1990. "A New Commonwealth in Need of British Support." *Times*, April 24, p. 16.

Hurd, Douglas. 1990. "The CSCE: Need for a New Magna Carta." Speech to the CSCE Ministerial Meeting, October 2, New York.

Isnard, Jacques. 1990. "Un entretien avec M. Chevènement." *Le Monde*, July 13, pp. 1, 9.

Isnard, Jacques. 1991. "La France accroîtrait sa participation à l'OTAN." *Le Monde*, December 4, p. 10.

Jeambar, Denis. 1990. "Un tiers des Français pour y croire." *Le Point*, December 3, pp. 22–23.

Joffe, Josef. 1984. "Europe's American Pacifier." *Foreign Policy*, 54:64–82.

Kohl, Helmut, and François Mitterrand. 1990. "La lettre commune be MM. Kohl et Mitterrand." *Le Monde*, December 10, p. 4.

"L'appartenance à l'OTAN est 'la destination naturelle' de l'Allemagne unie." 1990. *Le Monde*, May 13–14, p. 4.

"M. Giscard d'Estaing souhaite 'une solidarité' franco-allemand en matière de défense." 1990. *Le Monde*, April 3, p. 3.

Major, John. 1991. *Policy Statement 78/91*. New York: British Information Services, November 13, p. 2.

McEwen, Andrew. 1990. "Thatcher and Kohl at Odds Over Nuclear Missile Issue." *Times*, March 31, p. 16.

McEwen, Andrew. 1990. "Ministers Agree to Co-ordinate Naval Operations in Gulf." *Times*, August 22, p. 2.

Mitterrand, François. 1990. "M. Mitterrand: 'Pour l'instant le problème posé n'est pas de réduire le budget militaire.' " *Le Monde*, July 17, pp. 6–7.

Nagelschmitz, Helmut, ed. 1990. *Procedures, Programmes, Profiles: First All German Election*. Bonn: Inter Nationes, December.

"Number of Conscientious Objectors Doubled in 1991." 1992. *The Week in Germany*, January 31, p. 2.

"Open Your Arms." 1989. *Economist*, April 29.

O'Dwyer-Russell, Simon. 1990. "U.S. Troops Join Exercise in East–West Futility." *Sunday Telegraph*, January 21, p. 15.

Official Journal of the European Communities. 1989. Debates of the European Parliament, 1989–90 session, Sitting of Tuesday, 14 March, No. 2–376.

"Polls: Most Germans and Americans for German Unity." 1990. *The Week in Germany*, April 13, p. 2.

"Près de sept Européens sur dix sont favorables à une défense commune." 1990. *Le Monde*, December 13, p. 4.

Rosenzweig, Luc. 1990. "Un entretien avec le président de la RFA." *Le Monde*, March 8, p. 4.

Rupp, Rainer. 1989–90. "Europe 1992: Potential Implications for the North Atlantic Alliance." *NATO's Sixteen Nations*, December 1989–January 1990: 2–26.

Schmidt, Peter. 1989. "The Franco-German Defence and Security Council." *Aussenpolitik*, 40:360–371.

Schulte, Heinz. 1989. "Changing West German Stance Draws Concern." *Jane's Defence Weekly*, 12 (August 5):203.

Tebbitt, Norman. 1990. "No Fudging on This Euro Mould." *Times*, January 9, p. 12.

Thatcher, Margaret. 1990. "Shaping a New Global Community." Speech to the Aspen Institute, Aspen, Colorado, August 5.

"The Future for Britain." 1989. *Sunday Times*, November 19, p. B2.

Usborne, David. 1990. "Danes Attack British Hesitancy over Europe." *Independent*, February 20, p. 12.

U.S. Department of Defense. 1990. "Combined Annual Report to Congress on Standardization of Equipment With NATO Members and Cooperative Research and Development Projects with Allied Countries." Washington, DC: U.S. Department of Defense, June.

Vauzelle, Michel. 1990. "Paris, Berlin." *Le Monde*, March 7, p. 2.

PART III

THE 1992 PROJECT
AND THE FUTURE

12

The Future of Integration in Europe

Dale L. Smith and James Lee Ray

As defined in our introductory chapter, the 1992 Project refers to the attempt by the European Community to complete the single internal market by 1992. It seems clear, however, that this single market will *not* be completed by the end of 1992. All the new rules regarding the harmonization or mutual recognition of product standards, professional degrees, and capital movements will, in all probability, not have been agreed to in Brussels by the beginning of 1993; there will be an even larger backlog for getting these new regulations ratified by the national governments. And even the new standards that are in place will not apply to all member-states, because some will receive special dispensations, providing them a longer period to comply with the new regulations. Finally, some of the most contentious aspects of the single market, such as harmonization of the excise tax rates, will be pushed off until some future date, or patched over with "transitional" arrangements that will remain in place until the member-states can agree on a common policy.

Does the failure to fully complete the internal market by the end of 1992 imply that the Project has been a failure? We argue emphatically that is not the case. Up to this point, the 1992 Project has been a major success for the EC. Whether or not the Community will be a true common market by 1992 is less important than the fact that it is making progress toward that goal; 1992 was always more symbol than deadline. It was symbolic of Europe's renewed commitment to remove the final barriers and distortions that prevented the completion of the internal market. The importance of that commitment when it was made in 1985 must not be forgotten. The economic stagnation of the 1970s had carried over into the 1980s as the Europeans saw themselves fall further behind their main economic competitors, the Americans and the Japanese. The passage of the Single European Act in which the member-states pledged to complete the internal market by December 31, 1992, reinvigorated the process and changed perceptions in Europe from "europessimism" to "europhoria."

In this final chapter, we will review a range of new initiatives that are in large part a response to the success of the 1992 Project and that will shape the developments within the EC over the next decade. We will also provide an assessment of some probable consequences of the 1992 Project in terms of their effect on the future of integration in Europe.

New Initiatives: Plans for the Post-1992 EC

The enthusiasm among the member-states for the 1992 Project, along with other changes in Europe and beyond, stimulated the Community to begin preparing for what will come after the completion of the single market. Throughout 1991, two intergovernmental conferences—one on economic and monetary union (EMU), the other on political union—worked to provide a blueprint for the deepening of the integration process over the next decade. This blueprint came into reasonably clear focus in the historic Treaty on European Union that was signed by EC members at Maastricht, the Netherlands, in February 1992. In addition, changes in East–West relations have forced the EC to seriously reconsider its new role in this emerging world order and prepare for a wave of new membership applications. On the basis of these changes, we can point to five areas into which we see the Community moving in the coming years.

Economic and Monetary Union

According to the theory of economic integration, the establishment of a common market is followed by the creation of some form of economic and monetary union, and the Maastricht Treaty has put the Community well on its way to this next step in the integration process. By 1997, or 1999 at the latest, the member-states have agreed to establish a European Central Bank and introduce a common currency, the Ecu.[1] This is no mean accomplishment, since such a system will require that the national governments relinquish their monetary policy to Community control, and even have their budgets scrutinized by the other member-states.

Political Union: A Common Foreign and Defense Policy for Europe

With non-Communist governments and market-oriented reforms taking root in eastern Europe and the continuing, though sometimes halting, evolution of the former Soviet Union toward multiparty democracies and market economies, the EC faces a much different world today than it did a few years ago. The bipolar world into which the Community was born and in which it grew has disappeared. While this change in the international system obviously creates some problems, it also creates important new opportunities. The Maastricht Treaty developed a framework within which cooperation on foreign policy matters could be increased, up to the point of allowing certain issues to be decided within the Council of Ministers by qualified majority vote, rather than unanimity. The Treaty also calls for the strengthening of the Western European Union (WEU) as the foundation upon which to build toward the goal of a European defense policy. Only Denmark, Greece, and Ireland are not members of the WEU, and Greece has expressed an interest in joining by the end of 1992. The Treaty leaves undisturbed the commitments by the EC members to NATO. In short, the evolving structure of the post–cold war international system is likely to continue to push the Community toward increased coordination in the areas of foreign policy and national security.

A Community for All of Europe

The prospects of access to the single richest market in the world along with the end of the East–West division in Europe have created a flood of potential new members. Sweden and Austria, which have already applied, seem to be standing at the head of the queue, but other countries that are seriously considering membership stretch from Norway and Finland through Poland, Czechoslovakia, and Hungary.[2] Even historically neutral Switzerland seems intrigued by the economic advantages of membership. The expansion of the EC to include (almost) all of Europe presents a number of serious problems. It has long been assumed that there is a tradeoff between deepening the level of integration and expanding the geographic scope of the Community. The expansion of the EC from twelve to approximately twenty and the incorporation of these new members could well consume most of the energies of both the European Commission and Council for the foreseeable future. And what would it mean for the Community's plans for political union when many of these new, previously neutral members would want to "opt out" of any structure that appeared to be a military alliance? Most basically, however, the current structures of the Community could not handle a twenty-member EC without significant institutional reforms, which are not planned until the next round of treaty revisions in 1996 (*Economist*, 7/13/91).

Institutional Reforms

The Maastricht Treaty will also be important in determining the "shape" of this growing community. Will the current balance of power between the Commission, Council, and Parliament be maintained in the new areas of EMU and political union? This could well be the most important consequence of Maastricht, for the institutional dynamics of the new structure will play an important role in determining the direction and speed of future integration. There presently seem to be two competing "architectures" for the new Europe: pillars or branches. Those states who want to prevent, or at least slow, the evolution toward a federal community conceive of the EC as a number of separate pillars supporting a common roof. Under this conception, the institutional structure for political union could be considerably different from that for economic union. The Council, representing national interests, would be far more dominant, at the expense of the Commission, than in the current structure that governs economic affairs. This structure would also make it easier for members to pick and choose the community—economic, political, or social—to which they wanted to belong. The alternative architecture, favored by those supporting movement toward an ever-tighter federal union, looks much more like a tree. The branches, representing economic, security, or social affairs, would be structurally much more similar and integrated more directly through their common trunk. As the latest round in the debate between these two visions of Europe, the Maastricht Treaty looks, largely due to British insistence, more like pillars than branches. The new intergovernmental "pillars" of foreign policy and internal security will remain outside of the normal Community structure.

1992 and the Future of European Integration

In addition to the effect that the 1992 Project has had on stimulating some of these new initiatives, we can also point to other areas in which the consequences of 1992 are likely to be felt.

The Distribution of Costs and Benefits

Probably the most important consequence of the completion of the single market and the one that will most directly affect future integration is how the costs and benefits from the 1992 Project are distributed. As the barriers are removed, industry will attempt to exploit the economies of scale and improved efficiency that will be possible within the new single market. In the best-case scenario, the entire market for a specific product would expand and the manufacturers in each of the member-states would be able to increase output and employment. Even in this best-case scenario, it is likely that industrial sectors in certain states will gain more than their competitors in other states. All gain, but some gain more than others. However, it is much more probable that there will be absolute losses for industrial sectors in certain states and absolute gains in others. As the barriers that still exist within, for example, the pharmaceutical market disappear, will the Portuguese manufacturers in this capital and R&D-intensive sector win or lose as they are forced to compete more directly against the Germans, Dutch, and British? Gains and losses will be distributed asymmetrically across industrial sectors, regions, and nations, and how both the Community and the member-states respond to those asymmetries will be important for continued economic integration. The EC Commission has recognized this as a potential problem and has enlarged its regional funds and introduced new programs to prevent any increase in regional disparities that might occur from the 1992 Project.[3]

A People's Europe

With the progressive completion of the single market and further plans to expand Community powers into what might be broadly called social policy, the EC is moving closer to the everyday concerns of the European citizen. The eurostandards that the single market creates will increasingly lead the Community into issues of consumer protection and product control. The single market will also push the Community into growing involvement in workplace issues—worker consultation, working conditions, and equal opportunity (*Economist*, 7/6/91). Finally, decisions to mutually recognize professional degrees will filter down and provide a role for the EC in coordinating education policy across the member-states. The 1992 Project was about economic issues. The consequences of the completion of the single market will spill over into a broad range of social issues in the 1990s.

In chapter 4, Dalton and Eichenberg referred to a "permissive consensus" that in the past has given the national governments a relatively free hand in pursuing continued integration. At lower levels of integration this was possible, for neither the costs nor the benefits were large and the direct impact on peoples' lives and livelihood was fairly small. However, as Europe moves to a single market and that in turn spills over into increased European involvement in consumer, education, and workplace issues, it is likely that public involvement in the process will grow. As the process of integration continues to deepen, the Community will have an increasingly direct effect on the most important concerns of the individual citizen, and those individual citizens will be increasingly likely to speak out.

There are two channels through which increased citizen participation will affect the integration process. The first is through the national government. Our Level II game, as introduced in chapter 1, involves bargaining between the national government and subnational groups. By bringing pressure to bear on the national government these groups have the possibility of changing government policy toward integration. European farmers provide an important example of this sort of activism and pressure. No single group has been more directly affected by past integration than the farmers, and they have certainly not been hesitant in pressing their case with their national governments. As other groups become more directly affected by Community policies, it is likely that they too will press their concerns on their governments. The second path through which subnational groups will be able to affect the process of integration is through the European Parliament. Though still relatively ineffective, this institution is growing in power and may become an increasingly useful channel through which subnational groups can be heard at the Community level.

Positive versus Negative Integration

With the removal of the final distortions and barriers to the single market, the slope will become steeper—the process of integration more difficult. This might appear to be an uncommon view given the momentum for continued integration that the 1992 Project has created. However, it is a view based on the concepts of positive versus negative integration that are often employed by economists.[4] Put simply, negative integration refers to the removal of barriers and is associated with the economic liberalization that often accompanies integration. The dismantling of intracommunity obstacles to the free movement of goods, services, capital, and people are examples of negative integration. It involves the single decision to abolish some barrier, while positive integration requires more complex coordination of government policy over a long period of time and is assumed to be much more difficult to sustain. To explain the dynamics of this process, Molle (1990, 28–29) sees the liberalization of negative integration creating demands for positive integration in the form of harmonization and coordination policies. For example, the 1992 Project will remove obstacles to the free movement of capital (negative integration). However, for this program to work properly the member-states must also coordinate (positive integration) a number of national policies that either affect or are affected by the movement of capital. With the establishment of the single market, negative integration is basically complete, and future efforts to deepen the process, such as EMU and foreign and security policy coordination, can be characterized as mainly positive integration. Therefore, according to this view, a lot of the momentum the Community gained by completing the single market—removing the final barriers—will dissipate as it becomes involved in the much more difficult tasks of positive integration that lie ahead. The slope becomes steeper and progress toward the goal of union slower and more difficult.

Conclusion

A reading of the EC's current agenda for the rest of the 1990s would find that they plan to: (1) establish EMU; (2) increase cooperation in foreign and security policy; (3) accept two (or more) new members; (4) expand EC powers into new areas of social policy; and (5) reform their own institutions. This is an enormously ambitious agenda, especially when one remembers that it took the Community almost twenty-five years—one generation—to move from a customs union, established in 1968, to the single market. Therefore, we want to warn against the temptation of becoming discouraged with the pace of progress when we begin seeing some of these advances being pushed off beyond the year 2000. As we argued in chapter 2, this was a mistake an earlier generation of integration scholars made. Ernst Haas and Karl Deutsch, along with some of their students, originally saw the integration process in terms of years, rather than decades, and turned away from the study of integration when the process apparently stagnated in the 1970s. That decade was certainly a period of enormous international turbulence, and certain EC plans were definitely derailed by international shocks. However, the 1970s have been viewed by some as a period in which the Community consolidated important gains made in the 1960s and absorbed three new members. The 1990s may be a similar period of consolidation for Europe, and we may find that the Community's ambitious plans from the late 1980s and early 1990s require not a single decade to implement, but maybe two or three.

The importance of the 1992 Project is not to be found in the removal of barriers, the creation of Europewide standards, or even the institutional changes wrought by the Single European Act. The importance of 1992 is the fact that it is one step in the process of integration—a process that began almost forty years ago and could well take another forty or more to complete. But the significance is that progress toward the goal of economic and political union is being made. And just as the consequences of previous integration efforts influenced the 1992 Project, the completion of the single market will significantly affect the speed and direction in which the Community moves in the future. This is why 1992 is so important. Europe is engaged in a unique effort to build a new type of political community, and the consequences of the 1992 Project will have implications not only for the future of Europe, but also for other regions that see the process of political and economic integration as a way of enhancing the dual goals of peace and prosperity.

Notes

1. The United Kingdom and Denmark were given the right to "opt out" of the decision to adopt a common currency. The British government and Parliament will decide later whether to join, and Danish participation will depend on a referendum.

2. Where this list of applicants ends, of course, depends on how eastern Europe and the former Soviet Union evolve. The integration process in western Europe often seems to be mirrored by a process of disintegration in the East.

3. The Commission has also begun to study the issue as seen in a recent EC report (Buigues et al. 1990). See also Smith and Wanke (1991) for an attempt to assess the winners and losers from the 1992 Project.

4. Tinbergen (1954) is most often cited at the originator of these two concepts. They can also be found in work on the EC by Pelkmans (1980), Pinder (1989), Molle (1990).

References

Buigues, Pierre, F. Ilzkovitz, and J.-F. Lebrun. 1990. "The Impact of the Internal Market by Industrial Sector: The Challenge for the Member States." *European Economy (Social Europe)*, special edition. Brussels: Commission of the EC.

Economist. Various issues.

Molle, Willem. 1990. *The Economics of European Integration.* Aldershot, UK: Dartmouth.

Pelkmans, Jacques. 1980. "Economic Theories of Integration Revisited." *Journal of Common Market Studies*, 18:333–54.

Pinder, John. 1989. "The Single Market." In Juliet Lodge, ed., *The European Community and the Challenge of the Future.* London: Pinter.

Smith, Dale L., and Jürgen Wanke. 1993. "Completing the Single European Market: An Analysis of the Impact on the Member-states." *American Journal of Political Science*, 37.

Tinbergen, Jan. 1954. *International Economic Integration.* Amsterdam: Elsevier.

Index

EC. *See* European Community
ECE. *See* United Nations Economic
    Commisssion for Europe
Economic and Monetary Union
    (EMU), 110–24, 140, 220
  and defense cooperation, 206
  and European Monetary System, 98
  negotiation of treaty, 122
  structural and institutional
      implications of, 122–23
Economic development funds, 28
Economist (magazine), 24, 113, 114,
    204
ECSC. *See* European Coal and Steel
    Community
ECU. *See* European Currency Unit
Education policy, 83
EEZs. *See* Exclusive Economic Zones
EFA. *See* European Fighter Aircraft
Efficiency, economic, 58
EFTA. *See* European Free Trade
    Association
Elazar, Daniel, 95
Elite, financial-business, 117
Employment, 27–28
EMS. *See* European Monetary System
EMU. *See* Economic and Monetary
    Union
England. *See* Great Britain
Environmental quality, 61–62, 63, 88
  impact of majority voting on, 103
  internationalization of, 80–81
EPC. *See* European Political
    Cooperation
Equity, 56
ERDF. *See* European Regional
    Development Fund
ERM. *See* Exchange Rate Mechanism
ESA. *See* European Space Agency
Escape clause protection, 146
Euclid. *See* European Research and
    Technology Program
EUREKA, 185, 190, 202

European Atomic Energy
    Community, 23
European Business Roundtable, 9
European Coal and Steel Community
    (ECSC), 19, 23
European Commission, 120–21, 180,
    182, 183
European Community (EC), 19, 39–40
  academic analysis of, 30–38
  asymmetrical integration in, 92–105
  average annual growth rates, 28–29
  and defense cooperation, 208–10
  employment in, 27–28
  and evolution of complex
      governance, 45–64
  expansion of, 221
  financial systems in, 113
  growth rates of, 21–23
  industrial subsidies by, 157
  institutional development of, 23–25
  plans for post-1992, 220
  as policy actor, 93–96
  and postwar settlement, 126–40
  revisionist history of, 20–30
  U.S. state government responses to,
      164–76
  and world economy, 119–20
*The European Community: A
    Superpower in the Making*
    (Galtung), 34
European Community Monetary
    Committee, 114
European Council of Heads of State
    and Government, 25, 97–100,
    180, 183
European Court of Justice, 23–24,
    100–101, 104, 153
European Currency Unit (ECU), 25,
    114, 220
European Defense Community, 60, 82
European Economic Community, 23, 57
European Fighter Aircraft (EFA), 199,
    200